CHORAL MUSIC

ROUTLEDGE MUSIC BIBLIOGRAPHIES
Brad Eden, *Series Editor*

ISAAC ALBÉNIZ by Walter A. Clark
C. P. E. BACH by Doris Powers
SAMUEL BARBER by Wayne C. Wentzel
BÉLA BARTÓK by Elliot Antokoletz
ALBAN BERG by Bryan R. Simms
LEONARD BERNSTEIN by Paul R. Laird
BENJAMIN BRITTEN by Peter J. Hodgson
ELLIOTT CARTER by John F. Link
CENTRAL EUROPEAN FOLK MUSIC by Philip V. Bohlman
CARLOS CHÁVEZ by Robert L. Parker
FRÉDÉRIC CHOPIN by William Smialek
CHORAL MUSIC by Avery T. Sharp and James Michael Floyd
AARON COPLAND by Marta Robertson and Robin Armstrong
GAETANO DONIZETTI by James P. Cassaro
EDWARD ELGAR by Christopher Kent
GABRIEL FAURÉ by Edward R. Phillips
SCOTT JOPLIN by Nancy R. Ping-Robbins
JAZZ RESEARCH AND PERFORMANCE MATERIALS, 2ND EDITION
    by Eddie S. Meadows
ZOLTÁN KODÁLY by Michael Houlahan and Philip Tacka
GUILLAUME DE MACHAUT by Lawrence Earp
FELIX MENDELSSOHN BARTHOLDY by John Michael Cooper
NORTH AMERICAN INDIAN MUSIC by Richard Keeling
OPERA, 2ND EDITION by Guy Marco
GIOVANNI PIERLUIGI DA PALESTRINA by Clara Marvin
GIACOMO PUCCINI by Linda B. Fairtile
ALESSANDRO AND DOMENICO SCARLATTI by Carole F. Vidali
SERIAL MUSIC AND SERIALISM by John D. Vander Weg
JEAN SIBELIUS by Glenda Dawn Goss
TUDOR MUSIC by Richard Turbet
GIUSEPPE VERDI by Gregory W. Harwood
TOMÁS LUIS DE VICTORIA by Eugene Casjen Cramer
RICHARD WAGNER by Michael Saffle

CHORAL MUSIC
A RESEARCH AND
INFORMATION GUIDE

AVERY T. SHARP AND JAMES MICHAEL FLOYD

Routledge Music Bibliographies
ROUTLEDGE
NEW YORK AND LONDON

Published in 2002 by
Routledge
29 West 35th Street
New York, NY 10001

Published in Great Britain by
Routledge
11 New Fetter Lane
London EC4P 4EE

Routledge is an imprint of the Taylor & Francis Group.

Printed in the United States of America on acid-free paper.

10 9 8 7 6 5 4 3 2 1
Library of Congress Cataloging-in-Publication Data

Sharp, Avery T., 1942-
  Choral Music : a research and information guide / Avery T. Sharp and James Michael
  Floyd.   p. cm.
  ISBN 0-8240-5944-1 (acid-free paper)
1. Choral music--Bibliography. I. Floyd, James Michael. II. Title.

ML 128.C48 S53 2001
016.7825--dc21   2001019115

Contents

Acknowledgments

We sincerely appreciate the assistance of the following individuals and institutions.

Mr. Jeff Steely, Outreach Services Librarian, and the staff of the Resource Sharing Department, Baylor University. The interlibrary loan librarians and staffs at no less than one hundred other academic libraries around the United States. Ms. Donna Kennedy and Ms. Michelle Toon, the Information Technology Center, Baylor University. Mr. Darryl Stuhr, Fine Arts Library, Baylor University. Dr. Douglas W. Crow, Professor of German, Baylor University. The Baylor University Fine Arts Library student workers who assisted us: Patrick Buchta, Jennifer Campbell, Mun Hui Cho, Yvonne Bonnie Haines, Sun Lee, Andrea Malone, and Jason Villalba. Ms. Karen R. Little, indexer of Music Library Association *Notes*, for advice on indexing.

Avery T. Sharp
James Michael Floyd

Preface

Choral music may be defined as music written in parts designed to be performed with several voices on each part. It is a product of the mid-fifteenth century; during its long history the number of parts for which it was written has varied from two to a dozen or more, and the number of voices required for each part has been similarly unstandardized.—Homer Ulrich, "Introduction," *A Survey of Choral Music*

SCOPE

In the spirit of Ulrich's broad definition of choral music, this work describes book-length monographs and bibliographies, selected dissertations, worklists, choral and church music journals, some journal articles, electronic databases, and World Wide Web sites on choruses and choral music in the Western tradition. Information resources touching on all periods, genres, styles, and types of choral music are included, as are publications on choral music education.

1. Because the literature of choral music is less extensive than, for example, that of opera, the symphony, or chamber music, the decision was made to emphasize inclusiveness over the imposition of strict standards of scholarly quality.

2. With few exceptions, titles chosen for inclusion were published or reprinted between 1960 and 2000. A few landmark works that appeared earlier were, however, included. An example is Carl-Heinz Illing's *Zur Technik der Magnificat-Komposition des 16. Jahrhunderts*, published in 1936 and reputed to be the best treatment of its subject.

3. While emphasis was placed on compiling works in English, an attempt was made to identify important studies in German, French, Italian, and Spanish. A number of sources in German were identified and included, but few in French, Italian, and Spanish were found.

4. A few general music history series with significant information on choral music were included.

5. Studies exclusively on chant were excluded, although a few books that consider chant with other subjects were included. The presence of those works prompted inclusion of the term "chant" in the subject index.

6. Some studies of early madrigals, Masses, and motets were treated, because there is evidence of performance of works in those genres with more than one voice to a part.

7. Reference resources to the journal literature of choral music were included. Therefore, most of the individual articles annotated are choral worklists.

8. In addition to *Doctoral Dissertations in Musicology* and *Dissertation Abstracts International*, two extensive bibliographies of dissertations and theses—one on choral music, the other specifically on sacred music—appear in the guide. As a result, only selected individual dissertations were annotated. Dissertations on narrow topics (e.g., a single composer or a single choralwork) were excluded. The dissertations described are historical/stylistic studies of choral music genres, studies of particular nationalistic traditions during specified spans of time, works comparing the music of several composers, and repertory studies.

ORGANIZATION

The guide is divided into eight main sections, with each subdivided into several more specific headings:

     I. General Music Reference
     II. Choral Music Reference
     III. Choral and Church Music Periodicals
     IV. Choral Technique
     V. Surveys of Choral Music, Sacred and Secular
     VI. Studies of Choral Genres
     VII. Studies of Individual Composers and Works
     VIII. Choral Music Web Sites

Titles were placed in the category considered most descriptive of the content, with *See* references placed under other relevant sections to point readers to full annotations.

I

General Music Reference

DICTIONARIES AND ENCYCLOPEDIAS

1. Apel, Willi, ed. *Harvard Dictionary of Music.* 2nd ed., rev. and enlarged. Cambridge, Massachusetts: Belknap Press of Harvard University Press, 1969. xv, 935 p. SBN 674-37501-7   ML100 .A64 1969

   Music dictionary/encyclopedia. Some articles signed; brief bibliographies accompany longer articles. Musical examples and illustrations. Revised and expanded in 1986 as *The New Harvard Dictionary of Music,* edited by Don Michael Randel (item 6). Although Randel's edition updates scholarship, many articles were not carried over to the new edition.

2. Blume, Friedrich, ed. *Die Musik in Geschichte und Gegenwart: Allgemeine Enzyklopädie der Musik.* 2nd ed. Kassel, Germany: Bärenreiter; Stuttgart, Germany: Metzler, 1994–. ISBN 3-7618-1100-4 (Bärenreiter), ISBN 3-476-41022-6 (Metzler)   ML100 .M92 1994

   Authoritative music dictionary/encyclopedia published in German; comparable to the English *The New Grove Dictionary of Music and Musicians* (item 7). Universal in scope. First edition published between 1949 and 1979; second edition began publication in 1994 and is projected to include 20 volumes divided into two parts: subject and biographical. Numerous illustrations, photos, musical examples, charts, and graphs; selective bibliographies at end of most articles; some discographies. Indices.

3. Hitchcock, H. Wiley, and Stanley Sadie, eds. *The New Grove Dictionary of American Music.* London: Macmillan Press; dist. in United States by Grove's Dictionaries of Music, New York, 1986. 4 vols. ISBN 0-943818-36-2 ML101.U6 N48 1986

   Authoritative music dictionary/encyclopedia specifically about American music and musicians. More than 900 contributors. Unfortunately not indexed; however, information about choral music can be found in articles about specific genres, composers, stylistic periods, and cultural centers, among other topics. Numerous illustrations, photos, musical examples, charts, and graphs; selective bibliographies, discographies, and lists of works at end of most articles.

4. Jackson, Roland, ed. *Performance Practice Encyclopedia*. Fallbrook, California: Roland Jackson, 1997–. URL: http://www.performancepractice.com//

   Electronic information database; a continuation of the print journal *Performance Practice Review*. Provides summaries of research on performance practice. Sound excerpts will gradually be added, each illustrating a particular aspect of performance. Mode of access: World Wide Web.

5. Jones, F. O., ed. *A Handbook of American Music and Musicians: Containing Biographies of American Musicians and Histories of the Principal Musical Institutions, Firms and Societies*. Canaseraga, New York: F. O. Jones, 1886 ML106.U3 J7; reprint, New York: Da Capo Press, 1971. 182 p. SBN 306-70163-4   ML106.U3 J7 1971

   Unchanged reprint of the first edition. Invaluable source of information about American music, musicians (both native and foreign born), and musical subjects up to 1886. Brief entries for personal names, performing groups, individual compositions, concert halls and opera houses, musical societies, conservatories, publishers, periodicals, instrument manufacturers, music dictionaries, etc. Many entries not found in modern reference books. Few worklists in biographical entries; lists of performances under a few festivals and societies; few musical examples; no bibliographies; no index. Series: *Da Capo Press Music Reprint Series*.

6. Randel, Don Michael, ed. *The New Harvard Dictionary of Music*. Cambridge, Massachusetts: Belknap Press of Harvard University Press, 1986. xxi, 942 p. ISBN 0-674-61525-5   ML105 .H38

   Music dictionary/encyclopedia. Revision and expansion of the *Harvard Dictionary of Music* (2nd ed., 1969), edited by Willi Apel (item 1). Emphasis on the tradition of Western art music, but also includes coverage of non-Western and popular music and of musical instruments of all cultures. Some articles signed; brief bibliographies accompany longer articles. Musical examples and illustrations.

7. Sadie, Stanley, ed. *The New Grove Dictionary of Music and Musicians*. 2nd ed. London: Macmillian Reference; New York: Grove's Dictionaries, 2001. 29 vols. ISBN 0-333-60800-3, ISBN 1-56159-239-0   ML100 .N48 2001

Exceptional resource. Predecessor: *Grove's Dictionary of Music and Musicians*, edited by Eric Blom. Authoritative music dictionary/encyclopedia published in English; comparable to the German *Die Musik in Geschichte und Gegenwart* (item 2). Universal in scope. Two appendices: (1) index of terms used in articles on non-Western music, folk music, and kindred topics; and (2) list of approximately 2,500 contributors. Not indexed; however, information about choral music can be found in articles about specific genres, composers, stylistic periods, and cultural centers, among other topics. Numerous illustrations, photos, musical examples, charts, and graphs; selective bibliographies at end of most articles; some discographies. A second edition of the print version, and a new on-line version, were launched in January 2001. Mode of access: World Wide Web; URL: http://www.macmillan-reference.co.uk/grovemusic

8. Slonimsky, Nicolas, ed. *Baker's Biographical Dictionary of Musicians.* Centennial ed. New York: Schirmer Books, 2001. 6 vols. ISBN 0-02-865525-7   ML105 .B16 2001

Previously published as a single volume; the 2001 edition is a six-volume set, an enlargement of the eighth (1992) edition. An important biographical dictionary, with thousands of composer entries. Includes bibliographies and composer worklists.

BIBLIOGRAPHIES OF MUSIC LITERATURE

General Works

9. *American Reference Books Annual.* 1st ed. Littleton, Colorado: Libraries Unlimited, 1970–. (Annual) ISSN 0065-9959   Z1035.1 .A55

Excellent resource; reviews reference books in many subject disciplines, including music. Issued annually.

10. Brockman, William S. *Music: A Guide to the Reference Literature.* Littleton, Colorado: Libraries Unlimited, 1987. xv, 254 p. ISBN 0-87287-526-1 ML113 .B85 1987

Annotated bibliography of 841 music reference and research tools. Needs revision. Broadly organized into six divisions: general reference sources, general bibliographical sources, bibliographies of music literature, bibliographies of music, discographies, and supplemental sources (periodicals; associations, research centers, and other organizations). Author, title, and expansive subject indices.

11. Duckles, Vincent H., and Ida Reed. *Music Reference and Research Materials: An Annotated Bibliography.* 5th ed. Michael A. Keller, advisory editor; indexed by Linda Solow Blotner. New York: Schirmer Books, 1997. xviii, 812 p. ISBN 0-02-870821-0   ML113 .D83 1997

Invaluable reference resource. Annotated bibliography of more than 4,000 selected, published music reference and research tools. Broadly organized into 12 divisions, including dictionaries and encyclopedias; histories and chronologies; guides to musicology; bibliographies of music literature; bibliographies of music; reference works on individual composers and their music; catalogs of music libraries and collections; catalogs of musical instrument collections; histories and bibliographies of music printing and publishing; discographies and related sources; yearbooks, directories, and guides; electronic information resources; and bibliography, the music business, and library science. Each division is subdivided by subject. The expansive index is a valuable tool for locating items relating to choral music.

Indices of Music Literature and Music Periodicals

12. *International Index to Music Periodicals (Online).* Alexandria, Virginia: Chadwyck-Healey, 1997–. URL: http://iimpft.chadwyck.com/

Published as an electronic information resource; available to subscribers. Indexes more than 375 international music periodicals from over 20 countries with over 40 full-text titles; also indexes music articles and obituaries appearing in *The New York Times* and *The Washington Post.*

13. Meggett, Joan M. *Music Periodical Literature: An Annotated Bibliography of Indexes and Bibliographies.* Metuchen, New Jersey: Scarecrow Press, 1978. ix, 116 p. ISBN 0-8108-1109-X   ML128.P24 M43

Dated, yet useful reference tool. Annotated bibliography of 335 sources for (1) history of music periodicals in general, (2) history of music periodicals in the United States, (3) music periodical literature in general nonmusic indexes and bibliographies, (4) music periodical literature in special nonmusic sources, (5) music periodical literature in music indexes and bibliographies, and (6) lists of music periodicals. Includes annotated bibliography of nine other helpful reference tools. Indices for authors, editors, and compilers; subjects; and titles.

14. *The Music Index: A Subject-Author Guide to Music Periodical Literature.* Warren, Michigan: Harmonie Park Press, 1949–. ISSN 0027-4348 ML118 .M84

Print edition published monthly since 1949; accompanied by annually published complete subject heading list with cross references. First issue indexed 41 periodicals, all in English; now indexes over 350 periodicals published in some 20 countries. Subject heading list and monthly issues incorporated into annual volumes. Subjects include forms and types of music, personalities, and music compositions. Cites reviews of books and dissertations, music, music recordings, and performances.

The Music Index Online. Warren, Michigan: Harmonie Park Press, 1999–. URL: http://www.hppmusicindex.com/

Developed by Conway Greene Publishing Company. Cumulates entries from 1979 to 2001. Surveys over 655 international music periodicals.

The Music Index on CD-ROM. CD-ROM. Warren, Michigan: Harmonie Park Press, 2000. ISSN 1066-1514

Cumulates entries from 1979 to 2000. Annual, cumulative updates planned.

15. *RILM Abstracts of Music Literature.* 1–. 1967–. New York: RILM International Center. ISSN 0033-6955   ML1 .I83

    RILM Abstracts of Music Literature. New York: RILM, 1997–. URL: http://www.ohiolink.edu/cgi-bin/firstsearch.pl?rilm

    Abstracts of music literature. Inclusion based on quality. International in scope. All abstracts in English; foreign titles translated. Published quarterly, each issue has author index; fourth issue has author, title, and subject index for the year. Official journal of the International Repertory of Music Literature organization. Also published as an electronic information resource. Mode of access: World Wide Web.

Analysis

16. Diamond, Harold J. *Music Analyses: An Annotated Guide to the Literature.* New York: Schirmer Books; Toronto: Collier Macmillan Canada; New York: Maxwell Macmillan International, 1991. xi, 716 p. ISBN 0-02-870110-0   ML128.A7 D5 1991

    Annotated bibliography of 4,655 analytical writings about musical works. Various performing forces for compositions chosen, but many are choral. Arranged in alphabetical order by composer; composition titles listed in alphabetical order within each composer section. Index of distinctive titles.

17. Wenk, Arthur. *Analyses of Nineteenth- and Twentieth-Century Music: 1940–1985.* Boston: Music Library Association, 1987. xxvii, 370 p. ISBN 0-914954-36-9   ML113 .W45 1987

Wenk's fourth contribution to the *MLA Index and Bibliography Series* cumulates and updates indices originally published as series's numbers 13, 14, and 15. Stated purpose: "to provide rapid access to technical materials of an analytical nature contained in periodicals, monographs, festschriften, and dissertations." Analyses of works by 779 composers indexed in 5,664 entries by approximately 2,400 authors. Entries arranged in alphabetical order by composer and subdivided by genre or work when appropriate. Each entry gives composer, title, author, source of the analysis, and name of the work analyzed if that is not clear from the article's title. Author index. Series: *MLA Index and Bibliography Series*, no. 25.

Dissertations and Master's Theses

18. Adkins, Cecil, and Alis Dickinson, eds. *International Index of Dissertations and Musicological Works in Progress*. 1st ed. Philadelphia: American Musicological Society, 1977. 422 p.   ML128.M8 A43

    Adkins, Cecil, and Alis Dickinson, eds. *International Index of Dissertations and Musicological Works in Progress*. 7th North American ed., 2nd international ed. Philadelphia: American Musicological Society, International Musicology Society, 1984. 545 p.   ML128.M8 D62

    Adkins, Cecil, and Alis Dickinson, eds. *Doctoral Dissertations in Musicology: February 1984-April 1995*. 2nd cumulative ed. Philadelphia: American Musicological Society, International Musicology Society, 1996. ix, 406 p. ML128.M8 A4 1996

    Doctoral Dissertations in Musicology-Online. Philadelphia: American Musicological Society; Bloomington, Indiana: School of Music, Indiana University, 1996–. URL: http://www.music.indiana.edu/ddm/

    Listing of doctoral dissertations in musicology, completed and in progress. Entries classified by subject, including choral music, conducting, performance practice, sacred music, etc. Project began in 1952 under the direction of Helen Hewitt, but charge passed to Cecil Adkins in 1966, joined by Alis Dickinson in 1968. Supplements appeared in various publications, including *American Music Teacher*, *Acta Musicologica*, *The Journal of the American Musicological Society*, and were issued privately to society members by American Musicological Society. Cumulative editions have been published throughout the years, with the last being the February 1984 to April 1995 edition cited above. The print edition will no longer be issued in favor of the *Doctoral Dissertations in Musicology-Online* database. Mode of access: World Wide Web.

19. *Dissertation Abstracts International: A, The Humanities and Social Sciences*. Ann Arbor, Michigan: University Microfilms International, 1969–. (Monthly) Z5053 .D57

Author-prepared abstracts of doctoral dissertations from educational institutions throughout the world. Published monthly accompanied by an annual cumulative author index.

Dissertation Abstracts Ondisc. Ann Arbor, Michigan: University Microfilms, 1987–. Computer file. ISSN 1064-4687

Electronic database available to subscribers. Access to 1.5 million doctoral dissertations and master's theses. Provides citations only for dissertations from 1861 to June 1980; provides citations and abstracts for dissertations from July 1980 to the present.

20. Heintze, James R. *American Music Studies: A Classified Bibliography of Master's Theses.* Detroit, Michigan: Information Coordinators, 1984. xxv, 312 p. ISBN 0-89990-021-6   ML128.M8 H44 1984

Source for bibliographic control of master's theses "whose subject matter pertains to American music in an historical, sociological, or analytical manner." Almost 2,400 entries. Few entries are annotated. Excludes theses that examine instrumental or vocal programs in individual schools. Organized into seven subject categories: research and reference materials, historical studies (including composers, performance, secular music, sacred music, education), theory, ethnomusicology, organology, special topics (including philosophy, communications, and libraries), and related fields (theater and dance). Choral music figures most prominently in historical studies and theory sections. Three indices: author, subject, and expansive geographic index. Series: *Bibliographies in American Music*, no. 8.

Performance Practice

21. Jackson, Roland. *Performance Practice, Medieval to Contemporary: A Bibliographic Guide.* New York: Garland, 1988. xxix, 518 p. ISBN 0-8240-1512-6   ML128.P235 J3 1988

Annotated bibliography of 1,400 writings dealing with performance practice of the 9th through 20th centuries. Updates *Performance Practice: A Bibliography* (1971), edited by Mary Vinquist and Neal Zaslaw (item 22), the bibliography section of *The Interpretation of Early Music* (1974) by Robert Donington, and the bibliography in "Performing Practice" by Howard Mayer Brown and James W. McKinnon in *New Grove Dictionary of Music and Musicians* (item 7). Theorists, author, and expansive subject indices. Series: *Music Research and Information Guides*, vol. 9; *Garland Reference Library of the Humanities*, vol. 790.

22. Vinquist, Mary, and Neal Zaslaw, eds. *Performance Practice: A Bibliography.* New York: W.W. Norton, 1971. 114 p. ISBN 0-393-02148-3, ISBN 0-393-00550-X (pbk)   ML128.L3 V55

Annotated bibliography of 1,131 items. Most entries very briefly annotated. Information previously published in part in *Current Musicology* in 1969 and 1970. Criteria for inclusion: "problems of the 'how-to-do-it' kind." Majority of items cited limited to Western art music from approximately 1100 to 1900. Bibliography of 10 performance practice bibliographies included; expansive subject index.

Druesedow, John. *Performance Practice: A Supplemental Check-List*. Oberlin, Ohio: Conservatory Library, Oberlin College, 1975. xi p.   ML128.L3 V55 Suppl. 1975

Supplement to *Performance Practice: A Bibliography*, edited by Vinquist and Zaslaw, and previously published supplements in *Current Musicology* nos. 12/1971 and 15/1973. Cites about 130 books, articles, theses, and dissertations. Not annotated. Some titles are on choral subjects; most "items pertain to various aspects of Renaissance/baroque keyboard practice or to baroque practice in general."

Baker, Thomas W., and Robert Kline, eds. "Performance Practices Bibliography: Second Supplement." *Current Musicology*, 12 (1971), 129–149

Provides 195 additional titles. Not annotated. No index.

United States
23. Brookhart, Edward. *Music in American Higher Education: An Annotated Bibliography*. Warren, Michigan: Harmonie Park Press, 1988. ix, 245 p. ISBN 0-89990-042-9   ML120.U5 B77 1988

Briefly annotated bibliography of 1,300 writings limited to the history of music in American higher education from 1830 to 1985. Photos; author and expansive subject index. The subject index will best serve to locate sources about choral music, ensembles, and significant individuals in the field. Series: *Bibliographies in American Music*, no. 10.

24. Heintze, James R. *Early American Music: A Research and Information Guide*. New York: Garland, 1990. xii, 511 p. ISBN 0-8240-4119-4 ML120.U5 H46 1990

Annotated bibliography of 1,959 writings on early American music from its beginning to 1820. Includes critical and facsimile editions of music. Author/title index and subject index. Series: *Garland Reference Library of the Humanities*, vol. 1007.

25. Horn, David. *The Literature of American Music in Books and Folk Music Collections: A Fully Annotated Bibliography*. Metuchen, New Jersey: Scarecrow Press, 1977. xiv, 556 p. ISBN 0-8108-0996-6   ML120.U5 H7

Electronic version: Boulder, Colorado: NetLibrary, 1999. URL: http://www.netlibrary.com/summary.asp?ID=6613

Annotated bibliography of 1,388 writings about music and folk music collections published prior to 1976. A majority of the writings pertain to instrumental music and song; sections most likely to list studies on choral music are titled "church music," "hymnody," "psalmody," and "spirituals." As an appendix, 302 additional writings without annotation are listed. Expansive index. Also published as an e-book. Mode of access: World Wide Web.

Horn, David, and Richard Jackson. *The Literature of American Music in Books and Folk Music Collections: A Fully Annotated Bibliography: Supplement I*. Metuchen, New Jersey: Scarecrow Press, 1988. xvi, 570 p. ISBN 0-8108-1997-X   ML120.U5 H7 Suppl. 1

Electronic version: Boulder, Colorado: NetLibrary, 1999. URL: http://www.netlibrary.com/summary.asp?ID=6612

Supplement to David Horn's *The Literature of American Music in Books and Folk Music Collections: A Fully Annotated Bibliography* (1977). Annotated bibliography of 996 writings about music and folk music collections published between 1975 and 1980, including titles omitted from the previous compilation. Similar organization to its earlier counterpart. Sections most likely to list studies on choral music include "church music," "hymnody," "psalmody," and "spirituals." As an appendix, 323 additional writings without annotation are listed. Separate indices for subject, names, and titles. Also published as an e-book. Mode of access: World Wide Web.

Marco, Guy A. *The Literature of American Music III, 1983–1992*. Lanham, Maryland: Scarecrow Press, 1996. xviii, 451 p. ISBN 0-8108-3132-5 ML120.U5 M135 1996

Electronic Version: Boulder, Colorado: NetLibrary, 1999. URL: http://www.netlibrary.com/summary.asp?ID=6614

Continuation of David Horn's *The Literature of American Music in Books and Folk Music Collections: A Fully Annotated Bibliography* (1977) and its supplement (1988) by Horn and Richard Jackson. Annotated bibliography of 1,302 writings about music and folk music collections published between 1983 and 1993. Separate indices for titles, subjects, and authors. Also published as an e-book. Mode of access: World Wide Web.

26. Jackson, Richard. *United States Music: Sources of Bibliography and Collective Biography*. Brooklyn: Institute for Studies in American Music, Dept. of Music, Brooklyn College of The City University of New York, 1976. Rev. ed. vii, 80 p. ISBN 0-914678-00-0   ML120.U5 J2

Very selective, annotated bibliography of more than 90 writings on various aspects of music in the United States as well as sources of collective biographic information. Separate, brief section on church music; resources related to choral music can also be found among reference works and historical and regional studies. Index.

27. Krummel, Donald William. *Bibliographical Handbook of American Music.* Basingstoke: Macmillan, 1987. 269 p. ISBN 0-333-44631-3; Urbana: University of Illinois Press, 1987. 269 p. ISBN 0-252-01450-2   ML120.U5 K78 1987

Annotated bibliography of 760 resources in the area of American music, including bibliographies, worklists, discographies, indices, and electronic databases. Index.

28. Krummel, Donald William, Jean Geil, Doris J. Dyen, and Deane L. Root. *Resources of American Music History: A Directory of Source Materials from Colonial Times to World War II.* Urbana: University of Illinois Press, 1981. 463 p. ISBN 0-252-00828-6   ML120.U5 R47

Annotated bibliography of 1,689 resources of American music history before 1941. Surveys collections of manuscript and printed music, programs, catalogs, organizational and personal papers, iconography, and sound recordings (which includes piano rolls). Geographically limited to the United States, including Puerto Rico, Hawaii, and Alaska. Index.

II

Choral Music Reference

DICTIONARIES

29. Claghorn, Charles Eugene. *Women Composers and Hymnists: A Concise Biographical Dictionary*. Metuchen, New Jersey: Scarecrow Press, 1984. xiii, 272 p. ISBN 0-8108-1680-6   BV325 .C58 1984

    Biographical dictionary of 600 women hymnists and 155 women composers of church and sacred music from the Protestant, Roman Catholic, and Jewish traditions. Chronologically, ranges from 12th century to modern times; geographically, includes North America and Western Europe. Gives composer's name, dates, first line of well-known hymns, and brief biographical entry. Bibliography of 26 items; index by nationality.

30. Davidson, James Robert. *A Dictionary of Protestant Church Music*. Metuchen, New Jersey: Scarecrow Press, 1975. xvi, 349 p. ISBN 0-8108-0788-2   ML102.C5 D33

    Definitions of more than 300 terms, some brief, others lengthy essays. All but briefest entries include a bibliography. Protestant church interpreted as "any Christian church other than those of the Roman Catholic . . . or Eastern traditions." Emphasis on Lutheran subjects. Unavoidably, includes terms commonly used in Catholic worship. Cross references between entries. Expansive index.

31. Pooler, Frank, and Brent Pierce. *New Choral Notation: A Handbook*. 2nd ed., rev. and expanded. New York: Walton Music Corporation, 1973. xii, 84 p. MT35 .P6 1973

    Dictionary of more than 150 choral notation symbols frequently found in choral literature. Preliminary pages give the choral notation symbol with a brief description; following pages cite examples from the literature and provide additional information. Musical examples drawn from the works of 30-plus 20th-century composers, including Igor Stravinsky, Arnold Schonberg,

György Ligeti, Robert Morris, Pauline Oliveros, and Roger Reynolds. Notation symbols divided into the following categories: sung or voiced sounds, unvoiced (whispered) and synthetic sounds, tone clusters, glissando and vibrato, miscellaneous, and special effects.

BIBLIOGRAPHIES OF MUSIC LITERATURE

General Works

32. Thurman, Leon. "Invitation to a Bibliography . . Plus." *Choral Journal*, 19-9 (May 1979), 8–12

    Bibliography of 40 booklets and pamphlets related to choral conducting, 9 books related to voice production and voice pedagogy, and 49 research tools in the areas of choral training, choral program development, vocal production and pedagogy, choral techniques, and observational research.

33. Whitten, Lynn, ed. *A Classified, Annotated Bibliography of Articles Related to Choral Music in Five Major Periodicals through 1980*. Lawton, Oklahoma: American Choral Directors Association, 1982. xviii, 233 p. ML1500 .C63

    Classified, annotated bibliography of more than 1,000 choral-related articles in the following periodicals: *The American Choral Review* (1958–1980), *Church Music* (1966–1980), *The Journal of the American Musicological Society* (1948–1980), *Music and Letters* (1920–1980), and *The Musical Quarterly* (1915–1980). Authors and translators index and subject index. Series: *American Choral Directors Association*, no. 4.

    See also: Johnson, Craig R. "Choral Conducting Texts: An Annotated Bibliography" (item 176, no. 172); Laster, James, and Nancy Menk. "Literature on the Women's Chorus" (item 176, nos. 149, 150, 166); and Ramey, Jack. "Books, Periodicals, and Articles of Interest to Choral Directors in Schools" (item 176, no. 68).

Indices of Music Periodicals

34. Paine, Gordon. *The Choral Journal: An Index to Volumes 1–18*. Lawton, Oklahoma: American Choral Directors Association, 1978. xv, 170 p. ML1.C6563 P3

    Index to volumes 1–18 of *The Choral Journal*. Provides abstracts unless content is obvious from the title. Includes major articles, "Short Subjects," regular columns, book reviews and dissertation abstracts, and record reviews after September 1973. Excludes most American Choral Directors

Association organizational news and announcements, articles featuring individual choirs and tours by individual choirs, columns whose content does not lend itself to indexing, record reviews before September 1973 and all reviews of noncommercial recordings, and "Choral Review." Consists of two parts: (1) subject index (classified into 74 subjects) and (2) an expansive general index. General index is cross-referenced with subject index. Series: *American Choral Directors Association*: no. 3.

Special and Subject Bibliographies of Music Literature

Dissertations and Master's Theses

35. Anderson, Michael J. *A Classified Index of American Doctoral Dissertations and Dissertation Projects on Choral Music Completed or Currently in Progress through 1989*. Lawton, Oklahoma: American Choral Directors Association, 1990. xvii, 177 p.   ML128.C48 A53 1990

   Indexes 1,361 dissertations completed or in progress, 1938–1989. The majority of those listed have a choral orientation; some deal more specifically with vocal, church, or other related music subjects. Compiled from several sources including *Dissertation Abstracts International, Doctoral Dissertations in Musicology*, and university libraries's holdings. Attempts to be comprehensive. Organized by subject classifications, including, among others, choral conducting and techniques; forms of choral music; history and analysis of choral music; literature on, and music for, various types of choruses; performance practice; reference materials; and reviews. Bibliographic information includes title, author's name, type of degree, year degree awarded, institution awarding degree, number of pages, DAI, DDM, and UMI reference numbers where applicable, or library-assigned call numbers. Three indices: university index with address and phone numbers, author index, and expansive subject index. Series: *American Choral Directors Association*, no. 6.

36. Hartley, Kenneth R. *Bibliography of Theses and Dissertations in Sacred Music*. Detroit, Michigan: Information Coordinators, 1967. viii, 127 p. ML128.S2 H4

   Bibliography of approximately 1,500 master's theses and doctoral dissertations written in the United States dealing with aspects of sacred music. Organized alphabetically by state, then by educational institution. Provides author, title, degree earned, and date of completion. Not annotated. Several indices: author, biographies, works of individual composers, subject, and stylistic period. Series: *Detroit Studies in Music Bibliography*, no. 9.

Sacred Music

37. Heaton, Charles Huddleston. "A Church Music Bibliography." *Music: The Ago & RCCO Magazine*, 3 (Jan. 1969), 38–39; 3 (March 1969), 24–25; 3 (April 1969), 52–53

    Dated classified bibliography of approximately 400 writings. Items in English or English translations. Classifications: bells, choir and conducting, history, hymnal companions, hymnody, organ, periodicals, plainchant, and [performance] practice.

38. Jackson, Irene V. *Afro-American Religious Music: A Bibliography and a Catalogue of Gospel Music*. Westport, Connecticut: Greenwood Press, 1979. xiv, 210 p. ISBN 0-313-20560-4   ML128.34 J3

    First part: classified bibliography of 873 writings in six sections: (1) African American: general history, culture, anthropology, and sociology; (2) ethnomusicology, dance, and folklore; (3) African and African-American folksongs; (4) religious folksongs: spirituals, hymns, blues, and gospels; (5) African-American church/African-American religion; and (6) Caribbean: religion, music, culture, folklore, and history. Second part: catalog of gospel music published between 1937 and 1965, including the works of almost 500 composers. Entries supply composer, dates, titles of compositions, publisher, and sources of music. Two indices: (1) expansive index to bibliography and (2) index to catalog.

39. Powell, Martha C. *A Selected Bibliography of Church Music and Music Reference Materials*. Assisted by Deborah C. Loftis. Louisville, Kentucky: Southern Baptist Theological Seminary, 1977. v, 95, 9 p.   ML128.C54 P6

    Classified, annotated bibliography. Superseded in part by *Music Reference and Research Materials: An Annotated Bibliography* (1994), edited by Vincent H. Duckles and Ida Reed (item 11). Sections dealing with church music, choir training, choral-music bibliographies, and hymns, among others, should prove fruitful for research on choral music. Indices: (1) authors and editors and (2) titles. Includes nine-page supplement.

40. Von Ende, Richard Chaffey. *Church Music: An International Bibliography*. Metuchen, New Jersey: Scarecrow Press, 1980. xx, 453 p. ISBN 0-8108-1271-1   ML128.C54 V66

    Bibliography of literature about music in the Christian church, but also includes references to Jewish and Asian faiths. Broad coverage with 5,445 entries organized into 284 categories. International in scope, including citations in more than 25 different languages, but most are in English. Unfortunately, not annotated. Author, editor, and compiler index.

41. Yeats-Edwards, Paul. *English Church Music: A Bibliography.* With a Foreword by Erik Routley. London: White Lion Publishers, 1975. xviii, 217 p. ISBN 0-7284-0020-5   ML128.C54 Y4

    Annotated bibliography of 1,220 books, theses, pamphlets, and tracts in English printed from 1500 to the present; excludes periodical articles and music. Divided into nine sections: bibliographical, historical, biographical, choral, theological and theoretical, liturgical, musical, practical, and fictional. Introduced with a historical discussion of English church music and a chronological summary of events. Facsimiles of title pages and illustrations; expansive index.

    See also: DeVenney, David P. *American Masses and Requiems: A Descriptive Guide* (item 144); Hartley, Kenneth R. *Bibliography of Theses and Dissertations in Sacred Music* (item 36); Stevenson, Robert Murrell. "The English Service: A Bibliography of Editions and Literature" (item 176, no. 44)

United States

42. Orr, N. Lee, and W. Dan Hardin. *Choral Music in Nineteenth-Century America: A Guide to the Sources.* Lanham, Maryland: Scarecrow Press, 1999. ix, 135 p. ISBN 0-8108-3664-5   ML128.C48 O77 1999

    Selective bibliography of approximately 900 sources pertinent to choral music in the United States from the 1820s through the early years of the 20th century. Also includes individual chapters on leading 19th-century composers, e.g., Lowell Mason, Amy Beach, John Knowles Paine, etc. Index.

    See also: DeVenney, David P. *American Masses and Requiems: A Descriptive Guide* (item 144).

BIBLIOGRAPHIES OF CHORAL MUSIC

General Works

43. Berger, Melvin. *Guide to Choral Masterpieces: A Listener's Guide.* New York: Anchor Books, 1993. xiv, 365 p. ISBN 0-385-42248-2   ML1500 .B47 1993

    Guide to almost 100 choral works by 40 composers. Supplies brief biography of the composers and discussion of individual works. Texts for the Mass ordinary, Requiem, Te Deum, Stabat Mater, and Magnificat appended. Glossary of terms; discography listing a recording for each work; no index.

44. Charles, Sydney Robinson. *A Handbook of Music and Music Literature in Sets and Series.* New York: Free Press, 1972. 497 p.; London: Collier-Macmillan, 1973. 497 p. ML113 .C45

Describes the content and organization of 340 multivolume publications of music and music literature. Selective; intended to supplement, not duplicate such works as Anna Harriet Heyer's *Historical Sets, Collected Editions, and Monuments of Music* (1980) and Fred Blum's *Music Monographs in Series: A Bibliography of Numbered Monograph Series in the Field of Music Current since 1945* (1964). Four sections: (1) sets and series of music by several composers; (2) sets and series devoted to individual composers; (3) music literature monograph and facsimile series; and (4) music periodicals and yearbooks. Expansive index.

45. Daugherty, F. Mark, and Susan H. Simon, eds. *Secular Choral Music in Print.* 2nd ed. Philadelphia: Musicdata, 1987. 2 vols., xiii, 1322 p. ISBN 0-88478-020-1 ML128.V7 D3 1987

Revised edition of *Secular Choral Music* (1974), edited by Thomas R. Nardone, James H. Nye, and Mark Resnick. Bibliography of all secular choral music in print organized alphabetically by composer. Updated by 1991 and 1993 supplements. International in scope, though works published in the United States, Canada, and Western Europe are emphasized. Each entry provides composer, title, voicing, accompaniment, remarks, and pricing information (U. S. dollars). Heavily cross-referenced. Directory of publishers with addresses, noting distributors. Separately published arranger index and master index (composer and title). Series: *Music-in-Print Series*, vol. 2.

Secular Choral Music in Print, Second Edition: Arranger Index. Philadelphia: Musicdata, 1987. iii, 128 p. ISBN 0-88478-021-X ML128.V7 S37 1987

Arranger index lists in alphabetical order all arrangers cited in the *Secular Choral Music in Print* (1987), edited by Daugherty and Simon. Series: *Music-in-Print Series*, vol. 2c.

Daugherty, F. Mark, and Susan H. Simon, eds. *Secular Choral Music in Print: 1991 Supplement.* Philadelphia: Musicdata, 1991. xiii, 188 p. ISBN 0-88478-027-9 ML128.V7 D3 1987 Suppl.

1991 supplement to *Secular Choral Music in Print* (1987). Includes arranger index and directory of publishers with addresses, noting distributors. Series: *Music-in-Print Series*, vol. 2s.

Daugherty, F. Mark, and Susan H. Simon, eds. *Secular Choral Music in Print: 1993 Supplement.* Philadelphia: Musicdata, 1993. xiii, 223 p. ISBN 0-88478-031-7 ML128.V7 D3 1987 Suppl. 2

1993 supplement to *Secular Choral Music in Print* (1987). Includes arranger index and directory of publishers with addresses, noting distributors. Series: *Music-in-Print Series*, vol. 2t.

Secular Choral Music in Print: Master Index 1993. Philadelphia: Musicdata, 1993. vi, 365 p. ISBN 0-88478-032-5 ML128.V7 D33 1993

Composer and title index for *Secular Choral Music in Print* (1987) and the 1991 and 1993 supplements edited by Daugherty and Simon. Series: *Music-in-Print Series*, vol. 2x.

Cho, Robert W., Elisa T. Kahn-Ellis, Donald T. Reese, and Frank James Staneck, eds. *Secular Choral Music in Print: 1996 Supplement*. Philadelphia: Musicdata, 1996. xiii, 165 p. ISBN 0-88478-041-4 ML128.V7 D3 1987 Suppl. 3

1996 supplement to *Secular Choral Music in Print* (1987) and the 1991 and 1993 supplements edited by Daugherty and Simon. Includes arranger index and directory of publishers with addresses, noting distributors. Series: *Music-in-Print Series*, vol. 2u.

46. Library of Congress. National Library Service for the Blind and Physically Handicapped. *Braille Scores Catalog: Choral, 1979*. Washington: Library of Congress, 1979. 110 p. ML136.U52 M83

Dated. Bibliography of approximately 1,000 sacred and 600 secular choruses published in Braille and among the holdings of the National Library Service for the Blind and Physically Handicapped, Library of Congress. Supplies composer, title, voicing/accompaniment, and publisher. Series: *Music & Musicians*.

47. National Federation of Music Societies. *Catalogue of Choral Works*. London: National Federation of Music Societies, 1985. iv, 91 p. ML128.V7 N34 1985

Annotated bibliography of more than 1,000 choral works. Provides titles, voicing and accompaniment, duration, and publisher. Most works between 10 and 30 minutes in length; longer works also included. Four appendices: (1) list of stage works for concert performance; (2) list of works that can be performed with keyboard accompaniment only; (3) list of publishers with addresses; and (4) selected list of libraries with addresses.

48. Sharp, Avery T. *Choral Music Reviews Index, 1983–1985*. New York: Garland, 1986. x, 260 p. ISBN 0-8240-8553-1 ML128.C48 C5

Multiaccessed index to reviews of choral works in 16 English-language journals. Synopsizes reviews published 1983–1985 of more than 2,000 recently published or reissued octavos, choral collections, and extended choral works. Eight indices: composer, arranger, editor, use or special purpose, level of performing group, choral voicing, solo voicing, and accompanying instruments. Series: *Garland Reference Library of the Humanities*, vol. 674.

Sharp, Avery T. *Choral Music Reviews Index II, 1986–1988.* New York: Garland, 1990. xi, 397 p. ISBN 0-8240-4113-5   ML128.V7 S386 1990

Continuation of *Choral Music Reviews Index, 1983–1985.* Multiaccessed index to reviews of choral works in 14 English-language journals. Synopsizes reviews published 1986–1988 of more than 2,900 recently published or reissued octavos, choral collections, and extended choral works. Same indices as its companion with two added indices: (1) text source and (2) hymn-tune name or derivation of melody. Series: *Garland Reference Library of the Humanities*, vol. 962.

49. Snyder, Robert E. "Literature Forum: An Annotated Inventory of Easy Choral Music of the Classical Period." *Choral Journal*, 24–10 (June 1984), 33–36; 25–6 (Feb. 1985), 29–31; 25–9 (May 1985), 43–44

Annotated list of more than 70 works. Provides composer, title, translated title, performing forces, language of text, publisher, music number, duration, and comments.

50. Vogel, Emil. *Bibliothek der gedruckten weltlichen Vocalmusik Italiens: Aus den Jahren 1500–1700. Enthaltend die Litteratur der Frottole, Madrigale, Canzonette, Arien, Opern etc.* [Bibliography of Italian secular vocal music printed between the years 1500 and 1700]. Revised and enlarged by Alfred Einstein. Forewords by Emil Vogel and Alfred Einstein. Hildesheim, Germany: Georg Olms, 1945 (rep. 1962, 1972). 2 vols. xxiii, 530 p.; 832 p. ISBN 3-487-04200-2 (vol. 1, 1972), ISBN 3-487-04201-0 (vol. 2, 1972) ML120.I8 V8 1972

Text variously in German, Italian, and English. Originally published in 1892; updated in 1945. Extensive bibliography of Italian secular vocal music published between 1500 and 1700 arranged alphabetically by composer. Provides date of composition, title page information, physical details, contents of collections, dedicatory notes, known locations of scores, and additional remarks as needed. Separately lists printed collections in chronological order annotated in the same manner as the rest of the bibliography. Indices of titles, imprints, printers, publishers, and authors.

51. Vollen, Gene E. *The French Cantata: A Survey and Thematic Catalog*. Ann Arbor, Michigan: UMI Research Press, 1982. xii, 815 p. ISBN 0-8357-1281-8   ML1527 .V64 1982

First section surveys the origins, uses, music, text, and formal structure of the 18th-century French cantata. Second section is a thematic catalog which provides brief biographies of the composers, titles, sources, instrumentation and vocal ranges, authors of texts, and incipits of principal movements. Musical examples, tables, and illustrations; bibliography of approximately 230 items; three indices: (1) index of composers in catalog; (2) index of titles in catalog; and (3) expansive general index. Series: *Studies in Musicology*, no. 51.

See also: *Research Memorandum Series* (item 176)

Indices of Choral Music

52. Diehl, Katharine Smith. *Hymns and Tunes: An Index*. New York: Scarecrow Press, 1966. lv, 1185 p.   BV305 .D5 1966

Index to 78 hymnals. Five sections: (1) first lines and variants, (2) authors with first lines, (3) tune names and variants, (4) composers with tune names, and (5) solfeggio index to the melodies. Prefaced by historical information about hymns and hymnals. Several appendices, including an annotated bibliography of hymnals indexed. Also, bibliography of six relevant reference books.

53. Lincoln, Harry B. *The Italian Madrigal and Related Repertories: Indexes to Printed Collections, 1500–1600*. New Haven, Connecticut: Yale University Press, 1988. ix, 1,139 p. ISBN 0-300-03683-3   ML128.M2 L56 1988

Index to printed collections of the Italian madrigal, frottola, and lauda. Also includes aria, bicinium, canzona, canzonetta, giustiniana, greghesca, moresca, napolitana, oda, sonetto, strambotto, villanella, and villotta. Collection defined as a publication of works by more than one composer; excludes collections of works by a single composer. Four parts: (1) composer index with 38,000 melodic incipits in staff notation from 9,000 works, giving composer, first line of text, page or folio number, *Repertoire International des Sources Musicales* (RISM) number, genre, and comments if needed; (2) index to first lines; (3) thematic locator index to locate melodies by interval sequence; and (4) short title index to sources in RISM entry order with library or archive sigla.

54. Lincoln, Harry B. *The Latin Motet: Indexes to Printed Collections, 1500–1600*. Ottawa, Canada: The Institute of Mediaeval Music, 1993. x, 835 p. ISBN 0-931902-80-0   ML128.M67 L56 1993

Indexes more than 300 printed collections of the Latin motet. Collection defined as publication of works by more than one composer; excludes collections of works by a single composer. With few exceptions, excludes Latin Mass, Magnificat, lauda, and collections of responds. Five parts: (1) composer index with 19,000 melodic incipits in staff notation from 7,000 works, giving composer, first line of text, page or folio number, *Repertoire International des Sources Musicales* (RISM) number and comments if needed, and text incipits of about 400 instrumental pieces (settings for lute, organ, vihuela, guitar, or unspecified instrument); (2) index to first lines; (3) thematic locator index to locate melodies by interval sequence; (4) short title index to sources in RISM entry order with library or archive sigla; and (5) bibliography of about 300 modern editions. Cross references between sections where applicable. Series: *Wissenschaftliche Abhandlungen*, Bd. 59; *Musicological Studies*, vol. 59.

55. Oglesby, Donald. "Literature Forum: Index to Bach Cantata Scores: Locations in the *Bach Gesellschaft* Edition, *Neue Bach Ausgabe*, Hänssler/ Carus-Verlag Catalog, and Kalmus Catalog." *Choral Journal*, 35–8 (March 1995), 37–44

Index taken from the *Bach Cantata Database* available through the Miami Bach Society. Arranged by BWV number; also gives corresponding number in the *Bach Compendium* catalog (1985–1989). Provides location of cantatas in the four sources listed in the title of the article. Notes (lost, spurious, fragment, etc.) included as applicable.

56. Spencer, Donald Amos. *Hymn and Scripture Selection Guide: A Cross-Reference Tool for Worship Leaders*. Rev. and expanded. Grand Rapids, Michigan: Baker Book House, 1993. 315 p. ISBN 0-8010-8339-7   BV312 .S67 1993

Intended for "pastors, ministers of music, choir directors, and leaders of any church-related organization." Includes 380 hymns and 12,000 related scriptural references. Inclusion based on examining hymnals of 10 major denominations and five widely used interdenominational hymnals. Two sections: (1) alphabetical listing of hymn titles; (2) listing of scripture passages in biblical order. Cross references between the two sections. Index of hymn titles.

57. Wenk, Arthur. *Musical Resources for the Revised Common Lectionary*. Metuchen, New Jersey: Scarecrow Press, 1994. xvi, 614 p. ISBN 0-8108-2909-6   ML128.P7 W46 1994

Designed to assist ministers, organists, and choirmasters in the selection of hymns, organ music, and choral music appropriate to the lessons appointed for worship. Five main sections: (1) music for the church year; (2) scriptural index of hymn texts; (3) index of hymn preludes, including a brief list of melodic incipits; (4) scriptural index of anthems; and (5) indices of organ works and choral works cited.

Special and Subject Bibliographies of Choral Music

Choral Music for Children and Youth Choirs

General Works

58. Music Educators National Conference. *1985 Selective Music Lists: Vocal Solos, Vocal Ensembles.* With a Foreword by Paul F. Roe. Reston, Virginia: Music Educators National Conference, 1985. iii, 84 p.   ML132.V7 A15 1985

    Revision of earlier lists. Selective works for solo voice, junior high and senior high choral groups, jazz and show choir, and small vocal ensembles (madrigal singers and chamber choirs, treble voices, and male voices). Sections are subdivided by voicing (unison, two-part, three-part, SATB, etc.) and further grouped by classification (sacred, secular, folk/spiritual, Christmas, major works, etc.). Works are graded as easy, medium, or advanced. Information includes composer, title, and publisher/collection. Concludes with a directory of publishers; no index.

    See also: Rao, Doreen. "Selected Repertoire for Children's Chorus and Orchestra" (item 176, no. 142); and Saller, Paul H. "A Selective List of Sacred and Secular Music for Children's Voices" (item 176, no. 26)

Unison Choirs

59. "Literature Forum." *Choral Journal*, 19–5 (Jan. 1979), 48–49

    Annotated list of 17 sacred, 8 secular, and 6 Christmas works for unison choir. Gives title, composer, publisher, music number, performing forces, and comments.

Children's Choirs

60. Ferreira, Linda. "Classic Choral Music for Children's Voices." *Choral Journal*, 29–8 (Mar. 1989), 19–26

    Classified list of approximately 160 general works, 55 folk songs and spirituals, and 50 works for Christmas. Supplies composer/arranger, title, publisher, music number, and performing forces.

61. Music Educators National Conference. *Choral Music for Children: An Annotated List*. Preface by Doreen Rao. Reston, Virginia: Music Educators National Conference, 1990. ix, 166 p. ISBN 0-940796-80-5   ML128.J8 C5 1990

    Revision of Music Educators National Conference's (MENC) and American Choral Directors Association's (ACDA) *Music for Children's Choir: A Selective and Graded Listing* (1977; see item 62). Annotated list of approximately 300 titles. Entries arranged in alphabetical order by composer, providing title, publisher, music number, voicing, style (i.e., romantic, contemporary, American folk, etc.), language, descriptive notes, comment on pedagogical value, and level of difficulty (beginning, intermediate, advanced, and very young choirs (K–3)). Four indices: (1) composers or arrangers, (2) titles, (3) voicings (unison, two-part treble, three-part treble, and four-part treble), and (4) level of difficulty.

62. Music Educators National Conference, and American Choral Directors Association. *Music for Children's Choirs: A Selective and Graded Listing*. Reston, Virginia: Music Educators National Conference, 1977. 44 p. ML132.C5 M9

    Compiled under the direction of the Boy and Children's Choirs Standing Committee of the American Choral Directors Association; Donald W. Roach served as project coordinator. Approximately 700 titles. Broadly organized into unison, two-part, three-part, rounds and canons, and choral collections. Where applicable, further subdivided into secular, sacred, seasonal, two-part, three-part, etc. Works graded as easy, medium, or difficult. Information given includes composer/arranger/editor, title, publisher, and music number. Directory of publishers; no index. Revised in 1992 by the Music Educators National Conference as *Choral Music for Children: An Annotated List* (see item 61). However, the revision lists just 300 choral works.

63. Roach, Donald W. *Handbook for Children's and Youth Choir Directors*. Garland, Texas: Choristers Guild, 1987. 128 p.   MT915 .R65 1987

    Discussion of choir organization and administration, selection of music, and rehearsal technique. Classified list of approximately 860 choral works for children's and youth choirs, listing composer/arranger, title, voicing, publisher, and publication number, and 19 vocal-technique and sight-singing materials. Also, lists addresses for equipment and instrument sources (choir robes; music risers, stands, chairs, and music cabinets; choral music folios and filing supplies; handbell manufacturers; handbell supplies; Orff-type instruments; recorders, guitars, autoharps, percussion instruments; and choir pins, certificates, safety candles, posters, and other aids), addresses for 17 professional organizations and journals and 16 major handbell-music publishers. Classified bibliography of about 175 writings; no index.

64. Smith, Kathryn. "Focus: Commissioned Works: Works Commissioned for American Children's Choirs." *Choral Journal*, 33–8 (March 1993), 33–37

List of almost 150 published and unpublished works composed for children's choirs. Provides composer, title, performing forces, publication information (where applicable), and choir and conductor for whom the work was written. Works date from 1960s to 1990s.

65. Stultz, Marie. "Literature Forum: Selecting Music to Improve and Inspire Your Children's Choir: An Annotated List." *Choral Journal*, 34–5 (Dec. 1993), 35–40

Classified, annotated list of 26 works for children's choir. Classifications: music that builds headtone; tone building and diction; vocal tone and the mid-range; legato line; and the challenge of part-singing. Entries provide composer, title, performing forces, language of text, sacred or secular, duration, difficulty level (easy, accessible, medium, advanced), publisher, music number, and annotation. Composers include J. S. Bach, G. F. Handel, Franz Schubert, Ralph Vaughan Williams, Aaron Copland, Benjamin Britten, and John Rutter.

66. Tagg, Barbara, and Linda Ferreira. "Focus: Repertoire: Selected Literature for Children's Chorus." *Choral Journal*, 33–8 (March 1993), 41–54

Classified bibliography of musical works for children's chorus. Compiled with assistance from the National Committee on Children's Choirs. Gives composer, title, publisher, music number, and performing forces. Classifications: classic literature (100 works); Masses (6); folk song arrangements (40); jazz, gospel, and traditional American spiritual songs (14); seasonal works (40); solo repertoire suitable for unison singing (12); collections (13); extended works involving chorus, orchestra, and children (5); works for treble chorus and full orchestra or chamber ensemble (21); operas involving children (6); operas written for children (2); works for SATB chorus and children (11); and works using extended vocal techniques (18).

See also: Moore, Christopher. "A Bibliography of Contemporary Choral Music for High Voices, Performable by Children" (item 176, no. 36)

Junior High School Choirs

67. Allen, Sue Fay. "Literature Forum: Choosing Music for Ninth Grade Chorus." *Choral Journal*, 23–2 (Oct. 1982): 21–25

Recommends nearly 30 choral works for junior high choir. Gives title, com-
poser/arranger, performing forces, publication information, level of difficulty (easy to difficult), and annotation.

68. Chapman, Sandra. "Selected Choral Literature for Junior High Choirs."
    Choral Journal, 31–7 (Feb. 1991), 23–29

    Classified list (SA and two-part, SAB and three-part, SATB, SSA, and
    T(T)BB) of approximately 350 choral works suitable for junior high choirs.
    Gives title, composer/arranger, publisher, and music number.

69. Lovelace, Austin C. *The Youth Choir*. New York: Abingdon Press, 1964. 72
    p.   MT88 .L69

    Brief. Addresses organizing and maintaining a youth choir. Repertoire list
    recommends approximately 100 hymns, 8 collections, 20 cantatas, and
    about 150 anthems for unison, two-part, SAB, and SATB. Musical exam-
    ples; bibliography of 20 writings; index. Series: *A Basic Music Book*.

    See also: Mayer, Frederick D. "A Selected List of Music Suitable for Use at
    the Junior High School Level" (item 176, no. 37); Perinchief, Robert. "An
    Annotated Select List of Music for the Small Select Choir in the Music Pro-
    gram of the Intermediate Grades" (item 176, nos. 54, 59); Rhodes, Mark. "A
    Selective, Annotated List of Secular Renaissance Vocal Music Suitable for
    Junior-High-School Boys of Mixed Choruses" (item 176, no. 153); and
    Spencer, Helen Stott. "A Selected List of Music for Junior and Senior High
    School Women's Choruses" (item 176, no. 50)

Senior High School Choirs
70. Harris, Jerry Weseley. "An Analytical Inventory of Selected Contemporary
    S.A.T.B. Choral Compositions for High School Choirs." Ed.D. dissertation.
    University of Oregon, Eugene, 1966. 2 vols., ii, 837 p.

    Annotated list of 289 choral octavos performable by high school choirs
    composed by 20 selected composers "representative of the 'contemporary
    idiom'." Provides title, composer, voicing, accompaniment, publisher and
    music number, level of difficulty (range: 1–6), price, pagination, whether
    the work is sacred or secular, and comments on musical considerations,
    which includes voice ranges and tessitura, melody, harmony, rhythm, musi-
    cal texture, and text. Seventeen appendices, two of which function as
    indices, including listings of composers, titles, and several separate listings
    of titles indicating voicing classifications, ranges of difficulty, musical set-
    tings of choral text and specific compositional techniques, and melodic,
    harmonic, rhythmic, musical texture, and formal considerations. Music

notation representing voice ranges; bibliography of approximately 120 writings.

71. Hawkins, Margaret. *An Annotated Inventory of Distinctive Choral Literature for Performance at the High School Level*. Tampa, Florida: American Choral Directors Association, 1976. iv, 69 p.   ML128.V7 H37

Annotated bibliography of about 300 choral works and 60 anthologies appropriate for performance by high school mixed chorus. For individual works, provides composer, title, descriptive notes, voicing, language, publisher and publication number, and duration; for anthologies, provides anthology title, editor, publisher, and descriptive notes. No index. Series: *American Choral Directors Association*, no. 2.

72. May, James D. *Avant-Garde Choral Music: An Annotated Selected Bibliography*. Metuchen, New Jersey: Scarecrow Press, 1977. vii, 258 p. ISBN 0-8108-1015-8   ML128.V7 M43

Stated purpose: to "assist the high school choral director . . . with the selection, study, and performance of avant-garde choral music." Divided into three parts: first two define "avant-garde," discuss criteria for selection of compositions, and offer warm-up tips to aid in performance of avant-garde music; third part is annotated bibliography of about 240 choral works, giving composer, author or source of text, publisher, catalog number and pricing information (outdated), voicing, classification of difficulty (easy to difficult), timing, accompaniment, type of text (sacred, secular, vowel and consonant sounds, etc.), range and tessitura, description of avant-garde and traditional characteristics, and other supplementary information. Publishers's names and addresses are provided following the bibliography. Nine separate indices for works: SATB; SAB; SSA; TTB; two-part choir; unison choir; speaking chorus; electronic tape accompaniment; and a composer index. Brief bibliography of about 30 books and articles.

73. White, J. Perry. *Twentieth-Century Choral Music: An Annotated Bibliography of Music Suitable for Use by High School Choirs*. 2nd ed. Metuchen, New Jersey: Scarecrow Press, 1990. xi, 214 p. ISBN 0-8108-2394-2 ML128.C48 W53 1990

Annotated bibliography of 367 choral works; classified as SATB, SATB divisi, SAB, SSA, and TTBB. Provides composer, title, voicing, accompaniment, text, range, level of difficulty, style and general comments, publisher, duration, recommended usage (i.e., Christmas, festival, secular concert, etc.), date of composition, and recommended performance group (high school to college). Listing of publishers with addresses; separate composer and title indices.

See also: André, Don A. "Literature Forum: Orchestra and Chorus: Works for the Amateur or High School Performing Group" (item 115); Rayl, David. "Literature Forum: Thinking Small: Choral-Orchestral Works for the Small Choir with a Small Budget" (item 117); Spencer, Helen Stott. "A Selected List of Music for Junior and Senior High School Women's Choruses" (item 176, no. 50)

Choral Music for Adult Choirs

Choral Music for College and University Choirs
74. Bloesch, Richard J., and Weyburn Wasson. *Twentieth-Century Choral Music: An Annotated Bibliography of Music Appropriate for College and University Choirs.* Edited by Gordon Paine. Lawton, Oklahoma: American Choral Directors Association, 1997. xi, 289 p. ISBN 1-882648-09-9 ML128.C48 B56 1997

An annotated bibliography of approximately 700 20th-century choral works suitable for college and university choirs. Gives composer, title of work, performing forces, text source, language, duration, publisher, and descriptive notes. Provides listing of publishers and agents with addresses. Separate indices for composers, titles, accompaniment, language, voicing, and duration. Series: *American Choral Directors Association*, no. 9.

75. McCoy, Jerry. "Literature Forum: New Literature for College and University Choirs." *Choral Journal*, 28–7 (Feb. 1988), 31–37

Annotated bibliography of 39 choral works by American and Canadian composers. Purpose: "to create a compendium of new, unpublished, or obscure choral works that deserve performance." Selections organized into two groups: accompanied and unaccompanied. Provides title, composer, composer's address (if unpublished work), publication information (if published work), duration, language of text, performing forces, text source, and annotation, followed by name of choral conductor who recommended the work.

Choral Music for Men's Choirs
76. Crowell, Allen. "Literature Forum: Literature for the Three-Part Male Chorus." *Choral Journal*, 29–7 (March 1979), 38–40

List of approximately 80 works for men's chorus. Gives composer and dates, title, sections or movements, editor, voicing, and publication information.

77. Janower, David. "Male Chorus Music." *Choral Journal*, 27–2 (Sept. 1986), 36–40

    Supplements Raymond Miller's list of choral works (see item 79). Partially annotated bibliography of more than 80 works for "mature male voices." Gives composer/arranger, title, publisher, and music number.

78. Marvin, Jameson. "Music of the Renaissance: A Wealth of Literature for the Male Chorus." *Choral Journal*, 29–9 (April 1989), 5–21

    Selectively annotated bibliography of 198 sacred and 95 secular choral works written in the 15th and 16th centuries for men's voices. Gives composer, title, level of difficulty (easy to difficult), and publication/manuscript source. Provides annotations for the 30 most recommended works.

79. Miller, Raymond. "Keep Those Guys Singing with Choral Literature that is Enjoyable and Fun to Sing." *Choral Journal*, 26–2 (Sept. 1985), 27–30

    List of more than 80 compositions for male chorus. Gives composer/arranger, title, publisher, voicing, and music number. *See also* Janower, David. "Male Chorus Music" (item 77).

80. Roberts, Kenneth Creighton. *A Checklist of Twentieth-Century Choral Music for Male Voices*. Detroit: Information Coordinators, 1970. 32 p. ML128.V7 R6

    Annotated bibliography of nearly 300 works. Provides title, voicing and accompaniment, date of composition, pagination, publication information, and other descriptive notes. Series: *Detroit Studies in Music Bibliography*, no. 17.

81. Stam, Carl L. "Literature Forum: Male Chorus Repertoire Ideas: The Tip of the Iceberg." *Choral Journal*, 33–4 (Nov. 1992), 41–44

    Graded, annotated list of 52 recommended works for male chorus. Primarily includes original compositions, with some arrangements of folk songs and spirituals. Classified as follows: rather easy, medium difficult, rather difficult, and chant. Provides composer, title, publisher, music number, performing forces, and annotation.

82. Tortolano, William. *Original Music for Men's Voices: A Selected Bibliography*. 2nd ed. Metuchen, New Jersey: Scarecrow Press, 1981. 201 p. ISBN 0-8108-1386-6   ML128.V7 T66 1981

    Two parts. Part I contains a bibliography of 795 compositions and a number of collections of music for men's voices. Limited to original works for male chorus and based on "availability" and "practicality." Improvement on the first edition in size and organization of the bibliography. Provides basic bibliographic information, including publisher and catalog numbers, for each entry. Also provides a list of publishers, with addresses and telephone numbers, and a list of service and professional music organizations. Part II presents essays on a variety of topics, including "Learning a Song by the Barbershop Method" (Robert D. Johnson), "Intercollegiate Musical Council: A Bit of History" (Marshall Bartholomew), "The Male Choral Music of Franz Liszt" (James Fudge), "Mass Settings by Krenek, Harris, Harrison, and Langlais" (W. Tortolano), "Twentieth Century Male Choral Music Suitable for Protestant Worship" (John William Lundberg), and an article about legislation passed by Congress in 1975 entitled "Title IX and the Men's Glee Club" (Robert Grose). Brief bibliography appended, consisting mostly of catalogs and other listings of choral music. Two indices: index of authors and sources of texts; index of first lines and titles.

See also: Case, James H. "A List of Contemporary American Choral Music for Men's Voices" (item 176, no. 39); Hayes, Morris D. "A Select List of Music for Men's Voices" (item 176, nos. 42, 52, 75, 81, 83); Rasmussen, Mary. "A Bibliography of 19th- and 20th-Century Music for Male Voices with Wind- or Brass-Ensemble Accompaniment" (item 111); Van Camp, Leonard. "A Bibliography of Choral Music for Three-Part Male Chorus" (item 176, no. 92)

Choral Music for Women's Choirs

83. Anderson, Julia S. "Music for Women's Chorus and Harp: A Study of the Repertory and an Analysis and Performance of Selected Compositions." Ed.D. dissertation. Teachers College, Columbia University, New York, 1977. 224 p.

Offers a brief overview of the history of women's choruses, survey of the repertory for women's chorus and harp, and analysis of selected compositions. Annotated bibliography of 24 works for women's chorus and harp, 30 for women's chorus, harp, and other instruments, and 17 that can be transcribed for women's chorus and harp. Musical examples; bibliography of about 60 writings; no index.

84. Apfelstadt, Hilary. *Canadian Music for Women's Voices.* Greensboro, North Carolina: Spectrum Music Publishers, 1989. iv, 160 p.   ML120.C2 A64 1989

Annotated bibliography of approximately 230 choral works for women's voices by Canadian composers. Listed in alphabetical order by title. Suitable for advanced high school or university choirs. Provides title, composer, publisher, date of composition or publication, voicing, solos, language of text, level of difficulty (easy, medium-easy, medium-difficult, difficult), performance level (high school, college, church), accompaniment, vocal ranges, formal structure, musical style, vocal/technical challenges, and general comments. Three indices provide cross references: (1) sacred/secular works organized by composer; (2) extended works organized by composer; and (3) titles grouped by voicing.

85. Apfelstadt, Hilary. "Music of Canadian Composers for Women's Choruses." *Choral Journal*, 31–5 (Dec. 1990), 23–29

    Annotated bibliography of 32 extended choral works suitable for church or concert setting. Provides title, composer, date of composition, performing forces, duration, publishing information, level of difficulty, and descriptive remarks. Most works date from 1951 to 1987.

86. Breden, Sharon Ann. "Committee Report on Women's Choruses: Unison and SA." *Choral Journal*, 23–9 (May 1983), 37–41

    Breden, Sharon Ann. "Committee Report on Women's Choruses: Part II: Women's Chorus Literature." *Choral Journal*, 26–9 (May 1986), 23–33

    Annotated list of 80 works for treble choir. In two parts: part I lists general sacred works; part II lists Christmas and secular works. Provides title, composer/editor/arranger, publishing information, voice ranges, accompaniment, text, duration, movements, and annotation.

87. Burnsworth, Charles C. *Choral Music for Women's Voices: An Annotated Bibliography of Recommended Works*. Metuchen, New Jersey: Scarecrow Press, 1968. 180 p.   ML128.V7 B87

    Annotated bibliography of approximately 130 original compositions and 140 arrangements. Limited inclusion of folksongs and carols; excludes works intended exclusively for the Roman Catholic Church service. Gives composer/arranger, title, publisher and catalog number, number of vocal parts, grade of difficulty, approximate length, type of accompaniment, vocal range (lowest alto note to highest soprano note), and available editions. Six indices: (1) titles, (2) number of parts (SA, SSA, SSAA), (3) grade of difficulty (easy, medium, difficult), (4) works of extended length, (5) recommended collections, and (6) general index. Bibliography of 82 books, articles, and other items. List of publishers with addresses appended.

88. Guelker-Cone, Leslie. "Music for Women's Voices by Contemporary Women Composers of the United States and Canada." *Choral Journal*, 32–10 (May 1992), 31–40

Annotated list of 37 choral works. Level of difficulty ranges from simple two-part to complex works for numerous voices. Provides title, composer, performing forces, publisher, music number, text source, duration, level of difficulty, publication date, vocal ranges, and descriptive remarks.

89. Locke, Arthur Ware, and Charles K. Fassett. *Selected List of Choruses for Women's Voices.* 3d ed., rev. and enl. Northampton, Massachusetts: Smith College, 1964. xxiii, 253 p.   ML128.V7 L6 1964

Dated but useful. Previous editions in 1927 and 1946. Three sections: bibliography by composer, collections, and indices. The bibliography of over 4,000 titles by more than 350 composers restricted to works originally composed for treble or equal voices; with few exceptions, arrangements of folk songs omitted; unfortunately, many works composed for the Roman Catholic service are omitted because of their specialized nature. Bibliography arranged alphabetically by composer, giving composer's name and dates, title of composition, author of text, translator if applicable, voicing, accompaniment, duration, level of difficulty, and publisher with music number. Heavy use of abbreviations hampers usefulness (abbreviations explained in prefatory pages). Second section lists and annotates 18 collections of choruses for women, giving basic bibliographic information and full contents. Fewer abbreviations; much easier to use. Four indices: chronological list of composers; index of compositions by categories, including duration of compositions, compositions with accompaniment other than keyboard, and compositions with solos; index of authors and sources of texts; and index of first lines and titles.

90. Romza, Patricia-Andrea. "Female-Choir Music by French Composers: An Annotated Bibliography of Selected Works." D.M.A. dissertation. University of Georgia, Athens, 1997. vi, 207 p.

Prefaced by an overview of the history of French choral music. Annotated bibliography of 53 choral works for women's voices. Selected works range from the Renaissance to the present. Provides composer, title with English translation when appropriate, date of composition, movements, voicing, accompaniment, publisher and catalog number, ranges of voices, approximate difficulty, approximate length, manner in which score was obtained, textual information, sacred or secular designation, keywords, and annotation. As an appendix, Latin text with English translation of *Ave Maria, Ave verum corpus,* the feasts of Corpus Christi, *Laudate Dominum omnes gentes, Maria, Mater gratiæ,* the ordinary of the Mass, *O Salutaris, Pulchra es, Serve bone, Tantum ergo sacramentum, Tota pulchra es,* and *Veni Creator spiritus.* Musical examples; bibliography of 75 writings.

91. Thoburn, Crawford R. "Literature Forum: Christmas Music for Women's Voices." *Choral Journal*, 21–1 (Sept. 1980), 20–25

    Annotated bibliography of about 60 works. Four categories: (1) extended works or sets of pieces written originally for women's voices; (2) shorter works written originally for women; (3) works originally scored for mixed voices that have been arranged for women; and (4) works no longer in print or available in collected editions. Provides title, movements, composer, performing forces, publisher, music number, and descriptive remarks.

    See also: Case, James H. "A List of Contemporary American Choral Music for Women's Voices" (item 176, no. 43); English, Mary E. "A Select List of Music for Women's Voices" (item 176, no. 40); Kvam, Junrad. "A General List of Choral Music for Women's Voices" (item 176, no. 32); McChesney, Richard. "Music for Two-Part Women's Choir" (item 176, no. 89); Shenbeck, Lyn. "World Music for Treble Choirs" (item 176, no. 168); Spencer, Helen Stott. "A Selected List of Music for Junior and Senior High School Women's Choruses" (item 176, no. 50)

Choral Music with Dance

92. Tkach, Therees. "Literature Forum: Contemporary Choral Music with Dance and Movement." *Choral Journal*, 22–1 (Sept. 1981), 22–28

    Article in narrative form; cites many composers and titles of choral works incorporating dance and movement.

Choral Settings

Choral Settings of Hebrew Texts

93. Jacobson, Joshua R. "Literature Forum: A Selective List of Choral Music in Hebrew." *Choral Journal*, 22–1 (Sept. 1979), 13–16

    Annotated list of 33 nonliturgical and liturgical works. Almost all selections are 20th century. Gives title, composer/arranger, performing forces, publication information, source of text, duration, and brief comments.

94. Tischler, Alice. *A Descriptive Bibliography of Art Music by Israeli Composers*. Warren, Michigan: Harmonie Park Press, 1988. xxiii, 424 p. ISBN 0-89990-045-3   ML120.I75 T57 1988

    Annotated bibliography of approximately 3,200 musical works by 63 Israeli composers. Highly selective; limited to 20th-century works. Provides biographical sketch with sources, titles of compositions in English and Hebrew, performing forces, author and language of text, publication information, duration, location of score, performance information, discography, and notes. Four indices: (1) classification index, (2) author index, (3) transliterated Hebrew titles, and (4) multilingual titles. The classification index lists many choral works under the headings children's chorus, chorus, men's chorus, songs, and women's chorus. Series: *Detroit Studies in Music Bibliography*, no. 62.

Choral Settings of Poetry and Literature

95. Evans, May Garrettson. *Music and Edgar Allan Poe: A Bibliographical Study*. Baltimore: John Hopkins Press, 1939; reprint, New York: Greenwood Press, 1968. 97 p.   ML80.P65 E9

Specialized study of musical settings of Poe's texts. Needs to be updated. Contains annotated bibliography of musical settings, some of which are choral. Bibliography of 36 writings; no index.

96. Gooch, Bryan N. S., and David S. Thatcher. *Musical Settings of British Romantic Literature: A Catalogue*. Odean Long, editorial assistant. New York: Garland, 1982. 2 vols., lxxxiii, 1768 p. ISBN 0-8240-9381-X ML128.V7 G57 1982

Annotated bibliography of 12,907 musical settings of texts by British authors of the late 18th- and early 19th-century romantic period in literature. Entries arranged in alphabetical order by author, providing composer, title, publishing information, and performing forces. Lacks an index for subjects and for performing forces that would have been very beneficial. Three indices: authors, titles and first lines, and composers. Series: *Garland Reference Library of the Humanities*, vol. 326.

97. Gooch, Bryan N. S., and David S. Thatcher. *Musical Settings of Early and Mid-Victorian Literature: A Catalogue*. Odean Long, editorial assistant. New York: Garland, 1979. xxxvi, 946 p. ISBN 0-8240-9793-9 ML128.V7 G58

Annotated bibliography of nearly 6,000 musical settings of texts by British authors of the late 19th-century Victorian period in literature. Entries arranged in alphabetical order by author, providing composer, title, publishing information, and performing forces. Lacks an index for subjects and for performing forces that would have been very beneficial. Index of composers and of titles and first lines. Series: *Garland Reference Library of the Humanities*, vol. 149.

98. Gooch, Bryan N. S., and David S. Thatcher. *Musical Settings of Late Victorian and Modern British Literature: A Catalogue*. Odean Long, editorial

assistant. New York: Garland, 1976. xxiii, 1112 p. ISBN 0-8240-9981-8
ML128.V7 G59

Annotated bibliography of 7,728 musical settings of texts by British authors
of the late 19th-century Victorian period to the early 20th-century modern
period in literature. Entries arranged in alphabetical order by author, gives
date of composition, composer, title, publishing information, and performing forces. Lacks an index for subjects and for performing forces that would
have been very beneficial. Composer index. Series: *Garland Reference
Library of the Humanities*, vol. 31.

99. Gooch, Bryan N. S., and David S. Thatcher. *A Shakespeare Music Catalogue*. Odean Long, editorial assistant. Incorporating material collected and
contributed by Charles Haywood. Oxford: Clarendon Press, 1991. 5 vols.,
xcv, 2847 p. ISBN 0-19-812941-6 (vol. 1), ISBN 0-19-812942-4 (vol. 2),
ISBN 0-19-812943-2 (vol. 3), ISBN 0-19-812944-0 (vol. 4), ISBN 0-19-
812945-9 (vol. 5)   ML134.5.S52 G6 1991

Extensive, annotated bibliography of more than 21,000 musical settings of
the literary works of William Shakespeare. Entries arranged in alphabetical
order by title within five sections: (1) the plays; (2) the sonnets; (3) the
poems; (4) settings of commemorative pieces, apocryphal texts, etc.; and (5)
anthologies of Shakespeare music. Mostly instrumental music; includes
such vocal works as cantatas, choral symphonies and suites, motets, madrigals, glees, and part-songs. Provides composer, title, publication information or indicates manuscript, performing forces, first performance and
performers, and additional remarks as needed. Classified, annotated bibliography of 3,232 writings, comprising a single volume within the set.
Indices for bibliography of music: (1) Shakespeare's titles and lines; (2)
titles of musical works; (3) composers, arrangers, and editors; and (4) librettists and other writers. Indices for bibliography of writings: (1) Shakespeare's titles and (2) proper names.

100. Hovland, Michael A. *Musical Settings of American Poetry: A Bibliography*.
New York: Greenwood Press, 1986. xli, 531 p. ISBN 0-313-22938-4
ML128.V7 H67 1986

Annotated bibliography of 5,640 musical settings—art songs and choral
works—of American poetry. Entries arranged in alphabetical order by poet
and, typically, provides composer, title, publishing information, and performing forces. Unfortunately, lacks a suitable index for easily locating
choral works with various voicings and accompaniment. Index to composers and to titles of literary works. Series: *Music Reference Collection*,
no. 8.

101. Pollin, Burton Ralph. *Music for Shelley's Poetry: An Annotated Bibliography of Musical Settings of Shelley's Poetry*. New York: Da Capo Press, 1974. xxxiii, 175 p. ISBN 0-306-70640-7   ML80.S515 P6

Annotated bibliography of 1,309 musical settings of Shelley's poetry. Mostly songs; some are choral. Needs to be updated. Five separate indices: (1) composers, (2) poetry titles, (3) first lines of poetry, (4) chronological index of musical settings, and (5) languages used in the settings.

Choral Settings of Scriptures
102. Dovaras, John. *Choral Settings of the Scriptures with English Texts*. Dayton, Ohio: Roger Dean Publishing, 1988. ii, 62 p.   ML128.S2 D7 1988

Bibliography of approximately 3,000 choral works with English texts from the Old and New Testaments. Entries arranged in biblical order. Provides composer with dates, title, publisher, and additional notes when needed. Numerous cross references. Three appendices: (1) alphabetical listing of psalms in Latin, (2) numerical listing of psalms in Latin, and (3) English translations of 29 popular Latin texts, including *Ave Maria*, the Magnificat, and Te Deum. Composer index.

103. Wolverton, Vance D. "Literature Forum: Choral Settings of Psalm Twenty-Three in English: An Annotated Bibliography." *Choral Journal*, 35–9 (April 1995), 47–56; 35–10 (May 1995), 33–38

Annotated bibliography of English-language choral settings of Psalm 23. In two parts: (1) approximately 70 works for mixed voices, (2) nearly 40 for unison, treble, and men's voices. Each entry provides composer/arranger, title, performing forces, publisher, music number, estimated price, level of difficulty (easy to very difficult), and annotation.

See also: Herrema, Robert D. "Psalm Settings by 20th-Century Composers" (item 176, nos. 101/102, 104/105, 106/107, 109/110); Hutcheson, Robert J. "20th-Century Settings of the Passion: An Annotated Bibliography" (item 176, nos. 127, 129)

Choral Works with Instrumental Accompaniment

Electronic or Tape Accompaniment
104. Edwards, J. Michele. *Literature for Voices in Combination with Electronic and Tape Music: An Annotated Bibliography*. Ann Arbor, Michigan: Music Library Association, 1977. 194 p. ISBN 0-914954-09-1   ML128.E4 E37

Purpose: (1) "seeks to be a complete historical listing of compositions written for voices in combination with electronic and tape music . . . from earliest known works through 1975"; (2) bibliography "is a finding list of compositions currently available to performers." Cites 400 compositions, providing composer's full name, dates, and country of birth, title and date of composition, instrumentation, source or author of text, duration, notes about studio, audio information, technical equipment or personnel, publisher and/or availability of score and recordings, premiere performance, and bibliography of sources about the composition. Many works choral; also includes works for solo voice, instrumentalists who speak/sing, narrators, etc., all without choir. Limited to works for at least three live performers who sing or speak. Five appendices: publishers; nonpublisher score sources (alphabetical by country); foreign and hard-to-find record labels; studios (alphabetical by composer); and selected bibliography of sources, including 27 annotated books and articles and 40 recommended periodical titles. Expansive index by medium. Series: MLA *Index and Bibliography Series*, no. 17.

Guitar Accompaniment

105. Butts, David Leon. "Literature Forum: Twentieth Century Music for Chorus and Guitar." *Choral Journal*, 20–7 (March 1980), 29–32, 37

Annotated list of 21 choral works and collections. Criteria for selections: (1) 20th-century works and (2) composed guitar parts, rather than chord symbols or "ad lib." Includes works accompanied by guitar and works for guitar combined with other instruments. Entries provide title, composer, publisher, music number, performing forces, date, vocal ranges, and comments.

Harp Accompaniment

106. Archambo, Shelley Batt. "Choral Music with Harp Accompaniment." *Choral Journal*, 28–9 (April 1988), 23–27

List of almost 90 choral works with harp accompaniment. Includes accompaniment for harp combined with other instruments; excludes works for full orchestra containing harp with voices. Provides composer, title, performing forces, and distributor(s).

Chamber Ensemble Accompaniment

107. Bullock, William J. "Sacred Choral Works with Small Instrumental Ensemble: An Annotated List of Selected Twentieth-Century Works." New York: American Choral Foundation, 1982. 8 p.

Annotated bibliography of 20 sacred choral works accompanied by chamber ensembles of two to eight instruments. Gives composer, title with translation when appropriate, date of composition, occasion suitable for text, number of pages, duration, instrumental forces, and descriptive remarks. Series: *Research Memorandum/American Choral Foundation*, no. 134.

108. DeShera, Jan C. "Literature Forum: Choral Music Accompanied by Woodwinds: An Annotated List." *Choral Journal*, 33–7 (Feb. 1993), 39–46

Derived from the author's master's thesis. Classified, annotated list of 70
choral works with woodwind accompaniments, including woodwinds alone
or combined with horn, keyboard, or percussion. Provides composer/
arranger/transcriber/editor, title, performing forces, language of text, level
of difficulty (easy, medium, difficult), duration (occasionally), publisher,
music number, and annotation. Classified as follows: Renaissance, baroque,
classical, romantic, 20th-century sacred, 20th-century secular, and folk song
and carol arrangements. Bibliography of 13 writings from which the list
was derived.

109. Rasmussen, Mary. "A Bibliography of Choral Music with Horn Ensemble
Accompaniment, as Compiled from Eleven Selected Sources." *Brass Quarterly*, 5 (Summer 1962), 153–159

Bibliography of approximately 130 compositions. Provides composer with
dates, title, publication information (when applicable), voicing/scoring, and
source for citation.

110. Rasmussen, Mary. "A Bibliography of Choral Music with Trombone
Ensemble Accompaniment, as Compiled from Eleven Selected Sources."
Brass Quarterly, 5 (Spring 1962), 109–113

Bibliography of approximately 75 compositions. Provides composer with
dates, title, publication information (when applicable), voicing/scoring, and
source for citation.

111. Rasmussen, Mary. "A Bibliography of 19th- and 20th-Century Music for
Male Voices with Wind- or Brass-Ensemble Accompaniment." *Brass Quarterly*, 7 (Winter 1963), 67–77; 7 (Spring 1964), 124–132

Bibliography of more than 400 compositions. Provides composer with
dates, title, date of composition, publication information (when applicable),
voicing/scoring, and source for citation.

112. Rasmussen, Mary. "A Bibliography of 19th- and 20th-Century Music for
Mixed Voices with Wind- or Brass-Ensemble Accompaniment." *Brass
Quarterly*, 6 (Spring 1963), 120–130; 6 (Summer 1963), 179–186; 7 (Fall
1963), 34–44

Bibliography of approximately 600 compositions. Provides composer with
dates, title, publication information (when applicable), voicing/scoring, and
source for citation.

113. Vagner, Robert. "A Selective List of Choral and Vocal Music with Wind and Percussion Accompaniments." *Journal of Research in Music Education*, 14 (Winter 1966), 276–288.

     Vagner, Robert. *A Selective List of Choral and Vocal Music with Wind and Percussion Accompaniments*. S.l.: s.n., 1966. 13 p.

     Classified bibliography of some 200 choral and vocal works with wind and percussion accompaniments. Categories: mixed chorus and instrumental ensemble; mixed voices and a single obbligato instrument; treble or male voices with a single obbligato instrument; men's chorus with instrumental ensemble; women's chorus with instrumental ensemble; solo voice with ensemble; solo voices with flute and keyboard; solo voice with clarinet and keyboard; solo voice with oboe and keyboard; solo voice with horn and keyboard; published settings for children's voices; solo cantatas of Georg Philipp Telemann; and works of J. S. Bach. Information given includes composer with dates, title, publisher, and voicing/scoring.

114. Yoder, David Winston. "A Study and Performance of Extended Sacred Choral Works with Brass Instruments by Contemporary American Composers." D.M.A dissertation. University of Southern California, Los Angeles, 1973. vi, 226 p.

     Traces historical precedents of the use of brass ensembles in church services and presents analysis of six works: Randall Thompson's *A Feast of Praise*, Daniel Pinkham's *Christmas Cantata*, Ron Nelson's *The Christmas Story*, Fred Prentice's *The Day of Resurrection*, Halsey Stevens's *Te Deum*, and Norman Dello Joio's *Mass*. Musical examples and illustrations; bibliography of about 120 writings; bibliography of 41 choral works with brass.

     See also: Peress, Maurice. "A Selective List of Music for Voices and Brass Instruments" (item 176, no. 12); Whitwell, David. "Music for Voices and Brass Ensemble" (item 176, no. 53); Whitwell, David. "Music for Voices and Mixed Wind Ensembles" (item 176, no. 61); Whitwell, David. "Music for Voices and Trumpets; Music for Voices and Trombones; Music for Voices and Horns" (item 176, no. 56); Whitwell, David. "Music for Voices and Woodwind Instruments" (item 176, no. 64)

Orchestral Accompaniment

115. André, Don A. "Literature Forum: Orchestra and Chorus: Works for the Amateur or High School Performing Group." *Choral Journal*, 21–9 (May 1981), 50–56

Annotated list of 25 sacred and 6 secular works. Gives composer, title, performing forces, publication information, and duration.

116. Green, Jonathan D. *A Conductor's Guide to Choral-Orchestral Works.* Metuchen, New Jersey: Scarecrow Press, 1994. xiv, 307 p. ISBN 0-8108-2712-3   ML128.C48 G7 1994

Electronic Version: Boulder, Colorado: NetLibrary, 1999. URL: http://www.netLibrary.com/urlapi.asp?action=summary&v=1&bookid=3166

Green, Jonathan D. *A Conductor's Guide to Choral-Orchestral Works, Twentieth Century, Part II: The Music of Rachmaninov through Penderecki.* Lanham, Maryland: Scarecrow Press, 1998. xii, 300 p. ISBN 0-8108-3376-X   ML128.C48 G71 1998

Electronic version: Boulder, Colorado: NetLibrary, 1999. URL: http://www.netLibrary.com/urlapi.asp?action=summary&v=1&bookid=3165

Revision of the author's dissertation, "A Conductor's Guide to Twentieth-Century Choral-Orchestral Works in English" (1992). Part I: Annotated bibliography of 90 large-scale works for chorus and orchestra by 49 composers. Works chosen for inclusion are scored for mixed chorus and orchestra (containing a string section), contain some English text, are no less than 15 minutes in length, were composed between 1900 and 1972, and had performance materials commercially available at the time of publication. A biographical sketch is provided for each composer, along with a list of principal compositions and selected writings about the composer. Each annotated composition addresses duration, text source, performing forces, date of first performance, available editions, location of manuscript, performance issues, and relevant notes about the composition. A discography is provided for each work from the date of composition to 1993 along with additional readings about the composition. General bibliography of more than 80 writings.

Part II has similar format as previous volume. Includes 89 compositions by 31 composers. Includes shorter works and works that utilize nontraditional orchestras. Subtitle somewhat of a misnomer since the volume does not cover more recent composers than the previous volume.

Each volume includes a general bibliography of approximately 80 writings and two appendices: (1) sources, authors, and translators of texts; (2) music publishers and distributors. Each volume also published as an e-book. Mode of access: World Wide Web. Access may be limited to NetLibrary-affiliated libraries.

117. Rayl, David. "Literature Forum: Thinking Small: Choral-Orchestral Works for the Small Choir with a Small Budget." *Choral Journal*, 34–8 (March 1994), 43–52

Annotated bibliography of 73 choral works accompanied by small orchestra (usually strings and a few winds). Appropriate for high school choir. Entries grouped by style period (baroque to 20th century). Gives composer, title, performing forces, publisher, music number, and descriptive remarks.

See also: Rao, Doreen. "Selected Repertoire for Children's Chorus and Orchestra" (Item 176, no. 142)

Multicultural Music

118. Kean, Ronald M. "Literature Forum: Multicultural and Ethnically Inspired Choral Music: An Annotated List." *Choral Journal*, 33–10 (May 1993), 45–54

Classified, annotated list of approximately 50 non-Western choral works. Provides composer/arranger/editor, title, performing forces, language of text, duration, level of difficulty (easy, moderate, difficult), publisher, music number, and annotation. Classified by geographic area and includes sections on African-American gospel and Jewish music.

See also: Shenbeck, Lyn. "World Music for Treble Choirs" (item 176, no. 168); Tiemstra, Suzanne Spicer. "Anthologies, Collections, and Series of Latin American Choral Music" (item 176, no. 170)

Operas, Operettas, and Musical Shows

119. DeVenney, David P., and Craig R. Johnson. *The Chorus in Opera: A Guide to the Repertory*. Metuchen, New Jersey: Scarecrow Press, 1993. xv, 203 p. ISBN 0-8108-2620-8   ML128.C48 D47 1993

Annotated bibliography of nearly 600 opera choruses. Intentions: "to add to the body of choral repertory, and not necessarily to annotate opera scenes that make extensive use of chorus." Selection drawn from *Kobbé's Complete Opera Book* (1987). Citations include composer, title of opera, date of composition, librettist(s), publisher(s), act, scene, number, title or first line of text, performing forces, duration, level of difficulty (easy, medium, moderately difficult, and difficult), description of scene, and other notes as needed. Appended is a brief list of operas surveyed, but not annotated (operas without chorus or no excerptable chorus, scores unavailable for examination, and works not considered by the authors to be operas). Six indices: (1) titles of operas, (2) first lines and titles of scenes, (3) librettists, (4) choral performing forces, (5) difficulty level of excerpts, and (6) duration of excerpts.

120. Engel, Lehman. "A Select List of Choral Music from Operas, Operettas, and Musical Shows." New York: American Choral Foundation, 1963. 8 p.

   Classified, briefly annotated bibliography of more than 80 choral works. Provides composer, title and section, voicing, level (high school or college), publishers, and language. Directory of publishers appended. Series: *Research Memorandum Series*, no. 41.

121. Tiboris, Peter, and John Turner. "Literature Forum: Treasures for the Choral Program: The Opera Chorus." *Choral Journal*, 24–3 (Nov. 1983), 23–27

   Annotated list of 19 opera choruses "which could be adapted for concert use." Cites composer, chorus title, act and scene numbering, publisher of score being analyzed, page numbers, voicing, difficulty level (very easy to very difficult), accompaniment, solo parts, recommended translation, and comments. Works arranged in chronological order, from Henry Purcell to Aaron Copland.

Sacred Choral Music

General Works

122. Cornelius, Jeffrey M. "Literature Forum: The Classic Period: Accessible Repertoire for the Church Choir." *Choral Journal*, 22–3 (Nov. 1981), 13–18

   Article in narrative form; comments on works appropriate for church choir by Joseph Haydn and W. A. Mozart. Bibliography of nine writings.

123. Dupere, George Henry. "Sacred Choral Repertoire for Mixed Voices: A Recommended Listing." *Choral Journal*, 32–3 (Oct. 1991), 25–37

   Annotated list of about 280 choral works "appropriate for use in a variety of church situations." Criteria for selection: (1) SATB to SATB-divisi, (2) unaccompanied or keyboard accompaniment, and (3) no more than moderate difficulty. Provides title, composer, publisher, music number, subject (i.e., Christmas, general, praise, communion, etc.), and brief comments.

124. Eslinger, Gary S., and F. Mark Daugherty, eds. *Sacred Choral Music in Print*. 2nd ed. Philadelphia: Musicdata, 1985. 2 vols., xiii, 1322 p. ISBN 0-88478-017-1   ML128.V7 E78 1985

   Updates volume 1 of *Choral Music in Print* (1974), edited by Thomas R. Nardone, James H. Nye, and Mark Resnick; *Choral Music in Print: 1976 Supplement*, edited by Thomas R. Nardone; *Sacred Choral Music in Print: 1981 Supplement*, edited by Nancy K. Nardone; and *Music in Print Annual Supplement* (1982–1984). Bibliography of all sacred choral music in print organized alphabetically by composer. Updated by 1988 and 1992 supplements. International in scope, though works published in the United States, Canada, and Western Europe are emphasized. Each entry provides composer, title, voicing, accompaniment, remarks, and pricing information (U. S. dollars). Heavily cross-referenced. Directory of publishers with addresses, noting distributors. Separately published arranger index and master index (composer and title). Series: *Music-in-Print Series*, vol. 1.

Sacred Choral Music in Print, Second Edition: Arranger Index. Philadelphia: Musicdata, 1987. iii, 137 p. ISBN 0-88478-019-8   ML128.V7 E7837 1987

Arranger index lists in alphabetical order all arrangers cited in *Sacred Choral Music in Print* (1985), edited by Gary S. Eslinger and F. Mark Daugherty. Series: *Music-in-Print Series*, vol. 1c.

Simon, Susan H., ed. *Sacred Choral Music in Print: 1988 Supplement.* Philadelphia: Musicdata, 1988. xiii, 277 p. ISBN 0-88478-022-8 ML128.V7 E78 Suppl.

1988 supplement to *Sacred Choral Music in Print* (1985), edited by Gary S. Eslinger and F. Mark Daugherty. Includes arranger index and directory of publishers with addresses, noting distributors. Series: *Music-in-Print Series*, vol. 1s.

Daugherty, F. Mark, and Susan H. Simon, eds. *Sacred Choral Music in Print: 1992 Supplement.* Philadelphia: Musicdata, 1992. xiii, 304 p. ISBN 0-88478-029-5   ML128.V7 E78 1985 Suppl. 2

1992 supplement to *Sacred Choral Music in Print* (1985), edited by Gary S. Eslinger and F. Mark Daugherty. Includes arranger index and directory of publishers with addresses, noting distributors. Series: *Music-in-Print Series*, vol. 1t.

Sacred Choral Music in Print: Master Index 1992. Philadelphia: Musicdata, 1992. vi, 413 p. ISBN 0-88478-030-9   ML128.V7 S2 1992

Composer and title index for *Sacred Choral Music in Print* (1985), edited by Gary S. Eslinger and F. Mark Daugherty, the 1988 supplement edited by Susan H. Simon, and the 1992 supplement edited by F. Mark Daugherty and Susan H. Simon. Series: *Music-in-Print Series*, vol. 1x.

The Sacred Choral Sourcebook. Philadelphia: Musicdata, 1997. v, 467 p. ISBN 0-88478-046-5   ML128.V7 S23 1997

Derived from *Sacred Choral Music in Print* (1985) and its supplements (1988, 1992, 1996). Organized in two parts: composer listings and title listings. Information is minimal; provides composers, main titles of works, and publishers of editions. Publisher directory. Series: *Music-in-Print Series.*

125. Espina, Noni. *Vocal Solos for Christian Churches: A Descriptive Reference of Solo Music for the Church Year Including a Bibliographical Supplement of Choral Works*. 3d ed. Metuchen, New Jersey: Scarecrow Press, 1984. xiii, 241 p. ISBN 0-8108-1730-6   ML128.V7 E8 1984

Revision of second edition entitled *Vocal Solos for Protestant Services* (1974). Contents primarily dedicated to solo vocal music; also includes selected bibliography of almost 150 oratorios, Masses, Passions, cantatas, and extended anthems by 57 composers scored for solo voices and choir with or without accompaniment. Gives composer, title, scoring, language of text, and publisher. Three indices: occasions, music for solo voices, and titles.

126. Geck, Martin. *Deutsche Oratorien 1800 bis 1840: Verzeichnis der Quellen und Aufführungen* [German oratorios, 1800–1840: A catalogue of sources and performances]. Wilhelmshaven, Germany: Heinrichshofen, 1971. 105 p. ISBN 3-7959-0091-3   ML128.045 G43

German only. Three sections: (1) bibliography of approximately 350 oratorios with German text arranged in alphabetical order by composer; (2) list of premier and/or significant performances arranged by the names of German cities; and (3) list of performances arranged by year. Bibliography provides composer, title, date of composition, source of text, information about performances, and sources for the information. Series: *Quellen-Kataloge zur Musikgeschichte*, no. 4.

127. Jothen, Michael Jon. "Literature Forum: Choral Music for SAB Church Choirs." *Choral Journal*, 22–9 (May 1980), 43–51; 21–1 (Sept. 1980), 34–35

Annotated bibliography of 19 anthems, 18 arrangements, 10 extended works, and 11 collections for SAB or SSAB church choirs. Provides composer, title, publisher, language of text, duration, level of difficulty (easy to advanced), and comments.

128. Laster, James. *Catalogue of Choral Music Arranged in Biblical Order*. 2nd ed. Landham, Maryland: Scarecrow Press, 1996. vi, 711 p. ISBN 0-8108-3071-X   ML128.C54 L4 1996

Bibliography of more than 7,000 choral works arranged in biblical order. Divided into three main sections: Old Testament, the Apocrypha, and New Testament. Majority of the works are choral octavos. Extended works, with few exceptions, are excluded. Offers little in regard to Anglican Service music. Gives King James biblical reference: book, chapter, verse(s); additional scripture used, or author of paraphrased text, or translator; composer, arranger, or editor; title; voicing, solos, and accompaniment; and publication information. Cross-references texts from other biblical locations. Expansive composer and title indices.

129. Shafferman, Jean Anne. "Music for the Small Church Choir." *Choral Journal*, 31–4 (Nov. 1990), 19–24

Annotated bibliography of 114 octavos and four collections, arranged by voicing (SATB, SAB, two-part, unison). Up to 15 adult singers is considered a small church choir. Entries provide title, composer/arranger/lyricist, performing forces (majority for keyboard accompaniment), publisher and distributor, music number, price, and annotation.

130. Valentin, Erich. *Handbuch der Chormusik*. Rev. ed. Regensburg: Gustav Bosse, 1984. 2 vols.   ML128.V7 V3 1984

Unavailable for examination; annotation based on 1968 edition. German only. Immense, classified, annotated bibliography of choral music. Accompanied by critical commentary. Provides Latin text of the Mass, Requiem, Stabat Mater, Te Deum, *Ave Maria*, Magnificat, *Ave verum corpus*, Hymnus, and *Tenebrae factae sunt* with German translation and German text of *Herr Gott, dich loben wir* and *Grosser Gott*. Glossary of terms; discography; musical examples and illustrations; index of composers and titles.

See also: Bullock, William J. "Sacred Choral Works with Small Instrumental Ensemble: An Annotated List of Selected Twentieth-Century Works" (item 107); Collins, Walter S. "A Selected List of Renaissance and Baroque Choral Works with Sacred English Texts in Practical Editions" (item 176, no. 22); Dovaras, John. *Choral Settings of the Scriptures with English Texts* (item 102); Garcia, William Burres. "Church Music by Black Composers: A Bibliography of Choral Music" (item 155); Goucher, Louise Rogers. "Motets and Chorales of the Renaissance and Baroque Periods Written for Lent and Easter" (item 176, no. 62); Goucher, Louise Rogers. "Motets, Carols, and Chorales Suitable for the Christmas Season" (item 176, no. 51); Hayes, Morris D. "A Selected List of Sacred Music for Men's Voices" (item 176, no. 81); "A Selective List of 20th-Century English Church Music, Part I" (item 176, no. 108); Simmons, Morgan F. "Selected Lists of Sacred Choral Music" (item 176, no. 34); Somary, Johannes F. "A Selective List of Choral Music for Christmas" (item 176, nos. 17, 78); Thoburn, Crawford R. "Literature Forum: Christmas Music for Women's Voices" (item 91); Wolverton, Vance D. "Literature Forum: Choral Settings of Psalm Twenty-Three in English: An Annotated Bibliography" (item 103)

Jewish Synagogue Music
    See: Adler, Samuel. "A List of Music for American Synagogues" (item 176,
    no. 49); Galloway, Lane. "Jewish Choral Music for Concert Performance"
    (item 176, no. 158); Lindsley, Charles Edward. "Early Nineteenth-Century
    American Collections of Sacred Choral Music, 1800–1810" (item 153);
    Stevenson, Robert Murrell. "The English Service: A Bibliography of Edi-
    tions and Literature" (item 176, no. 44)

Protestant Church Music
131. Britton, Allen Perdue, Irving Lowens, and Richard Crawford. *American
    Sacred Music Imprints, 1698–1810: A Bibliography*. Worcester: American
    Antiquarian Society, 1990. xvi, 798 p. ISBN 0-912296-95-X   ML128.H8
    B68 1989

    Extensive, annotated bibliography of sacred music, mostly tunebooks,
    printed in the British-American colonies and United States between 1698
    and 1810. For each main item, provides transcription of title page. For each
    specific item, gives pagination, page size, method of printing, date of publi-
    cation, and other relevant notes. When applicable or known, gives identifi-
    cation of engraved plates, notes about the music, attributions of composers
    and sources, first printings, origin of the music (American or non-Ameri-
    can), the number of "Core Repertory" pieces (the 101 sacred compositions
    most frequently printed in America during the cited period) in each book,
    citations of works found in important bibliographies, location of copies, and
    additional notes, including cross references, as warranted. Describes con-
    tents of each according to its main divisions. Includes compilers's prefatory
    statements (often quoted in part), which includes the compilers's advertise-
    ments, endorsements, forewords, introductions, and prefaces. Five appen-
    dices: (1) chronological list of imprints; (2) sacred sheet music, 1790–1810;
    (3) list of composers and sources; (4) the "Core Repertory"; and (5) geo-
    graphical directory of engravers, printers, publishers, and booksellers. Two
    expansive indices: (1) prefatory statements and (2) general index.

132. Bullock, William J. *Bach Cantatas Requiring Limited Resources: A Guide
    to Editions*. Lanham, Maryland: University Press of America, 1984. viii, 49
    p. ISBN 0-8191-3863-0   ML134.B1 B9 1984

    Annotated list of available editions of 47 church cantatas by J. S. Bach "that
    choral organizations of limited means would usually seek to perform." Criteria
    for selection: (1) cantatas that include at least one choral number other than
    "customary" concluding chorale and (2) cantatas that require no more than a
    string ensemble plus two woodwind instruments, not excluding those works
    that employ additional instruments that merely double other parts. Entries

provide German title with English translation, date of composition, occasion for which cantata was composed, number of pages of the *Bachgesellschaft* edition, and duration. Also provides information about language, instrumentation, voicing, and available editions. Lists publishers with addresses. Three indices: (1) title, (2) solo voice requirements, and (3) occasion.

133. Dykes Bower, John, and Allan Wicks. *A Repertory of English Cathedral Anthems.* London: Church Music Society/Oxford University Press, 1965. 35 p.   ML128.S2 B67

    Classified list (anthems for the seasons of the church's year, saints's days and red letter days, dedication festival, missions, evening, holy communion, funerals and memorial services, weddings, the queen's accession, harvest, hospitals, and general) of approximately 575 anthems by English composers. Gives composer (with dates), title, publishers, series, and page numbers, where applicable. No index.

134. Evans, Margaret R. *Sacred Cantatas: An Annotated Bibliography, 1960–1979.* Jefferson, North Carolina: McFarland, 1982. xviii, 188 p. ISBN 0-89950-044-7   ML128.C15 E9 1982

    Three main divisions: brief history of the sacred cantata, bibliography, and indices. History subdivided into two parts, 1900–1960 and 1960–1979, limited to cantatas in England and America; bibliography of 16 books and journal articles. Bibliography of more than 400 sacred cantatas. Criteria for inclusion: work or edition written for SATB choir, with occasional sectional divisions and occasional soloists; English text or English translation; copyrighted after 1959 and before 1980; 7 to 30 minutes duration; text appropriate for use in a Protestant worship service. Excludes settings of traditional Mass text and new editions of cantatas by J. S. Bach. Entries provide names of composer, titles of works, description of required forces, publisher, selling agent, place, publisher's number, copyright date, approximate performance time, availability of scores and parts, source of text, plan of the work, vocal ranges, and other descriptive notes; includes journal reviews, listings of works in periodicals and journals, and recordings; comments included on stylistic characteristics and level of difficulty. Three indices: title index; main index of composers, giving title, level of difficulty, appropriate church-year season, and soloists if required; special occasions index, which lists cantatas appropriate for specific days or occasions, excluding Christmas and Easter (included in the main index).

135. Protestant Episcopal Church in the U. S. A. Joint Commission on Church Music. *Music for Church Weddings.* New York: H. W. Gray, 1963. 12 p. ML128.W4 P7

Pamphlet that is dated but still useful. Suitable in any Christian church. Recommends about 30 hymns and 30 choral works appropriate for church weddings. No secular works. Also lists organ works and vocal solos and duets. Entries give composer, title, and publisher. Concludes with a dated list of publishers with addresses; no index.

136. Protestant Episcopal Church in the U. S. A. Joint Commission on Church Music. *Music for Funerals.* New York: H. W. Gray, 1963. 12 p. ML128.C54 P73

    Pamphlet for amateur church musicians. Dated but still useful in any Christian church. Recommends about 10 hymns in addition to those designated as "For the Departed" and 35 anthems appropriate for funeral and memorial services. Also lists organ works and vocal solos and duets. Composer, title, and publisher listed for each work. Dated list of publishers with addresses. No index.

137. Protestant Episcopal Church in the U. S. A. Joint Commission on Church Music. *Service Music and Anthems: For the Nonprofessional Choir.* New York: H. W. Gray, 1963. 54 p.   ML128.P7 P75 1963

    Pamphlet for amateur church musicians. Dated but still useful in any Christian church. Recommends approximately 170 works for service, 525 anthems, and 15 collections. Works classified by "The Holy Communion," "Morning Prayer," "Evening Prayer," and by liturgical year. Composer, title, and publisher listed for each work. Dated list of publishers with addresses; no index.

138. Steere, Dwight. *Music for the Protestant Church Choir: A Descriptive and Classified List of Worship Material.* Richmond, Virginia: John Knox Press, 1955. ix, 229 p.   ML128.V7 S84

    Annotated bibliography of 644 choral works. Criteria for selection limited to works for the Protestant worship service and works for mixed chorus, excluding mixed quartets and works for men's voices and women's voices. Bibliography, now quite dated, divided into four classifications: standard list, a cappella standard list, current list, and a cappella current list. Basic bibliographic information included for each work with brief annotation. Four helpful indices: topical index of the church year; first lines; composers, arrangers, musical sources; and authors, translators, textual sources.

139. Walker, Diane Parr, and Paul Walker. *German Sacred Polyphonic Vocal Music between Schütz and Bach: Sources and Critical Editions.* Warren,

Michigan: Harmonie Park Press, 1992. vii, 434 p. ISBN 0-89990-054-2
ML128.S2 W34 1992

Bibliography of "all extant German sacred music for three or more voices"
from 1648 to about 1700. Contains 6,000 entries from manuscripts and published works, including music from Austria, Switzerland, and German-
speaking parts of Eastern Europe. Includes music of foreign-born
composers who spent their careers in German-speaking countries. Excludes
music of Heinrich Schütz, Johann Kuhnau, and Johann Joseph Fux (major
compositional activity dates before 1648 or after 1700). No attempt to dis-
tinguish works for soloists from works for choral performance. Entries list
composer, title, performing forces, liturgical occasion, source location,
number in *Repertoire International des Sources Musicales* (RISM) and/or
Wolfgang Reich's *Threnodiae sacrae: Katalog der gedruckten Kompositio-
nen des 16.–18. Jahrhunderts in Leichenpredigsammlungen innerhalb der
Deutschen Demokratischen Republik* (1966), format (score and/or parts),
availability on microfilm, modern editions, and appropriate additional
notes. Four indices: title and first lines, performing forces (based on the
number of voices and ranges), liturgical occasions, and manuscript sources.
Series: *Detroit Studies in Music Bibliography*, no. 67.

See also: Dakers, Lionel. *Making Church Music Work* (item 233);
Kroeger, Karl. *American Fuging-Tunes, 1770–1820: A Descriptive Catalog* (item 152)

Roman Catholic Church Music

140. Kirsch, Winfried. *Die Quellen der mehrstimmigen Magnificat- und Te
Deum-Vertonungen bis zur Mitte des 16. Jahrhunderts* [The sources of the
polyphonic Magnificat and Te Deum settings up to the middle of the 16th
century]. Tutzing, Germany: Hans Schneider, 1966. 588 p. ML128.M3 K6

German only. Annotated bibliography of 950 Magnificats and 65 Te Deums
composed before 1550, thus excluding the works of Giovanni Pierluigi da
Palestrina and Orlando di Lasso and English-language Magnificats.
Includes instrumental and vocal works. Lengthy introductory essay. Bibliography organized into four sections: (1) chronological list of manuscripts
and prints; (2) alphabetical list of manuscripts and prints with relevant
pieces cited and secondary literature noted; (3) works organized by composer; and (4) thematic catalog with melodic incipit of vocal Magnificats
and Te Deums, omitting instrumental works. Bibliography of almost 300
books and articles.

141. Maggs, John Anderson. "Literature Forum: Original Settings of the Ordinary for Choir and Organ." *Choral Journal*, 23–9 (May 1983), 11–16

Annotated bibliography of 11 works. Shorter Masses. Gives composer, title, publishing information, performing forces, language of text, duration, movements, and comments.

142. Ward, Tom R. *The Polyphonic Office Hymn, 1400–1520: A Descriptive Catalogue.* S.l.: American Institute of Musicology; Neuhausen-Stuttgart, Germany: Hänssler, 1980. 315 p   ML169.8 .R46 no.3

Annotated bibliography of more than 755 polyphonic settings of Office hymns found in manuscripts between 1400 and 1520. Arranged alphabetically by first stanza. Gives incipit, sources, remarks, and editions. Four indices: (1) alphabetical listing of texts with cross references, (2) cantus firmi used, (3) alphabetical listing by composer (few are attributed works), and (4) alphabetical listing according to sigla of all sources. Two tables: hymns of the Italian tradition and hymns of the German tradition. Series: *Renaissance Manuscript Studies*, no. 3.

See also: Davis, Oma Grier. "A Selected, Annotated Bibliography of Te Deums in the Library of Congress, and a History of This Hymn in Ceremonial Music since 1600" (item 446); DeVenney, David P. *American Masses and Requiems: A Descriptive Guide* (item 144); Mac Intyre, Bruce C. *The Viennese Concerted Mass of the Early Classic Period* (item 418)

United States

General Works

143. DeVenney, David P. *American Choral Music since 1920: An Annotated Guide.* Berkeley, California: Fallen Leaf Press, 1993. xviii, 278 p. ISBN 0-914913-28-X   ML128.C48 D45 1993

Completes DeVenney's four-volume bibliographic survey of this repertory. Annotated bibliography of almost 2,000 choral works by 76 composers active in the United States between 1920 and 1993, along with an annotated bibliography of more than 200 selected writings. With few exceptions, excludes hymns, folk songs and spirituals, works written specifically for stage, choruses published separately from larger works, works written for an ensemble of solo voices rather than choral ensemble, and arrangements other than those made by the composer. Information given, when applicable and known, includes composer, title, opus number, date of composition or copyright, author or source of text, duration, publisher, and location of manuscript. Entries in bibliography of music are cross-referenced to bibliography of selected writings. Five indices: titles, authors and sources of texts, performing forces, durations, and an expansive index to the bibliography of selected writings. Series: *Fallen Leaf Reference Books in Music*, no. 27.

144. DeVenney, David P. *American Masses and Requiems: A Descriptive Guide.* Berkeley, California: Fallen Leaf Press, 1990. xvii, 210 p. ISBN 0-914913-14-X   ML128.C2 D4 1990

Annotated bibliography of over 1,000 Catholic Masses, Requiems, and individual Mass movements by composers active in the United States between 1776 and 1990, with an annotated bibliography of almost 150 writings on American Masses and Requiems. Bibliography of music divided into two parts: (1) 28 significant American Masses and Requiems and (2) 935 other Masses and Requiems. As applicable, includes composer, title, date of composition, performing forces, duration, textual notes, movements, publishing information and/or location of manuscript, commissioning agent, and cross references to relevant citations in the bibliography of writings. Some reviews of compositions are cited. Eight indices; most are expansive. Separate indices for men's voices, women's voices, children's voices, and unison voices. Also, indices for Requiem settings, titles, nonliturgical texts and authors, and the bibliography of writings. Series: *Fallen Leaf Reference Books in Music*, no. 15.

145. DeVenney, David P. *Early American Choral Music: An Annotated Guide.* Berkeley, California: Fallen Leaf Press, 1988. xx, 149 p. ISBN 0-914913-09-3   ML128.V7 D43 1988

Annotated guide to American choral music from 1670 to 1825. Three main sections: bibliography of music, bibliography of writings, and indices. Bibliography of music contains known choral works by 32 composers, giving opus number, date of composition, performing forces, author of text, duration of work if over 10 minutes, published editions, name of collection, and location of composer's manuscript. Bibliography of 127 writings. Six indices: (1) compositions by genre (extended works for mixed voices; other works for mixed voices; and works for men's and women's voices); (2) sacred works; (3) secular works; (4) titles; (5) texts, authors, translators; and (6) an expansive index to the bibliography of writings. Series: *Fallen Leaf Reference Books in Music*, no. 10.

146. DeVenney, David P. *Nineteenth-Century American Choral Music.* Berkeley, California: Fallen Leaf Press, 1987. xxi, 182 p. ISBN 0-914913-08-5 ML128.C48 D48 1987

Major research tool on 19th-century American choral music. Three main sections: bibliography of music, bibliography of writings, and indices. Annotated bibliography of music contains almost 1,300 choral works written by composers active in the United States during the 19th century and through World War I. Composers who primarily wrote popular music

excluded. Also excluded: stage works, hymns, hymn tunes, melodies borrowed from folk tunes, arrangements of other composers's works, separately published choruses, choruses intended for didactic purposes, and
songs with optional choral endings or refrains. Entries provide, if known,
opus number, date of composition, performing forces, author of text, duration, published editions, and location of the manuscript. Lacks qualitative
remarks. Entries conclude with cross references to articles in the bibliography of writings. Annotated bibliography of over 130 writings that present
historical, theoretical, and analytical examinations of the works or performance practice and interpretation of the composers's music. Ten indices:
five indices of compositions organized by genre and voicing; sacred works;
secular works; titles; authors and translators; and index to the bibliography
of writings. Series: *Fallen Leaf Reference Books in Music*, no. 8.

147. Dox, Thurston J. *American Oratorios and Cantatas: A Catalog of Works
Written in the United States from Colonial Times to 1985.* Metuchen, New
Jersey: Scarecrow Press, 1986. 2 vols., 1330 p. ISBN 0-8108-1861-2
ML128.O45 D7 1986

Excellent annotated bibliography of over 3,450 oratorios and cantatas composed in the United States by more than 1,000 composers. Spans more than
200 years from colonial times to 1985. Grouped into four categories: oratorio, choral cantata, ensemble cantata, and choral theater. Information given,
if known, includes title; publishing information; date of composition; termi-
nological designation; required vocal and instrumental forces; characters
designated in the work; source of text; approximate performing time; length
in pages; number of parts, sections, acts, or movements; location of published score or manuscript; Online Computer Library Center (OCLC) number; date and place of first performance; and reviews of premiere or later
performances. Title, author, and topical indices.

148. Eagon, Angelo. *Catalog of Published Concert Music by American Composers.* 2nd ed. Metuchen, New Jersey: Scarecrow Press, 1969. viii, 348 p.
SBN 8108-0175-2   ML120.U5 E23 1969

Eagon, Angelo. *Catalog of Published Concert Music by American Composers: Supplement to the Second Edition.* Metuchen, New Jersey: Scarecrow Press, 1971. viii, 150 p. ISBN 0-8108-0387-9   ML120.U5 E23 1969
Suppl.

Eagon, Angelo. *Catalog of Published Concert Music by American Composers: Second Supplement to the Second Edition.* Metuchen, New Jersey:
Scarecrow Press, 1974. viii, 148 p. ISBN 0-8108-0728-9   ML120.U5 E23
1969 Suppl. 2

Annotated catalog of concert music by American composers. Originally intended to list works available for purchase; now dated. Organized by medium; includes many works for mixed, women's, and men's voices. Two supplements provide additional titles. Each volume includes addresses for publishers and author and composer indices.

149. Fuld, James J., and Mary Wallace Davidson. *18th-Century American Secular Music Manuscripts: An Inventory*. Philadelphia: Music Library Association, 1980. xiii, 225 p. ISBN 0-914954-16-4   ML120.U5 F93

    Annotated bibliography of 85 18th-century American secular musical manuscripts. The manuscripts, held by 20 libraries and private individuals, comprised approximately half of the located secular manuscripts known at time of publication. Expansive index. Series: *MLA Index and Bibliography Series*, no. 20.

150. Heintze, James R. *American Music before 1865 in Print and on Records: A Biblio-Discography*. Preface by H. Wiley Hitchcock. Rev. ed. Brooklyn: Institute for Studies in American Music, Conservatory of Music, Brooklyn College of the City University of New York, 1990. xiii, 148 p. ISBN 0-914678-33-7   ML120.U5 H458 1990

    Listing of pre-1865 American music "in-print" at the time of the publication of this resource. Based on the collections of The American University, the Library of Congress, and the University of Maryland at College Park. Organized in three parts: (1) annotated bibliography of printed music; (2) music in facsimile reprints; and (3) discography. Printed music classified broadly by performing forces, including a separate section of 94 choral works. Provides basic bibliographic information about each work along with annotative remarks. Discography arranged in alphabetical order by composer; less convenient arrangement for seeking choral titles. Two expansive indices: (1) recording manufacturer index and (2) composers, compilers, and titles. Series: *I.S.A.M. Monographs*, no. 30.

151. Jackson, Richard. *U. S. Bicentennial Music*. [Vol.] I. Brooklyn: Institute for Studies in American Music, Department of Music, School of Performing Arts, Brooklyn College of the City University of New York, 1977. iv, 20 p. ISBN 0-914678-06-X   ML120.U5 J18

    Annotated bibliography published at the time of the Bicentennial of the American Revolution. In addition to approximately 200 choral works, it includes band music; organ and piano music; chamber and miscellaneous instrumental music; orchestral music; songs; stage works; popular music in collections and sheet music; reprints, facsimile editions, and collections;

music of Charles Ives published 1970–1976. Criteria for selection: music on American subjects, patriotic music, and folk-music settings. Titles range from 18th to 20th century. Publisher directory. Series: *I.S.A.M. Special Publications*, no. 1.

152. Kroeger, Karl. *American Fuging-Tunes, 1770–1820: A Descriptive Catalog*. Westport, Connecticut: Greenwood Press, 1994. xvi, 220 p. ISBN 0-313-29000-8   ML120.U5 K76 1994

Descriptive bibliography of nearly 1,300 fuging-tunes published during the late 1700s and early 1800s. Brief biographical information about each composer. Provides tune name, numerical incipit, structure, duration, number of fuges, fuge length, order of vocal entry, rhythmic profile, fuge ending and entry distance, date and collection for the earliest printing of tune, poetic meter, first line of text, source of text, and annotative notes. Heavy use of abbreviations (abbreviations explained in prefatory pages). Separate indices for tune names, structure, fuge order of entry, fuge rhythm, text coordination and fuge time interval, date of first publication, alphabetical listing of sources, chronological listing of sources, meter, first lines, poetic sources, geographic index of composers, and tunes with multiple fuges. Series: *Music Reference Collection*, no. 41.

153. Lindsley, Charles Edward. "Early Nineteenth-Century American Collections of Sacred Choral Music, 1800–1810." Ph.D. dissertation. University of Iowa, Iowa City, 1968. x, 272 p.

Two parts: (1) historical survey of tune-book production to 1810; (2) annotated bibliography of more than 100 tune-books, 1800–1810. Bibliography attempts to be comprehensive and is based on the holdings of 78 U. S. library collections. Bibliography arranged in chronological order and provides composer/compiler with dates, complete title-page description, physical details of the book, an outline of content, and, if applicable, information regarding further editions. Facsimile; bibliography of almost 75 writings; index of composers/compilers.

See also: Britton, Allen Perdue, Irving Lowens, and Richard Crawford. *American Sacred Music Imprints, 1698–1810: A Bibliography* (item 131); Case, James H. "A List of Contemporary American Choral Music for Men's Voices" (item 176, no.39); Case, James H. "A List of Contemporary American Choral Music for Women's Voices" (item 176, no. 43); Case, James H. "A List of Contemporary American Choral Music for Mixed Voices" (item 176, no. 46); Dox, Thurston. "American Concert Oratorios" (item 176, no. 163); Evans, Margaret R. *Sacred Cantatas: An Annotated Bibliography, 1960–1979* (item 134); Guelker-Cone, Leslie. "Music for Women's Voices by Contemporary Women Composers of the United States and Canada" (item 88); McCoy, Jerry. "Literature Forum: New Literature for College and University Choirs" (item 75)

African-American Music

154. Cloud, Lee V. "Literature Forum: Choral Works by African-American Composers." *Choral Journal*, 33–2 (Sept. 1992), 44–48

Graded bibliography of approximately 200 choral works by African-American composers. Provides composer names and dates, title, performing forces, publisher and music number, and degree of difficulty (easy, medium, difficult). Includes original compositions and folk song arrangements or hymns; excludes arrangements of spirituals or gospel music.

155. Garcia, William Burres. "Church Music by Black Composers: A Bibliography of Choral Music." *The Black Perspective in Music*, 2–2 (1974): 145–157

Bibliography of choral music for the church by 41 African-American composers. Lists composer with dates, title, voicing/scoring, publication information, catalog number, pagination, and price. Includes a list of recommended books on African-American music and a list of publishers with addresses. Information dated.

156. Trice, Patricia Johnson. *Choral Arrangements of the African-American Spirituals: Historical Overviews and Annotated Listings.* Westport, Connecticut: Greenwood Press, 1998. xiii, 235 p. ISBN 0-313-30211-1 ML128.V7 T75 1998

Survey of choral arrangements of the African-American spiritual. Traces the development of the spiritual and analyzes its musical characteristics. Includes annotated list of approximately 380 arrangements, providing publisher, ranges, subject, key, meter, tempo, form, treatment, and comments. Also includes an impressive annotated list of nearly 100 arrangers, citing general biographical information along with information about training, awards, career, and repertoire. Separate expansive title, arranger, and subject indices. Series: *Music Reference Collection*, no. 66.

157. White, Evelyn Davidson. *Choral Music by African American Composers: A Selected, Annotated Bibliography.* 2nd ed. London: Scarecrow Press, 1996. viii, 226 p. ISBN 0-8108-3037-X ML128.C48 W5 1996

Annotated list of compositions by 102 African-American composers and arrangers. Entries are graded for difficulty. Information provided includes title, copyright date, number of pages, voicing and soloists, vocal ranges, range of difficulty, accompaniment (if applicable), publisher, and catalog number. Also includes a selected listing of 25 collections of Negro spirituals and brief biographical sketches of 84 composers. Three appendices: selected source readings; selected discography, including a catalog of selected *Voice of America Recordings*; and addresses of publishers and composers. Title index.

See also: Jackson, Irene V. *Afro-American Religious Music: A Bibliography and a Catalogue of Gospel Music* (item 38)

DISCOGRAPHIES

158. Bloesch, Richard J. "Choral Recordings: Resources for Discography." *Choral Journal*, 30–8 (March 1990), 5–16

    Annotated bibliography of 38 resources. Six sections: (1) journals devoted primarily to reviews of sound recordings; (2) other music journals containing some record reviews; (3) journals devoted primarily to discography; (4) books on discography; (5) record catalogs from the United States, England, Germany, and France; and (6) indexes of record reviews and other resources.

159. Blyth, Alan, ed. *Choral Music on Record*. Cambridge, England: Cambridge University Press, 1991. viii, 309 p. ISBN 0-521-36309-8   ML156.4.V7 C54 1990

    Collection of reviews of recordings of 25 major choral works. Provides ample historical information about the composer and work. Classified discographies by composer and title of more than 600 recordings. Works discussed: Claudio Monteverdi's *Vespro della Beata Vergine* (1610); J. S. Bach's *St. John Passion*, *St. Matthew Passion*, and *Mass* in B Minor; G. F. Handel's *Messiah*; W. A. Mozart's *Requiem*; Joseph Haydn's *The Creation* and *The Seasons*; Ludwig van Beethoven's *Missa Solemnis*; Felix Mendelssohn's *Elijah*; Gioacchino Rossini's *Stabat Mater* and *Petite Messe solennelle*; Hector Berlioz's *Grande Messe des morts, Te Deum*, and *L'Enfance du Christ*; Giuseppe Verdi's *Requiem*; Johannes Brahms's *A German Requiem*; Gabriel Fauré's *Requiem*; Edward Elgar's *The Dream of Geronitus*; William Walton's *Belshazzar's Feast*; Michael Tippett's *A Child of Our Time*; Benjamin Britten's *War Requiem*; Igor Stravinsky's *Svadebka* (The Wedding) and *Symphonie de Psaumes*; and Leoš Janáček's *Msa Glagolskaja* (Glagolitic Mass). Expansive index.

160. Day, Timothy. *A Discography of Tudor Church Music*. London: British Library, 1989. 317 p. ISBN 0-7123-0503-3   ML156.4.R4 D4 1989

Attempts to list all commercial recordings along with BBC Transcription Service discs and tapes of BBC broadcasts. Covers 1921–1988. Includes original compositions as well as adaptations. Main section is chronological list of commercial discs or broadcasts transmissions. Entries provide composers, title of works, performers, recording company, date, and music number. For more significant recordings, notes recording dates and locations, inclusion of program notes, texts and translations noted, and important reviews. Three sections refer to the main section: (1) alphabetical list of composers and their works with recordings arranged chronologically within each section; (2) index of choirs and solo performers; and (3) chronological list of recorded talks and feature programs related to Tudor music. Preface is a 34-page essay, "Tudor Church Music in the Twentieth Century."

161. Laster, James. *A Discography of Treble Voice Recordings.* Metuchen, New Jersey: Scarecrow Press, 1985. vii, 147 p. ISBN 0-8108-1760-8 ML156.4.V7 L4 1985

    Discography of approximately 11,000 recordings of works for treble voices, including women's voices, girl's voices, and unchanged male voices. Organized in alphabetical order by composer. Gives composer/arranger, title, performers, and publication information. No indices.

162. Tagg, Barbara, and Linda Ferreira. "Focus: Technology." *Choral Journal*, 33–8 (March 1993), 57–62

    Classified list of about 80 compact discs and almost 20 videos and videodiscs of musical works for children's choirs. Includes extended works (i.e., operas, works involving full orchestra and chamber ensembles, etc.). Provides composer, title, performers, publisher and music number.

    See also: Berger, Melvin. *Guide to Choral Masterpieces: A Listener's Guide* (item 43); *Garland Composer Resource Manuals* (item 450); *Greenwood Press, Bio-Bibliographies in Music* (item 451); Heintze, James R. *American Music before 1865 in Print and on Records: A Biblio-Discography* (item 150); *Stabat Mater Dolorosa: The Stabat Mater, a Musical Journey through the Ages . . .* (item 511)

TEXTS AND TRANSLATIONS

163. Bausano, William. *Sacred Latin Texts and English Translations for the Choral Conductor and Church Musician: Propers of the Mass.* Westport, Connecticut: Greenwood Press, 1998. 278 p. ISBN 0-313-30636-2 ML54.8 .S23 1998

Offers poetic English translations of more than 900 Latin propers of the Mass for the entire church year as used in the Roman Catholic Mass prior to the Second Vatican Council. Provides cross-referencing and listings of propers for various feasts and seasons of the year. Series: *Music Reference Collection*, no. 68.

164. Jeffers, Ron. *Translations and Annotations of Choral Repertoire. Vol. 1, Sacred Latin Texts*. Corvallis, Oregon: Earthsongs, 1988. 279 p. ISBN 0-9621532-0-6, ISBN 0-9621532-1-4 (pbk)

Volume 1: Literal word-by-word English translation of more than 100 Latin texts, including the Roman and Requiem Mass, along with prose rendering in order to restore proper word order and clarify meaning within the appropriate liturgical context. Several additional features: description of the liturgical year and Hours of Divine Office; glossary of terms; Latin pronunciation guide which includes Austro-German variants; and selected settings of Latin texts with cross references of settings of texts by composers, styles, and voicings. Index of titles and first lines.

Jeffers, Ron. *Translations and Annotations of Choral Repertoire. Vol. 2, German Texts*. Edited and annotated by Gordon Paine. Corvallis, Oregon: Earthsongs, 2000. xi, 366 p. ISBN 0-9621532-2-2, ISBN 0-9621532-3-0 (pbk)

Volume 2: Literal word-by-word English translation of nearly 170 German texts. Translations compiled by Jeffers; Gordon Paine edited and annotated each. Several additional features: discussions of the German Lutheran Bible and J. S. Bach's sacred cantatas; German pronunciation guide; glossary of terms; selected settings of German texts, demonstrating the variety of composers and voicings associated with each. Separate indices for authors and for titles and first lines.

165. Terry, Charles Sanford. *Joh. Seb. Bach: Cantata Texts, Sacred and Secular: With a Reconstruction of the Leipzig Liturgy of His Period*. London: Constable, 1926; reprint Holland Press, 1964. xx, 656 p.   ML410.B13 T38

Provides English translations of Bach's sacred and secular cantatas, including three oratorios. Cantata texts presented in relation to the Leipzig liturgy. Musical examples; three indices: cantatas listed by BWV number; index of titles; index of people.

III

Choral and Church Music Periodicals

166. *American Choral Review: Bulletin of the American Choral Foundation.* 1–. 1958–. Washington, DC: Chorus America. (Quarterly)

   Newsletter format; now published with *Voice of Chorus America* (pullout); brief article(s); reviews of choral performances, recent publications, recent recordings.

167. *The American Organist.* 1–. 1967–. New York: American Guild of Organists. (Monthly)

   News of American Guild of Organists (AGO) and Royal Canadian College of Organists members, events, competitions, etc.; interviews; articles; departments include "Choral Old and New" and "New Choral Music."

168. *Choir & Organ.* 1–. 1993–. Harrow, Middlesex, England: Orpheus Publications. (Quarterly)

   Monthly section "Cantus in Choro" includes choral music news, events, brief articles, reviews of new music, etc.; reviews of choral music and CDs, organ music and CDs; organ recital lists.

169. *The Choral Journal.* 1–. 1959–. Lawton, Oklahoma: American Choral Directors Association. (10 issues a year, Aug.–May)

   Association news and events; three to four substantive articles per issue; reviews of CDs, books; 25-plus reviews of choral works in each issue; research reports; "Literature Forum" a regular feature (e.g., J. S. Bach cantatas; 20-century settings of Psalm 150). Absorbed *Texas Choirmaster*, Aug./Sept. 1964. Separately prepared index of the first 18 volumes. *See also* Paine, Gordon. *The Choral Journal: An Index to Volumes 1–18* (item 34).

170. *The Chorister.* 1–. 1949–. Garland, Texas: The Choristers Guild. (10 issues a year)

Focuses on music with young people; articles, news releases, reviews, and study plans for choral compositions; announcements and news of the members and activities of the guild.

171. *Chorus!* 1–. 1989–. Atlanta, Georgia: Norcross Music Associates. (Monthly)

    For the choral enthusiast; tabloid format; interviews, articles, reviews, concert calendar.

172. *Church Music Quarterly.* 1–. 1963–. Westhumble, Dorking, England: Royal School of Church Music. (Quarterly)

    Royal School of Church Music (RSCM) news and events; articles; reviews of choral music, organ music, CDs, books; choirmaster/organist job announcements.

173. *International Choral Bulletin.* 1–. 1981–. Chicago, Illinois: International Federation for Choral Music. (Quarterly)

    International Federation for Choral Music (IFCM) founded by the seven main national choral organizations of the world; *International Choral Bulletin* published quarterly in four languages: English, French, German, Spanish; regular feature titled "Dossier" presents several brief articles on a topic or theme (e.g., children's choirs, choral singing for the blind, Polish choral music, Puerto Rico); IFCM news and choral world news; repertoire lists; occasional book and CD reviews; information on festivals, workshops, competitions.

174. *Pastoral Music.* 1–. 1976–. Washington, DC: National Association of Pastoral Musicians. (Bimonthly)

    Published by the National Association of Pastoral Musicians, an organization of musicians and clergy dedicated to fostering the art of music liturgy; articles; reviews; professional concerns; music ministry positions advertisements; calendar of events; music industry news.

175. *Reformed Liturgy & Music.* 1–. 1963–. Louisville, Kentucky: Office of Theology and Worship, Congregation Ministries Division, Presbyterian Church (U. S. A.). (Quarterly)

    Goal is to develop an understanding of Reformed piety, corporate worship, and the role of music in the church; each issue planned around a theme (e.g., celebrating the Iona Community, praying alone and in common, music in the service of God); articles; occasional reviews of books and music collections;

lectionary aids for the Sundays of each quarter of the Christian year (i.e., recommended scriptures, suggested hymns, choral music, children's music, organ music, handbell music, piano music, vocal solos).

176. *Research Memorandum Series*. 1–. 1959–. New York: The American Choral Foundation. (Irregular)

Newsletter format; irregularly issued. Published in affiliation with the American Choral Directors Association. Variously administered by the American Choral Foundation, the Association of Professional Vocal Ensembles, and Chorus America (APVE). Majority of issues are annotated bibliographies of music, bibliographies of music literature, or discographies. A classified bibliography of the *Research Memorandum Series*, nos. 1–158 (1959–1990), was published in January 1991 as issue no. 159. The following are selected titles:

No. 12. Peress, Maurice. "A Selective List of Music for Voices and Brass Instruments." (February 1960)

No. 13. Greenberg, Noah. "A Selective List of XV- and XVI-Century Netherlandish Choral Music Available in Practical Editions." (March 1960)

No. 15. Hickock, Robert. "A Selective List of Baroque Choral Works in Practical Editions." (June 1960)

No. 17. Somary, Johannes F. "A Selective List of Choral Music for Christmas." (October 1960)

No. 22. Collins, Walter S. "A Selected List of Renaissance and Baroque Choral Works with Sacred English Texts in Practical Editions." (March 1961)

No. 23. Saller, Paul H. "A Selective List of Sacred and Secular Music for Children's Voices." (April 1961)

No. 24. Larue, Jan, and John Vinton. "A Selective List of Choral Compositions from the Classical Period in Practical Editions." (June 1961)

No. 27. Hillis, Margaret. "A Select List of Choral Music for Festivals." (December 1961)

No. 31. Brothers, Richard. "Anthems Suitable for Use in the Worship of Unitarian and Other Liberal Churches." (April 1962)

No. 32. Kvam, Junrad. "A General List of Choral Music for Women's Voices." (June 1962)

No. 34. Simmons, Morgan F. "Selected Lists of Sacred Choral Music." (October 1962)

No. 35. Hosmer, Helen M. "Select List of Choral Music for Festivals." (November 1962)

No. 36. Moore, Christopher. "A Bibliography of Contemporary Choral Music for High Voices, Performable by Children." (December 1962)

No. 37. Mayer, Frederick D. "A Selected List of Music Suitable for Use at the Junior High School Level." (January 1963)

No. 39. Case, James H. "A List of Contemporary American Choral Music for Men's Voices." (March 1963)

No. 40. English, Mary E. "A Select List of Music for Women's Voices." (April 1963)

No. 42. Hayes, Morris D. "A Select List of Music for Men's Voices." (August 1963)

No. 43. Case, James H. "A List of Contemporary American Choral Music for Women's Voices." (September 1963)

No. 44. Stevenson, Robert Murrell. "The English Service: A Bibliography of Editions and Literature." (October 1963)

No. 46. Case, James H. "A List of Contemporary American Choral Music for Mixed Voices." (January 1964)

No. 49. Adler, Samuel. "A List of Music for American Synagogues." (April 1964)

No. 50. Spencer, Helen Stott. "A Selected List of Music for Junior and Senior High School Women's Choruses." (May 1964)

No. 51. Goucher, Louise Rogers. "Motets, Carols, and Chorales Suitable for the Christmas Season." (July 1964)

No. 52. Hayes, Morris D. "A Selected List of Music for Men's Voices." (September 1964)

No. 53. Whitwell, David. "Music for Voices and Brass Ensemble." (December 1964)

Nos. 54, 59. Perinchief, Robert. "An Annotated Select List of Music for the Small Select Choir in the Music Program of the Intermediate Grades." (February 1965, July 1965)

No. 56. Whitwell, David. "Music for Voices and Trumpets; Music for Voices and Trombones; Music for Voices and Horns." (April 1965)

No. 61. Whitwell, David. "Music for Voices and Mixed Wind Ensembles." (December 1965)

No. 62. Goucher, Louise Rogers. "Motets and Chorales of the Renaissance and Baroque Periods Written for Lent and Easter." (February 1966)

No. 64. Whitwell, David. "Music for Voices and Woodwind Instruments." (May 1966)

No. 68. Ramey, Jack. "Books, Periodicals, and Articles of Interest to Choral Directors in Schools." (January 1967)

No. 71. Beckwith, R. Sterling. "The Choral Tradition of the Russian Church." (September 1967)

No. 72. McChesney, Richard. "Music for the Inexperienced Choir." (October 1967)

No. 75. Hayes, Morris D. "A Selected List of Folk Songs for Men's Voices." (January 1968)

No. 76. Klyce, Stephen. "A List of 20th-Century Madrigals." (February 1968)

No. 78. Somary, Johannes F. "A Selective List of Choral Music for Christmas." (September 1968)

No. 79. McChesney, Richard. "Music for the Chorus without Tenors." (October 1968)

No. 81. Hayes, Morris D. "A Selected List of Sacred Music for Men's Voices." (December 1968)

No. 83. Hayes, Morris D. "A Selected List of Secular Music for Men's Voices." (April 1969)

Nos. 84, 90. Van Camp, Leonard. "A Bibliography of Rounds and Canons." (May 1969, December 1969)

Nos. 88, 91. Van Camp, Leonard, and Diana Rawizza. "A Bibliography of Polychoral Music." (October 1969, April 1970)

No. 89. McChesney, Richard. "Music for Two-Part Women's Choir." (November 1969)

No. 92. Van Camp, Leonard. "A Bibliography of Choral Music for Three-Part Male Chorus." (May 1970)

Nos. 93, 94, 99. Van Camp, Leonard. "A Bibliography of Choral Music for Six-Part Mixed Voices": "Renaissance Music" (June 1970); "Baroque and Romantic Music" (October 1970, February 1971)

Nos. 97, 103. "A List of 20th-Century Madrigals: Madrigals on German Texts." (December 1970, December 1971)

Nos. 101/102, 104/105, 106/107, 109/110. Herrema, Robert D. "Psalm Settings by 20th-Century Composers." (October/November 1971, January/February 1972, October/November 1972, January/February 1973)

No. 108. "A Selective List of 20th-Century English Church Music, Part I." (December 1972)

No. 114. Hays, Alfreda. "Passion Settings of the German Baroque: A Guide to the Printed Editions." (October 1974)

Nos. 127, 129. Hutcheson, Robert J. "20th-Century Settings of the Passion: An Annotated Bibliography." (March 1979, November 1979)

Nos. 135, 136. White, Arthur Carlton. "Published Moravian Choral Music." (November 1983, July 1984)

No. 141. Gilbert, Nina. "Who's Who in Arcadia: A Glossary of Italian and English Madrigals from the 16th and 17th Centuries." (May 1986)

No. 142. Rao, Doreen. "Selected Repertoire for Children's Chorus and Orchestra." (August 1986)

No. 144. Gilbert, Nina. "Choral Music for Dedications." (May 1987)

No. 145. Reynolds, Robert D. "Textless Choral Music." (August 1987)

Nos. 149, 150. Laster, James, and Nancy Menk. "Literature on the Women's Chorus." (July 1988, October 1988)

No. 153. Rhodes, Mark. "A Selective, Annotated List of Secular Renaissance Vocal Music Suitable for Junior-High-School Boys of Mixed Choruses." (July 1989)

No. 158. Galloway, Lane. "Jewish Choral Music for Concert Performance." (October 1990)

No. 163. Dox, Thurston J. "American Concert Oratorios." (July 1993)

Nos. 166, 175. Laster, James, and Nancy Menk. "Literature on the Women's Chorus." (January 1995, Summer 1999)

No. 167. Ward, Robert J. "Compositions for Speaking Chorus." (July 1995)

No. 168. Shenbeck, Lyn. "World Music for Treble Choirs." (January 1996)

No. 169. Gresham, Mark. "Music for Unison Chorus." (June 1996)

No. 170. Tiemstra, Suzanne Spicer. "Anthologies, Collections, and Series of Latin American Choral Music." (January 1997)

No. 172. Johnson, Craig R. "Choral Conducting Texts: An Annotated Bibliography." (January 1998)

Nos. 173, 174. Wyss, Jane. "Vocal Pedagogy Texts of Interest to Choral Conductors": "Part I: Books" (Summer 1998); "Part II: Recent Articles, Videotapes, and Dissertations" (Fall 1998)

177. *Sacred Music.* 1–. 1874–. Grand Rapids, Michigan: Church Music Association of America. (Quarterly)

Incorporates *Caecilia* and *Catholic Choirmaster*; academic/scholarly publication.

178. *The Voice of Chorus America*. 1–. 1978–. Washington, DC: Chorus America. (Quarterly)

Focus is on the business side of establishing and maintaining professional and volunteer choruses; news and features of interest to chorus board members, conductors, managers, fundraisers, marketers, and arts advocates; regularly features lists of professional and volunteer members's concerts.

IV

Choral Technique

GENERAL WORKS

179. Althouse, Jay. *168 Non-Musical Ways to Improve Your Band or Choral Program.* East Stroudsburg, Pennsylvania: Music in Action, 1986. 85 p. MT10 .A5 1986

    168 individually numbered tips regarding public relations, administrative duties, new materials and teaching resources, developing associations with colleagues, organizations to join, rehearsals, and performances. No bibliography; no index.

180. American Choral Directors Association. National Committee on High School Choral Music. *Guide for the Beginning Choral Director.* With a Foreword by Gordon H. Lamb. Tampa, Florida: American Choral Directors Association, 1972. iii, 41 p.   MT85 .A4 1972

    Aimed toward the college senior and beginning choral director. Topics: student teaching; organizing the choral program and its role in the total school program; choral auditions and preparation for the first rehearsal; selection of music for high school choir; contests and clinics; and choosing and securing a choral teaching position. Contributors: Louis H. Diercks, Florian N. Douglass, Richard Gaarder, Ernest Hisey, Lee Kjelson, Jack A. Learned, Hardy Lieberg, and Gordon H. Lamb. Annotated bibliography of 13 items; no index.

181. Christy, Van Ambrose. *Evaluation of Choral Music: Methods of Appraising the Practical Value of Choral Compositions with Reference to Music Generally Available in the United States.* New York: Bureau of Publications, Teachers College, Columbia University, 1948 ML1151.N5 C5 1948; reprint, New York: AMS Press, 1972. x, 107 p. ISBN 0-404-55885-2 ML1151.N5 C5 1972

Title self-explanatory. Dated yet interesting study. Numerous tables; bibliography of 55 writings; no index. Series: *Columbia University, Teachers College, Contributions to Education*, no. 885.

182. Christy, Van Ambrose. *Glee Club and Chorus: A Handbook of Organizing, Conducting, and Maintaining Glee Club and Choral Organizations, with Selected, Graded, and Classified Lists of Octavo Music and Texts.* New York: G. Schirmer, 1940. viii, 149 p.   MT88 .C54

Out of date, but of historical interest. Two sections: (1) eight-chapter discussion of methods of choral conducting, organizing choirs, rehearsals, musical interpretation, concert tours and radio broadcasting, contests and festivals, and program building and materials; and (2) graded, classified list of approximately 1,500 octavo choral works for men's and women's glee clubs and a cappella mixed choruses. List of octavos broadly divided into three sections: music for mixed voices, men's voices, and treble voices. Each section classified by subject (e.g., folk songs, spirituals, and songs for special occasions). Each subject further classified by national origin, special occasion, or other descriptive groupings (hunting songs, drinking songs, chanteys, and novelties). Entries list composer and/or arranger, title, octavo number, price (outdated), publisher, number of parts, grade of difficulty (easy, medium, difficult), highest and lowest notes (men's voices and treble voices only), duration, and general remarks. Brief bibliography of 17 books and collections of music. Index.

183. Collins, Don L. *Teaching Choral Music.* 2nd ed. Upper Saddle River, New Jersey: Prentice Hall, 1999. xvii, 509 p. ISBN 0-13-081356-7   MT930 .C58 1999

Suitable as a textbook; intended for use in secondary schools. Organized into three sections: introductory; how to teach; and administration and organization. Study projects, discussion questions, and bibliographies included at the end of each chapter. Numerous musical examples, illustrations, and photos. Several appendices, including: (1) suppliers of choral music, materials, and equipment; (2) classified list of approximately 600 choral works and collections for choirs in middle-level grades; (3) classified list of about 180 multicultural choral works; (4) 25 sight-reading materials; (5) 34 Web sites useful to choral music educators. Expansive index.

184. Corp, Ronald. *The Choral Singer's Companion.* Rev. and updated. London: Batsford, 2000. 224 p. ISBN 0-9052-1063-8   MT875 .C68 2000

The 2000 edition not available for examination; annotation based on 1987 editions (London: Batsford; New York: Facts on File Publications). Six main sections: (1) practical guides to singing, sight reading, conducting, running a choir, planning programs, and obtaining music; (2) brief biographical entries on over 140 composers; (3) titles of more than 140 compositions with brief information about work, voicing and scoring, and duration; (4) definitions of over 100 choral-related terms; (5) texts often set to music by composers with English translations, including sections of the Mass and Requiem Mass, Te Deum Laudamus, and Stabat Mater; and (6) lists of works suggested as a starting point for building choral programs. Latter section, with over 500 titles, subdivided into numerous sections: 20th-century choral works by British composers, secular choral works, choir and strings, works without strings, choir and organ, choir and piano, works with harp, Christmas music, Easter music, stage works for concert performance, works for female voices, works for male voices, children's voices, the Masses of Haydn, concert programs given by the BBC Club Choir over the first 10 years of its existence, orchestration of various works, and a list of addresses of various music organizations. Composers and works show a British bias. Bibliography of 15 items; index. The 2000 edition includes a chapter on singing by Barbara Alden.

185. Gordon, Lewis. *Choral Director's Complete Handbook*. West Nyack, New York: Parker, 1977. 220 p. ISBN 0-13-133363-1   MT88 .G78

For the experienced choral director. Practical handbook to building a successful choral program. Abundant illustrations, charts, and musical examples; no bibliography; expansive index.

186. Grunow, Richard F., and Milford H. Fargo. *The Choral Score Reading Program*. Chicago: G.I.A. Publications, 1985. 66 p. + audiocassette MT85.G78 C4 1985

Program, consisting of audiocassette and workbook, designed to develop skills in analyzing a choral score and detecting errors in choral ensemble performance. Provides 60 musical excerpts. Test format; answer key provided.

187. Hammar, Russell A. *Pragmatic Choral Procedures*. Metuchen, New Jersey: Scarecrow Press, 1984. xviii, 359 p. ISBN 0-8108-1698-9   MT875 .H18 1984

Based upon author's 40 years of experience in choral music. Four sections: Part I: brief history of conducting, music education through the choral experience, and the conductor's role in regard to serving the singer's needs; Part II: vocal and musical development of the choral singer; Part III: technical, interpretative, and rehearsal considerations for the conductor; Part IV: church choir orientations and contemporary church music concepts. Amply documented; numerous illustrations and musical examples; review questions at the end of each chapter. Classified bibliography of over 130 entries; index.

188. Harris, Ernest E. *Music Education: A Guide to Information Sources.* Detroit: Gale, 1978. xvii, 566 p. ISBN 0-8103-1309-X   ML19 .H37

Annotated bibliography of resources in the area of music education. Seventy-four sections organized under five headings: (1) general reference; (2) music education; (3) subject matter areas; (4) special uses of music; and (5) technology, multimedia resources, and equipment. Separate section on choral and vocal music; resources in choral music easily found in other sections of the bibliography. Two appendices: (1) supplemental listing of holdings in certain libraries and (2) list of periodicals. Author, title, and subject indices. Series: *Gale Information Guide Library: Education Information Guide Series*, vol. 1.

189. Hylton, John Baker. *Comprehensive Choral Music Education.* Englewood Cliffs, New Jersey: Prentice Hall, 1995. x, 325 p. ISBN 0-13-045287-4 MT875 .H95 1995

Suitable for use with secondary school, college, church, and community choral ensembles. Topics include building tone, rehearsal techniques, developing conducting skill, performance considerations, the score, style in choral singing, administration of the choral music education program, planning for special events and specialized ensembles, comprehensive choral music education, and the choral profession. Discussion questions and bibliographies included at the end of each chapter. Latin texts with English translations of the Mass Ordinary and Requiem Mass. Recommended lists of choral works interspersed throughout text (mixed chorus, women's voices, men's voices, and multicultural titles). List of music publishers and distributors; musical examples, illustrations, and photographs; expansive index.

190. Kerr, Anita. *Voices.* With complete recorded examples. New York: MCA Music, 1972. xi, 130 p.   MT875 .K4

Thirty-one chapters; content primarily musical examples with intermittent discussion; accompanying sound disc with recorded examples. Offers practical voice ranges, chords and voicing, aspects of arranging, organizing a choir, conducting, and rehearsal methods. Musical examples and illustrations; bibliography of the *Anita Kerr Choral Series*; no index.

191. Kjelson, Lee, and James Elwin McCray. *The Conductor's Manual of Choral Music Literature.* Melville, New York: Belwin Mills, 1973. 272 p. M1548.K52 C6

Kjelson, Lee, and James Elwin McCray. *The Singer's Manual of Choral Music Literature.* Melville, New York: Belwin Mills, 1973. vi, 196 p. MT875 .K53 1973

Five chapters: Renaissance, baroque, classical and early American, romantic, and 20th century. Each chapter presents four to five music selections in full SATB voicing with keyboard accompaniment. Each selection preceded by biographical information about the composer. The *Conductor's Manual* presents discussion of musical characteristics and performance considerations for each composition; this information is not included in the *Singer's Manual.* Recommended readings, topics for discussion, and discussion questions for high school students for each chapter. Two appendices: (1) suggested Latin pronunciation guide and (2) glossary of approximately 300 terms. No index.

192. Lamb, Gordon H. *Choral Techniques.* 3rd ed. Dubuque, Iowa: Wm. C. Brown, 1988. xii, 302 p. ISBN 0-697-00612-3   MT85 .L3 1988

Three parts: (1) "The Score and the Conductor" discusses conducting techniques, score study, interpreting choral music, English and Latin choral diction, and choral tone; (2) "Rehearsal Techniques" addresses selection and placement of voices, selection of repertoire, building a concert program, and other rehearsal considerations; (3) "Organization and Management" covers management of a choral department, advice for organizing small ensembles, student teaching, professional ethics and teacher relationships, and clinics, festivals, and contests. Includes a classified list (mixed voices, women's voices, and men's voices) of approximately 275 compositions and directory with addresses of music publishers, music dealers, concert apparel dealers, manufacturers of choral risers, recording companies, and professional organizations. Musical examples, illustrations, and tables; bibliography of about 70 items; expansive index.

193. Miller, Kenneth E. *Handbook of Choral Music Selection, Score Preparation and Writing.* West Nyack, New York: Parker, 1979. 240 p. ISBN 0-13-372532-4   ML1500 .M6

Topics include guidelines for selecting choral music, maintaining a choral library, score preparation and the choral conductor, suitability of text, training of the conductor, composers of American choral music, musical practices for the choral writer (arranging, editing, and composing), modern musical techniques, and nontraditional notation (includes examples and descriptions of notation). Chapter 2: forty-five annotated recommended choral works under the headings mixed choir, female choir, male choir, and chamber choir. Three appendices: compliance with copyright law; selected publishers of choral music; and a selected list of about 350 choral works under the headings mixed choir, female choir, male choir, chamber choir, and choral music with electronic tape. Musical examples, model concert programs, and charts; bibliography of about 40 items; expansive index.

194. Neidig, Kenneth L., and John W. Jennings, eds. *Choral Director's Guide.* West Nyack, New York: Parker, 1967. vii, 308 p.   MT88 .N3

Thirteen chapters by different authors: (1) "Personal and Professional Development" (Wiley L. Housewright); (2) "Public Relations" (Louis H. Diercks); (3) "The Voice Class" (Louis Nicholas) includes a list of approximately 90 "teaching songs"; (4) "The Chamber Ensemble" (Rose Marie Grentzer) addresses organizing and costuming, rehearsal techniques, programming, performance, and conducting; includes a classified list of more than 100 works suitable for chamber ensemble; (5) "Choosing Music for Performance" (Harold A. Decker) includes a dated list of approximately 225 publishers of choral music with addresses and a classified (according to appropriate audience) and graded (easy, medium, difficult) list of choral music; (6) "A Practical Guide to Style" (Hugh Thomas) also includes about 50 recommended choral-collection recordings and classified, graded lists of recommended choral compositions (48 Renaissance, 31 baroque, 13 classical, 52 romantic, 135 contemporary, and 123 arrangements of folk music, Christmas music, and hymns); (7) "Contests and Festivals" (Dallas Draper) gives practical advice and includes a classified, graded list of choral compositions for junior and senior high school festivals compiled by the Southern California Vocal Association (senior high school: 180 for mixed choir, 180 women's voices, 200 men's voices, and 65 madrigals; junior high school: 20 unison, 125 women's voices, 25 treble or boys's voices, 125 mixed or boys's voices, and 13 boys's voices; lists without indicating graded difficulty: 45 collections, 35 state music texts; and 60 supplementary music texts); (8) "The Summer Choral Workshop" by the officers of the North Carolina Summer Choral Workshop; (9) "Junior High School—The Pivotal Point" (Robert Knauf); (10) "Physical Facilities and Equipment" (Wayne S. Hertz); (11) "Practical Rehearsal Techniques" (Warner Lawson); (12) "The Challenge of Performance" (Hugh Ross); and (13) "Establishing a Program of Permanent Value" (Thomas Hilbish). Musical examples, photos, illustrations, and charts; expansive index.

195. Page, Robert, Louise Greenberg, and Fred Leise, eds. *The Chorus Handbook: Chorus 101: The How-To Book for Organizing and Operating a Professional or Volunteer Choral Ensemble.* Washington, DC: Chorus America, 1999. vi, 176 p. MT88 .C56 1999

Fifteen chapters written by 21 contributors. Covers all aspects of organizing a professional or volunteer choral ensemble. Chapters: "The Legal Aspects of Establishing Your Chorus" (Floyd Farmer); "Volunteer and Professional Singers; Auditions; Performance Schedules" (Paul Hill); "House Management" (Mary Elizabeth Schruben); "Music Resources, Purchase and Handling" (Lawrence Bandfield); "The Board of Directors" (Constance J. Bernt); "Staffing" (Jan Eimstad); "Budgeting and Accounting" (Eimstad, Fred Leise); "Public Relations and Marketing for Your Chorus" (Nicole E. De Nigro); "Finding the Funding for Your Future" (Terry Knowles); "Creating Educational Programs" (Mary Deissler); "Support Groups/Guilds/Auxiliaries" (Mary Lyons); "Multiculturalism and Diversity: Awareness of Our Cultural and Environmental Interconnectedness" (Albert J. McNeil); "Multiculturalism and Diversity: A Brief History of the Gay and Lesbian Choral Movements" (Dennis Coleman); "Commissioning of Compositions" (Dale Warland); "Commissioning a Musical Work" (Alice Parker); "The Art of Choral Recording" (Almeda and Jackson Berkey, Cletus Baker); "Domestic Touring" (Nancy Plum, Alison Hankinson); "Tour Guide" (Barry K. Miller). Musical examples; expansive index.

196. Paine, Gordon, ed. *Five Centuries of Choral Music: Essays in Honor of Howard Swan.* Stuyvesant, New York: Pendragon Press, 1988. ix 389 p. ISBN 0-918728-84-3 ML1500 .F5 1988

A festschrift on the occasion of Howard Swan's 80th birthday. Includes the following essays: "A Biographical Conversation with Howard Swan" and "Tactus, Tempo, and Praetorius" (Gordon Paine); "The 'Conductor's Process' " (Jameson Marvin); "Integrity in the Teaching and Performing of Choral Music" (Lynn Whitten); "The Creative Experience: Some Implications for the Choral Conductor" (Allen Lannom); "The Art and Craft of Choral Arranging" (Lloyd Pfautsch); "Understanding Male Adolescent Voice Maturation—Some Significant Contributions by European and American Researchers" (John Cooksey); "The Reconstruction of the Evening Service for Seven Voices by Thomas Weelkes" (Walter S. Collins); "Some Puzzling Intabulations of Vocal Music for Keyboard, ca. 1600, at Castell' Arquato" (H. Colin Slim); "Rhythm: The Key to Vitalizing Renaissance Music" (John B. Haberlen); "The Opus Ultimum: Heinrich Schütz's Artistic and Spiritual Testament" (Ray Robinson); "Bach's Motets in the Twentieth

Century" (Wesley K. Morgan); "Handel's Funeral Anthem for Queen Caroline: A Neglected Masterpiece" (Harold A. Decker); "Aspects of Performance Practice during the Classic Era" (Dennis Shrock); "The Vocal Quartets of Brahms (Op. 31, 64, and 92): A Textual Encounter" (G. Roberts Kolb); "The Text of Britten's *War Requiem*" (Robert Shaw). Extensive index. Series: *Festschrift Series*, no. 6.

197. Richmond, John W. "Selecting Choral Repertoire as Pre-Curriculum: 'Planned Serendipity'." *Choral Journal*, 30-10 (May 1990), 23–30

Suggests criteria-based models for selecting choral music. Concludes with a list of repertoire search tools: 41 books and 16 repertoire articles.

198. Robinson, Ray, and Allen Winold. *The Choral Experience: Literature, Materials, and Methods.* New York: Harper & Row, 1976. ISBN 0-06-161419-X MT88 .R7; reprint, Prospect Heights, Illinois: Waveland Press, 1992. xvi, 510 p. ISBN 0-88133-650-5   MT88 .R7 1992

Four parts: (1) "The Choral Experience" gives a historical perspective of choral music and discusses choral conducting and vocal production; (2) "Rehearsal Technique" considers choral sound, diction, and rehearsal and performance problems; (3) "Basic Musicianship" presents music elements of rhythm, pitch, harmony and texture, and form; and (4) "Performance Practices" covers the Renaissance through the 20th century. Of special interest is the separate section on Latin, Italian, Spanish, German, and French diction in Chapter 5, "Choral Diction." Many musical examples, illustrations, photographs, tables, and charts; recommended reading lists at the end of most chapters; expansive index.

199. Roe, Paul F. *Choral Music Education.* 2nd ed. Englewood Cliffs, New Jersey: Prentice-Hall, 1983. ISBN 0-13-133322-4   MT930 .R65 1983; reprint, Prospect Heights, Illinois: Waveland Press, 1994. x, 355 p. ISBN 0-88133-807-9   MT930 .R65 1994

Suitable as a text for undergraduate music education. Three main divisions: Chapters 1, 2, and 3 suggest promotional activities and make recommendations for scheduling and curriculum, selecting and organizing singers, and practical administrative procedures; Chapters 4, 5, 6, and 7 address vocal fundamentals, sight-reading, general music, and common problems experienced in junior high, such as the changing voice; Chapters 8, 9, 10, 11 examine conducting, rehearsal techniques, style, and performance. Topical bibliographies at the end of most chapters; appendix with recommendations about applying for a teaching position; expansive index.

200. Swan, Howard. *Conscience of a Profession: Howard Swan, Choral Director and Teacher*. Edited by Charles Fowler. Chapel Hill, North Carolina: Hinshaw Music, 1987. x, 197 p. ISBN 0-937276-07-3   MT85 .S898 1987

A collection of 21 addresses delivered between 1945 and 1986 by the distinguished choral conductor, Howard Swan. Organized into five sections: (1) Howard Swan, the man and his philosophy; (2) the church musician; (3) the conductor; (4) the choral professional; and (5) Howard Swan, the historian. Musical examples, illustrations, and photos; bibliography of nearly 50 writings by and about Swan.

20TH-CENTURY MUSIC

201. Lorentzen, Bent. *New Choral Dramatics: Dimensions in Choral Speech and Movement*. Translated by Bent Lorentzen. Rev. and edited by Frank Pooler and Steven Porter. New York: Walton Music Corp., 1973. 44 p.   MT948 .L674

Describes and illustrates nontraditional notation. Intended for ensembles and choral groups. Presents 30 exercises/compositions in four sections: sound forming, aleatoric performance, noise forming, and choral dramatics. No bibliography; no index.

202. Robison, Richard William. "Reading Contemporary Choral Literature: An Analytical Study of Selected Contemporary Choral Compositions with Recommendations for the Improvement of Choral Reading Skills." Ph.D. dissertation. Brigham Young University, Provo, Utah, 1969. xiii, 363 p.

Purpose: "to identify through analysis specific musical features peculiar to contemporary choral music; to relate these features to skills required by singers to perform the music; and to devise methods to help the singer solve the problems presented by this literature." Presents analysis of selected choral works by Samuel Barber, Aaron Copland, Norman Dello Joio, Lukas Foss, Charles Ives, Vincent Persichetti, Daniel Pinkham, and William Schuman. Includes three enlightening excerpts from letters written by Dello Joio, Persichetti, and Pinkham. Abundant musical examples and tables; bibliography of 75 books and dissertations, catalogs, periodical articles, scores, and recordings.

203. Strommen, Carl. *The Contemporary Chorus: A Director's Guide for the Jazz-Rock Choir*. Sherman Oaks, California: Alfred, 1980. x, 126 p. ISBN 0-88284-111-4   MT875 .S88

Topics include stylistic elements of harmony and rhythm, the rhythm section, vocal ensemble with jazz band, sound system, rehearsal, improvisation, and composing, arranging, and publishing. Includes two additional articles: "Perfectionist Carmen McRae" by Harvey Siders and "The Backup Singers: High Reward for a Privileged Few" by Don Heckman. Musical examples and illustrations; bibliography of about 50 writings; discography of about 150 recordings.

ARRANGING AND COMPOSITION

204. Ades, Hawley. *Choral Arranging*. 2nd ed., expanded. Delaware Water Gap, Pennsylvania: Shawnee Press, 1983. vi, 304 p.   MT70.5 .A3 1983

Basic principles of choral arranging. Numerous musical examples and a list of supplementary examples for each chapter; bibliography of 22 writings; expansive index.

205. Bone, David L. *52 Instant Hymn Anthems*. Nashville, Tennessee: Abingdon Press, 1995. 144 p. ISBN 0-687-00798-4   MT88 .B775 1995

Practical guide for adapting hymns found in common hymnals for use as anthems. Charts and musical examples; glossary of terms.

206. Davison, Archibald T. *The Technique of Choral Composition*. New York: Mills Music, 1945; reprints, Cambridge, Massachusetts: Harvard University Press, 1951, 1955, 1960, 1963. xiii, 206 p.   MT70.5 .D35

Written in 1945 with several reprints. Practical guide covering musical and technical fundamentals, idiomatic choral practices, polyvocal writing, accompaniment, special choirs, text, and form. Three appendices: (1) dated list of publishers; (2) index of 31 collections; and (3) index of about 135 composers and more than 300 compositions. Indices also function as work-lists, providing title, composer/editor, publication information, and date or music number. Numerous musical examples; documented with footnotes.

207. Jothen, Michael Jon. "The Development and Utilization of Guidelines for Use as an Aid in Composing Choral Music for Elementary School Age Choirs." Ph.D. dissertation. Ohio State University, Columbus, 1978. x, 223 p.

Presents guidelines for use as an aid in composing choral music for elementary school age choirs. Charts, tables, and musical examples; bibliography of 40 writings and nine scores.

208. Ostrander, Arthur E., and Dana Wilson. *Contemporary Choral Arranging*. Englewood Cliffs, New Jersey: Prentice-Hall, 1986. xv, 320 p. ISBN 0-13-169756-0   MT70.5 .O87 1986

Similar in content to Hawley Ades's *Choral Arranging* (item 204); in addition, Ostrander and Wilson's guide addresses jazz, country, rock, and pop vocal styles and accompaniment. Well-organized, addressing fundamentals and providing arranging exercises at the conclusion of most chapters. Numerous musical examples; expansive index.

See also: Kerr, Anita. *Voices* (item 190).

CHILDREN AND YOUTH CHOIRS

General Works

209. Bartle, Jean Ashworth. *Lifeline for Children's Choir Directors.* Rev. ed. Toronto: Gordon V. Thompson Music, 1993. viii, 215 p.   MT85 .B3 1993

Chapters 1–6 discuss positive attitude, professional organizations for choral conductors, developing the child's voice, the uncertain singer, diction, musicianship, and conducting children's choirs. Chapters 7–10 address recruitment, organization, rehearsal techniques, teaching plans, suitable repertoire, concerts and performances, and the role of piano accompanists for school primary choir, school junior choir, junior church choir, and the community or professional children's choir, respectively. Repertoire lists give composer, title, publisher, music number, and voicing. Musical examples (some in graphic notation), sample programs, and illustrations; bibliography of 39 writings; no index.

210. Brinson, Barbara A. *Choral Music Methods and Materials: Developing Successful Choral Programs (Grades 5 to 12).* New York: Schirmer Books; London: Prentice Hall International, 1996. xi, 319 p. ISBN 0-02-870311-1 MT930 .B82 1996

Intended for undergraduate choral methods courses. Topics include philosophical foundations, recruitment and retention of singers, auditions and placement of singers, development and evaluation of a choral curriculum, repertoire, programming music, musical analysis and score preparations, the rehearsal, behavior management in rehearsal, vocal techniques and musicianship skills, the changing voice, pop ensembles and musical productions, and management of a choral program. Suggested projects and recommended readings at the end of each chapter. List of almost 200 graded choral works for mixed voices, treble voices, and tenor-bass choirs, and nearly 100 works for pop ensembles, providing composer/arranger, title, voicing, and publisher. Photos, musical examples, charts, and illustrations; expansive index.

211. Jacobs, Ruth Krehbiel. *The Children's Choir.* Philadelphia: Fortress Press, 1958. iv, 299 p. ISBN 0-8006-0222-6; Rock Island, Illinois: Augustana Book Concern, 1958. vii, 311 p.   MT88 .J17

Collection of the materials published in the *Choristers Guild Letters* between September 1949 and June 1957. Covers methods; discipline; primary choir, including a nine-month study plan for developing musicianship; projects and special activities; special worship services; Christmas with poetry, games, discussion of traditions, etc.; the child in relation to church and home; hymns and hymn study; and spirit of the leader. Fortress Press edition has no bibliography; Augustana Book Concern edition offers a list of materials (classified bibliography of about 150 writings and 200 anthems, carols, cantatas, and works for special occasions; classified discography of approximately 100 recordings; and classified list of over 30 audiovisual materials). Illustrations and musical examples; expansive index.

Tufts, Nancy Poore. *The Children's Choir.* Vol. II. Foreword by Nita Akin. Philadelphia: Fortress Press, 1965. ix, 309 p.   MT898 .T83 1965

Vol. II contains materials published in the *Choristers Guild Letters* after June 1957. Topics include the value of children's choirs and good leadership; primary, junior, boys, youth, and handbell choir; projects and special activities; religious drama and choral speaking; hymns and hymn study; special worship services and festivals; the Christmas season; and materials (classified bibliography of approximately 200 writings and 500 anthems, cantatas, works for handbells, and collections of music). Illustrations, charts, and musical examples; expansive index.

212. Jacobs, Ruth Krehbiel. *The Successful Children's Choir.* S.l.: H. T. FitzSimons, 1995. 63 p. ISBN 0-9646552-2-5   MT915.J24 S9 1995

Brief. Addresses organizing and training a children's choir, with special emphasis on religious education. Classified list of approximately 200 sacred works for children's choirs and 43 recommended writings. No index.

213. Lundstrom, Linden J. *The Choir School: A Leadership Manual.* Rev. ed. Minneapolis, Minnesota: Augsburg Publishing House, 1963. 88 p.   MT88 .L8 1963

First published in 1938. Consists of two primary parts: (1) historical survey of the choir school from the 14th century to the present and (2) plan for training children's choirs. Photos; documented with end notes; no index.

214. Sample, Mabel Warkentin. *Leading Children's Choirs.* Nashville, Tennessee: Broadman Press, 1966. vii, 127 p.   MT88.S14 L4

Practical advice for organizing, selecting music, rehearsing, and performance considerations for children's choir. Emphasis on music education in the church and religious education through music. Classified bibliography of over 100 general books on children, church music, child psychology, public school music education, worship and religious education, voice training, and selected periodicals. Five appendices: enrollment card forms, selected repertoire, suggested teaching aids, companies furnishing children's choirs robes, and professional organizations. No index.

215. Stultz, Marie. *Innocent Sounds: Building Choral Tone and Artistry in Your Children's Choir: A Personal Journey.* Fenton, Missouri: MorningStar Music Publishers, 1999. xii, 180 p. ISBN 0-944529-30-5   MT915 .S88 1999

Invaluable handbook for choral directors of children's choirs. In three parts: (1) training the young singer; (2) techniques for building good intonation; and (3) selecting and evaluating fine choral literature. Includes suggested lesson plans, vocal exercises, and special activities for choral students. Several separate listings of choral titles throughout (26 titles for building diction; 25 for building pure vowels; 62 baroque, 59 contemporary, 27 canonic works to develop accuracy; annotated list of 49 titles to build beautiful tone; annotated list of 222 works for treble voices published between 1991 and 1997); lists are classified by genre, performing forces, and level of difficulty. Numerous musical examples, illustrations, and photos. No bibliography.

See also: Roach, Donald W. *Handbook for Children's and Youth Choir Directors* (item 63)

Preschool Choirs

216. Bedsole, Betty. *Effective Music Activity Teaching in Preschool and Children's Choirs.* Nashville, Tennessee: Convention Press, 1992. 63 p. MT915 .B38 1992

Addresses activity teaching in preschool and children's choirs. Musical examples and illustrations; no bibliography.

217. Bedsole, Betty, Derrell Billingsley, and G. Ronald Jackson. *Leading Preschool Choirs.* Nashville, Tennessee: Convention Press, 1985. 128 p. MT915 .B4 1985

First in a series of three books (*see also* Talmadge Butler's *Leading Younger Children's Choirs* (item 220) and Martha Kirkland's *Leading Older Children's Choirs* (item 223)). Instructional book for volunteer preschool choir leaders in Southern Baptist churches. Language is simple for the nonprofessional church musician. Purpose: to aid preschool children in developing skills in listening, singing, moving, and playing instruments through musical activities. Several charts correlate levels of understanding and singing goals of preschool, younger, and older children; short glossary (11 terms); no index.

218. McRae, Shirley W. *Directing the Children's Choir: A Comprehensive Resource.* New York: Schirmer Books, 1991. xiv, 232 p. ISBN 0-02-871785-6   MT915 .M49 1991

Eight chapters with cross references. Provides practical advice for promoting and organizing children's choirs; presents the historical, theological, and educational basis for Christian children's choirs; examines characteristics of children, ages 4–11, providing insights and suggesting goals; presents the Kodály and Orff approaches to singing and methods of applying each to children's choirs; discusses organizational, musical, and budgetary considerations; gives pedagogical advice for working with the child's voice; offers guidelines for rehearsal; and makes suggestions for enriching the program. Five appendices: list of professional organizations; bibliography of over 100 books, collections of music, journals, and videocassettes; additional bibliography of approximately 20 recordings of children's choirs, audiovisuals, and books for children along with addresses of musical instrument vendors; a guide to abbreviations in Orff arrangements; and an essay entitled "The Church Musician and the Copyright Law." Photos, musical examples, graphs, illustrations; expansive index.

Children's Choirs

219. Bostock, Donald. *Choirmastery: A Practical Handbook.* London: Epworth Press, 1966. viii, 128 p.   MT88 .B78

Directed toward the church choral director. Addresses choir organization, conducting, rehearsal techniques, voice production and enunciation, interpretation, repertoire, and the junior choir. Includes brief survey of the evolution of church music. Offers a classified list of nearly 200 choral works and collections. Musical examples, tables, and illustrations; no bibliography; index.

220. Butler, Talmadge, G. Ronald Jackson, and Betty Woodward. *Leading Younger Children's Choirs.* Nashville, Tennessee: Convention Press, 1985. 128 p.   MT88 .B95 1985

Second in a series of three books (*see also* Betty Bedsole's *Leading Preschool Choirs* (item 217) and Martha Kirkland's *Leading Older Children's Choirs* (item 223)). Instructional book for volunteer younger children's choir leaders in Southern Baptist churches. Provides activities for younger children (grades 1–3) for the development of "spiritual, musical, and church music understandings." Language is simple for the nonprofessional church musician. Short glossary (22 terms); numerous illustrations, chart, and musical examples; no index.

221. Coleman, Henry, and Hilda West. *Girls' Choirs*. London: Oxford University Press, 1962. viii, 65 p.   MT88 .C694

    Discusses girls's choirs in English schools and communities. Topics include organizing a choir, vocal training, selection of repertoire, and rehearsal. Chapter 3, "Choosing What to Sing," includes a classified bibliography of about 50 choral compositions that highlight various vocal techniques. Musical examples and illustrations; dated list of publishers with addresses; no index.

222. Ingram, Madeline D. *Organizing and Directing Children's Choirs*. Foreword by Austin C. Lovelace. New York: Abingdon Press, 1959. 160 p. MT88 .I5

    A practical guide to organizing and directing primary, junior, and junior high choirs based upon recorded classroom lectures of Madeline Ingram. Appended are listings of materials for primary, junior, and junior high choirs, consisting primarily of songs and anthems; listings of anthems for combined choirs, Christmas, Lent, and Easter; and a separate listing of hymnals and songbooks. Bibliography of almost 50 items further subdivided into the following categories: choir organization and children's choirs; books about hymns; worship and the arts; vocal training and teaching music; music in Christian education; child psychology; rhythms for children. Expansive index.

223. Kirkland, Martha, Jo Ann Butler, and Terry Kirkland. *Leading Older Children's Choirs*. Nashville, Tennessee: Convention Press, 1985. 123 p. MT88 .K58 1985

    Third in a series of three books (*see also* Betty Bedsole's *Leading Preschool Choirs* (item 217) and Talmadge Butler's *Leading Younger Children's Choirs* (item 220)). Instructional book for volunteer older children's choir leaders in Southern Baptist churches. Provides activities for older children (grades 4–6) which emphasize the development of singing skills, building of hymn repertoire, and use of the hymnal. Language is simple for the non-professional church musician. Short glossary (26 terms); numerous illustrations, charts, and musical examples; no index.

224. Swears, Linda. *Teaching the Elementary School Chorus*. West Nyack, New York: Parker, 1985. xiii, 209 p. ISBN 0-13-892514-3   MT930 .S9 1985

Addresses fundamental aspects of organizing and maintaining an elementary choral program. Three sections: "Building a Choral Music Program for Children," "Achieving a Good Choral Sound," and "Planning for Successful Rehearsal and Performance." Musical examples and illustrations; bibliography of 31 recommended choral works; bibliography of approximately 20 writings; list of publishers with addresses; expansive index.

See also: Bedsole, Betty. *Effective Music Activity Teaching in Preschool and Children's Choirs* (item 216); McRae, Shirley W. *Directing the Children's Choir: A Comprehensive Resource* (item 218)

Junior High School Choirs

225. Roach, Donald W. *Complete Secondary Choral Music Guide*. West Nyack, New York: Parker, 1989. xvi, 302 p. ISBN 0-13-162538-1   MT88 .R68 1989

Organized into four parts: (1) administration of junior and senior high school choruses; (2) the conductor and the choral score; (3) developing choral musicianship in students; and (4) planning rehearsals and performances. Eighteen appendices, including repertoire lists, music theater sources and materials, equipment and instrument sources, and other published materials. Musical examples, illustrations, and charts; classified bibliography of 120 writings; expansive index.

Senior High School Choirs

226. Boyd, Jack. *Teaching Choral Sight Reading*. Champaign, Illinois: Mark Foster Music Company, 1981. 209 p. ISBN 0-916656-17-9   MT870.B785 T4

Series of sight-singing exercises for high school choir. Addresses chromatic intervals, key-oriented melodies, rhythms, and contemporary notation. Four appendices draw examples from original compositions and provide additional information on basics of sight reading, rounds and canons, the C clef, and contemporary sounds. No bibliography; no index.

227. Jipson, Wayne R. *The High School Vocal Music Program*. West Nyack, New York: Parker Publishing, 1972. 224 p. ISBN 0-13-387902-X   MT3.U5 J56

Five parts: (1) sequential choral program; (2) the high school voice; (3) physical needs, such as adequate choral facilities and developing a choral library; (4) performances; and (5) evaluation and promotion of the choral program. Chapter 7, "Developing and Maintaining a Choral Library," presents a classified, annotated list (beginning choir, SATB; intermediate choir; girl's choir; concert choir; extended works for advanced choir; and Mass numbers) of approximately 100 musical works, giving title, composer/ arranger, music number and publisher, and comments. Musical examples, illustrations, and tables; no bibliography of writings; expansive index.

228. Poe, Frances R. "The Development of Instructional Materials for Teaching and Performing Renaissance Choral Music." Ph.D. dissertation. Indiana University, Bloomington, 1978. viii, 289 p.

Develops a conductor's manual and self-instructional performer's workbook for teaching and performing Renaissance choral music. Designed for senior high school choral ensembles and college choral ensembles composed primarily of non–music majors. Genres studied: French chanson, madrigal, German Lied, Mass, anthem, and chorale motet. Musical examples and tables; bibliography of about 80 writings.

229. Shewan, Robert. *Voice Training for the High School Chorus.* West Nyack, New York: Parker, 1973. 224 p. ISBN 0-13-943571-9   MT930 .S52

Practical guide for senior high school choral conductor. Discusses developing tone concepts through speech and guiding voices by singing in the imagination. Other topics: registers and vocal timbres; aural-image placement and resonance; expressive singing and choral intonation and blend; breathing; diction; classifying voices and selecting music for the high school chorus; learning and interpreting the score; and rehearsing. Many musical examples, graphs, and illustrations; no bibliography; expansive index.

230. Wolverton, Vance D. "Classifying Adolescent Singing Voices." Ph.D. dissertation. University of Iowa, Iowa City, 1985. x, 158 p.

Study of voice range, tessitura, quality, and register change among senior high school choral students. Musical examples and tables. Bibliography of 47 writings.

See also: Roach, Donald W. *Complete Secondary Choral Music Guide* (item 225)

ADULT CHOIRS

Church Choirs

231. Churchill, John. *Congregational Singing: The Congregation's Part in Public Worship.* Croydon, England: Royal School of Church Music, 1966. 26 p. ML3100 .C53

Brief guide offers practical suggestions for the improvement of congregational singing. Discusses hymns, Psalms, Versicles, and Responses. Bibliography of 26 writings; no index.

232. Coleman, Henry. *The Amateur Choir Trainer*. With a Foreword by Harvey Grace. London: Oxford University Press, 1932 (rep. 1936, 1944, 1950, 1954, 1959). xi, 143 p.   MT88 .C69

Coleman, Henry. *The Church Choir Trainer*. London: Oxford University Press, 1964. 182 p.   MT88 .C69 1964

Primarily of historical interest. British church choir training guide. Revised in 1964 under the title *The Church Choir Trainer*. Coleman, former Master of the Music at Peterborough Cathedral, presents his system for training choirs of boys and men. Offers practical advice for the nonprofessional choirmaster. Topics include choir organization, elementary voice training, enunciation, expression, balance, blend, text considerations in psalms and hymns, common vocal faults and their remedies, the boy's changing voice, the alto part, discipline, the organ and its use and abuse, the congregation, and general principles for teachers. *The Amateur Choir Trainer*: no bibliography; no index. *The Church Choir Trainer*: appendix of vocal exercises; brief bibliography; no index.

233. Dakers, Lionel. *Making Church Music Work*. Catalog of anthems compiled by David Patrick. London: Mowbrays, 1978. 218 p. ISBN 0-264-66470-1 MT88 .D27

Addresses interpretation and performance of church music. Includes annotated listing of approximately 340 anthems classified by church occasion. Musical examples; no bibliography; no index.

234. Etherington, Charles L. *The Organist and Choirmaster*. New York: Macmillan, 1952. xiii, 178 p.   MT88 .E85

Guide for organists and choirmasters "who, unfamiliar with Anglican services and traditions, find themselves called upon to prepare music for the services of that church." Six chapters offer information about the duties of the choirmaster, organist, and choristers; a description of the seasons of the church, the music, and aspects of the Anglican service; problems concerning equipment and organization; concludes with a brief chapter on choir etiquette. Non-Anglican church musicians should also find this volume helpful. Tables of the church calendar and a few musical examples; no bibliography; expansive index.

235. Nordin, Dayton W. *How to Organize and Direct the Church Choir.* West
     Nyack, New York: Parker, 1973. 214 p. ISBN 0-13-425207-1   MT88 .N74

     Ten-chapter discussion of planning, organizing, managing, and directing a
     successful church music program. Includes an annotated bibliography enti-
     tled "Church Music for Every Occasion" with approximately 150 choral
     works classified by the church year. Entries provide title, composer, pub-
     lisher, and required voices. Expansive index.

236. Rhys, Stephen, and King Palmer. *ABC of Church Music.* With a Foreword
     by Thomas Armstrong. Boston: Crescendo, 1967. 206 p. SBN 87597-025-7
     ML3131 .R5; London: Hodder and Stoughton, 1967. 212 p.   ML3131 .R5
     1967b

     For church organists and choir directors. Topics: place of music in worship;
     prose and verse set to music; the organ and organist; the choir and choir-
     master; the choral library; human relationships and official bodies; and pat-
     terns of ritual in services. Discussion too general to offer much to
     experienced church musicians. Classified list of approximately 250 anthems
     and larger sacred works. Entries graded and provide composer, title, and
     publisher. Selection shows British bias. Recommends collections of Roman
     Catholic church music, carols, and anthems. Two appendices: (1) classified
     bibliography of approximately 50 books on various aspects of church
     music; and (2) 100 "stirring" tunes with first line, tune, and location in
     hymn books; expansive index.

237. Routley, Erik. *Church Music and the Christian Faith.* Foreword by Martin
     E. Marty. Carol Stream, Illinois: Agape, 1978. vi, 153 p. ISBN 0-916642-
     10-0   ML3001 .R83; reprint, London: Collins, 1980. 156 p. ISBN 0-00-
     599650-3   ML3001 .R83 1980

     Revision of earlier writing published as *Church Music and Theology*
     (1959). Routley shares his insights on musical esthetics, theological issues,
     and practical matters for choirs, directors, and organists. Two appendices:
     (1) annotated bibliography of five varied organ accompaniments, along with
     fragments and examples, and (2) specification of the organ in University
     College Chapel, Oxford and in St. James's Church, Newcastle upon Tyne.
     Musical examples; bibliography of 28 writings; expansive index.

     See also: Hammar, Russell A. *Pragmatic Choral Procedures* (item 187)

College and University Choirs

   See: Poe, Frances R. "The Development of Instructional Materials for
   Teaching and Performing Renaissance Choral Music" (item 228)

Men's Choirs

238. Eckhardt, Andreas. *Männerchor: Organisation und Chorliteratur nach 1945.* Mainz: Schott, 1977. 205 p. ISBN 3-7957-2625-5   ML2660 .E25 1977

    German only. Discusses organizational development of the male chorus and the development of choral literature for the ensemble in post-1945 Germany. Identifies four stylistic directions found in male-chorus literature. Musical examples; classified bibliography of about 250 writings; index of names.

Women's Choirs

See: Anderson, Julia S. "Music for Women's Chorus and Harp: A Study of the Repertory and an Analysis and Performance of Selected Compositions" (item 83)

CHORAL NOTATION

239. Fleming, Larry Lee. "Contemporary Choral Notation." Ph.D. dissertation. University of Minnesota, Minneapolis, 1976. viii, 273 p.

    Presents a system of choral notation with specific emphasis on pitch and timbre. Musical examples and illustrations; bibliography of approximately 175 writings.

240. Hicks, Val J. "Innovative Choral Music Notation: The Semantics, Syntactics and Pragmatics of Symbology." Ph.D. dissertation. University of Utah, Salt Lake City, 1971. viii, 160 p.

    Study of "avant-garde" music notation found in vocal and choral music. Musical examples; bibliography of 155 writings and 68 vocal scores.

CHORAL REHEARSALS

241. Boyd, Jack. *Rehearsal Guide for the Choral Director.* 2nd ed. Champaign, Illinois: Mark Foster Music Company, 1977. 228 p. ISBN 0-916656-03-9 MT88.B82 R4 1977

    For beginning and experienced conductors. Guide to selecting music, planning programs, tryouts, and rehearsals. Final chapter examines stylistic characteristics and rehearsal problems in five choral works from different periods of music. Numerous musical examples and illustrations; expansive index.

242. Crowther, Duane S. *Teaching Choral Concepts: Simple Lesson Plans and Teaching Aids for In-Rehearsal Choir Instruction.* Bountiful, Utah: Horizon, 1981. 447 p. ISBN 0-88290-119-2   MT875 .C78

Conceptual approach to teaching choral singing with 35 brief lessons organized into four units. Musical examples, illustrations, graphs, and tables; bibliography of about 160 writings; no index.

243. Eberhardt, Carl. *A Guide to Successful Choral Rehearsals.* Translation by Kurt Michaelis. Frankfurt: Henry Litolff's Verlag; C. F. Peters, 1973. 40 p. MT85 .E22

Issues addressed include seating arrangement, discipline, general voice training, warm-up exercises, and rehearsal considerations. Abundant musical examples and illustrations; no bibliography; no index.

244. Gordon, Lewis. *Choral Director's Rehearsal and Performance Guide.* West Nyack, New York: Parker Publishing, 1989. xiii, 256 p. ISBN 0-13-133398-4 MT85 .G74 1989

Informative guide to establishing and developing a choral program in school, church, or community settings. Written with beginning and experienced choral directors in mind, although more beneficial to the former. Thirteen chapters subdivided into easy-to-follow sections. Topics include: establishing a choir, selecting music and planning programs, business procedures and financial considerations, conducting techniques, conducting rehearsals, and performance evaluation. Numerous illustrations and examples; index.

CONDUCTING

245. Adler, Samuel. *Choral Conducting, An Anthology.* 2nd ed. New York: Schirmer Books, 1985. xvii, 604 p. ISBN 0-02-870070-8   MT85 .C44 1985

Anthology of about 150 compositions from the pre-Renaissance to the late 1960s. Generally for four-part mixed chorus. Improvement over first edition in that it contains more works while eliminating difficult works and those requiring large forces. Many are excerpts rather than complete works. Stated purposes: (1) "to provide a large body of choral music for use in conducting classes" and (2) "to suggest a structured curriculum . . . for the acquisition of solid technique in the field of choral conducting." Instructional chapters inserted between examples (right-hand techniques; development of left hand; special choral problems). Three indices: publishers, composers, and titles.

246. Busch, Brian R. *The Complete Choral Conductor: Gesture and Method.*
     New York: Schirmer Books, 1984. xii, 275 p. ISBN 0-02-870340-5   MT85
     .B925 1984

     Choral conducting manual; over 130 conducting diagrams. Organized into
     three parts: (1) mechanics of conducting, (2) advanced conducting gestures,
     and (3) conductor as organizer and teacher. Two appendices: (1) basic inter-
     national phonetic alphabet sounds found in English pronunciation and (2)
     bell vowel chart. Numerous musical examples, illustrations, and photos; no
     bibliography; expansive index.

247. Dahlin, Walter O. *Basic Choral Conducting.* Nashville, Tennessee: Conven-
     tion Press, 1972. 80 p.   MT88 .D24

     Practical, basic study course for the inexperienced church choir director.
     Several brief chapters on aspects of conducting technique alternate with
     chapters on music fundamentals, vocal principles, rehearsal techniques, the
     worship service, music selection, and helpful hints. Annotated bibliography
     of 17 books on church music, conducting, choir training, and diction. No
     index.

248. Davison, Archibald T. *Choral Conducting.* Cambridge, Massachusetts: Har-
     vard University Press, 1940 (rep. 1948, 1950, 1954, 1956, 1959, 1962, 1965,
     1968, 1971, 1980). 73 p. ISBN 0-674-128001 (1980)   MT85.D28 C4

     An instructional book by the distinguished American educator. Topics
     include developing necessary skills for a conductor, the art of conducting,
     limitations and attributes of various choral combinations, organizing suc-
     cessful rehearsals, and choral technique. Illustrations and musical exam-
     ples; no bibliography; no index.

249. Decker, Harold A., and Colleen J. Kirk. *Choral Conducting: Focus on Com-
     munication.* Englewood Cliffs, New Jersey: Prentice Hall, 1988. ISBN
     0-13-133380-1   MT85 .D315 1988; reprint, Prospect Heights, Illinois:
     Waveland Press, 1995. x, 374 p. ISBN 0-88133-876-1   MT85 .D315 1995

     Aspects of choral conducting. Illustrations, photographs, tables, and numer-
     ous musical examples, including 26 representative musical works from the
     Renaissance to the 20th century. Partially annotated bibliography of 350
     choral works for children's chorus, adolescent voices, treble chorus, male
     chorus, and church choir. Pronunciation guides; glossary of terms; bibliog-
     raphy of more than 100 writings; expansive index.

250. Decker, Harold A., and Julius Herford, eds. *Choral Conducting Symposium.*
     2nd ed. Englewood Cliffs, New Jersey: Prentice Hall, 1988. xii, 290 p.
     ISBN 0-13-133372-0   MT85 .C444 1988

Collection of articles on aspects of choral conducting. Howard Swan's "The Development of a Choral Instrument" addresses choral tone and diction and categorizes six "schools" of choral singing in America (created by John F. Williamson, William Finn, Olaf and Paul Christiansen, Fred Waring, Joseph Klein, and Robert Shaw). Swan presents practical applications of techniques from each "school" and offers his own methodology. Lloyd Pfautsch's "The Choral Conductor and the Rehearsal" discusses planning and execution of successful rehearsals. Walter S. Collins's "The Choral Conductor and the Musicologist" deals with choral editing and performance practice and suggests critical editions, monographs, dictionaries and encyclopedias, periodicals, bibliographies, and discographies. Daniel Moe's "The Choral Conductor and Twentieth-Century Choral Music" examines problems associated with performing contemporary music and includes a representative list of 153 20th-century choral works. Julius Herford's "The Choral Conductor's Preparation of the Musical Score" discusses score analysis with selected examples from Requiems by W. A. Mozart, Hector Berlioz, Johannes Brahms, and Gabriel Fauré. As a companion to Herford's article, Jan Harrington's "Contributor's Notes" presents an analysis of the Introit and Kyrie movements from Giuseppe Verdi's *Messa da Requiem*. James G. Smith contributes a classified bibliography of more than 350 books, periodicals, articles, and other items. Numerous graphs, charts, and musical examples; expansive index.

251. Ehmann, Wilhelm. *Choral Directing*. Translated by George D. Wiebe. Minneapolis, Minnesota: Augsburg Publishing House, 1968. xi, 214 p.   MT85 .E413

Translation of *Die Chorführung, Band II, Das künstlerische Singen*, originally published in 1949. Two parts: first half discusses choral posture and choral breath; voice, speech, and ear training; body movement and choral singing; and conducting patterns and choral gestures. Second half discusses preparation by the choral director, artistic unison and canon singing, and multivoiced choral singing, and concludes with remarks about the final rehearsal and performance. Codifies the ideas of a leading exponent of the German music education movement of the 1920s and 1930s. Musical examples and charts; no bibliography; no index.

252. Ehret, Walter. *The Choral Conductor's Handbook*. London: Augener, 1959. 55 p.   MT85 .E43 1959a; New York: Edward B. Marks Music Corp., 1959. 55 p.   MT85 .E43

Concise, pithy advice for all choral directors regardless of the experience or the skill of their groups. Sixteen chapters, each covering one problem area.

Topics include rehearsal procedures, presenting a new choral work, flatting, dynamics, tempo, rhythm, blend and balance, diction, vowels, consonants, diphthongs, tone color, staging, criteria for selection of choral music, audio aids, and program and performance suggestions. Musical examples; no bibliography; no index.

253. Ericson, Eric, Gösta Ohlin, and Lennart Spångberg. *Choral Conducting.* Translated and edited by Gunilla Marcus and Norman Luboff. Stockholm: Sveriges Körförbunds, 1974; English ed., New York: Walton Music, 1976. 176 p.   MT85 .E74 1976

Originally published in Swedish. First chapter addresses conducting technique; following chapters present articles by various writers on aspects of choral music and choral singing: "Rehearsing Methods" (Eric Ericson); "The Sounds of a Choir" and "Intonation" (Gösta Ohlin); "Improvising the Tone to Exercise the Reaction" (Jürgen Jürgens); "Intonation Exercises" (Richard Berg, Ingegerd Persson, and Agneta and Stefan Sköld); "Playing the Score" (Lennart Spångberg); "Of Choirs and Instruments" (Helge Lidén); and "Means of Expression in Contemporary Choir Music" (Gunnar Eriksson). List of music publishers classified by country and list of Walton Music publications appended. Abundant musical examples and illustrations; brief bibliography of books on conducting; index.

254. Finn, William J. *The Art of the Choral Conductor.* Foreword by Joseph R. Foley. Preface by Leopold Stokowski. Evanston, Illinois: Summy-Birchard, 1960. 2 vols. 292 p.; 302 p.   MT85 .F52 1960

Two volumes entitled "Choral Technique" and "The Conductor Raises His Baton" respectively. Addresses choral musicianship, diction, dynamics, tempo, conducting, sight reading, and counterpoint, among other topics. Musical examples and illustrations; sparsely documented with footnotes; expansive index.

255. Garretson, Robert L. *Conducting Choral Music.* 8th ed. Upper Saddle River, New Jersey: Prentice Hall, 1998. xvii, 427 p. ISBN 0-13-775735-2 MT85.G175 C6 1998

First edition published in 1961. Treats in some detail most of the problems a choral conductor is likely to meet. Chapters on conducting techniques, tone and diction, maintaining vocal health, children's voices and the boy's changing voice, style and interpretation, rehearsal techniques, programs and concepts, and planning and organization. Selective bibliography, including a separate videotape listing, at the end of each chapter. Numerous music examples, illustrations, tables, and photos. Impressive 103-page appendix lists choral composers (ca. 1200–1992), choral octavo publications, choral collections, extended choral works, music publishers/distributors, national retail music dealers/distributors, manufacturers of music equipment, and choir travel/tour services. Expansive index.

256. Green, Elizabeth A. H. *The Modern Conductor.* 6th ed. Upper Saddle River, New Jersey: Prentice Hall, 1997. xvii, 286 p. ISBN 0-13-251481-8   MT85 .G785 1997

College textbook based on the technical conducting principles of Nicolai Malko. Discusses both instrumental and choral aspects of conducting. Musical examples and illustrations; appendices include stage layout for choral groups and a list of terms; bibliography of nearly 100 writings. Separate expanded indices for subjects, musical examples, and music for performance.

257. Haberlen, John B. *Mastering Conducting Techniques.* With supplementary exercises by Charles Knox. Champaign, Illinois: Mark Foster, 1977. ix, 60 p. ISBN 0-916656-01-2   MT85 .H15

Consists of brief exercises, organized into 22 units, which highlight basic conducting techniques. Among the topics treated are meter patterns, preparatory motion, dynamics, cueing, independence of hands, tempo changes, syncopation, and the fermata. Musical examples; no bibliography.

258. Heffernan, Charles W. *Choral Music: Technique and Artistry.* Foreword by Howard Swan. Englewood Cliffs, New Jersey: Prentice-Hall, 1982. xi, 161 p. ISBN 0-13-133330-5   MT875 .H33 1982

Exceptional book on choral singing and conducting. Organized into five chapters. Topics include essential vocal and conducting techniques and choral artistry. Numerous graphs and musical examples; classified bibliography of 160-plus items; expansive index.

259. Holst, Imogen. *Conducting a Choir.* London: Oxford University Press, 1973 (rep. 1990, 1991, 1993, 1995). x, 161 p. ISBN 0-19-313407-1 MT85 .H73

Originally published in 1973; reprinted with corrections. A guide for beginning conductors. Musical examples, illustrations, and photographs; bibliography of 18 writings and a few recommended collections of music. Indices of first lines of musical examples and expansive general index.

260. Kaplan, Abraham. *Choral Conducting.* New York: W. W. Norton, 1985. xvi, 203 p. ISBN 0-393-95375-0   MT85 .K3278 1985

Generally successful and flexible contribution to the literature on conducting technique. Concise and succinct. Useful with undergraduate conducting
classes. Badly drawn conducting patterns. Diction section based on work of
Madeleine Marshall. No bibliography; no index.

261. Manson, John L. *Interpretive Choral Singing*. Nashville, Tennessee: Broad-
     man Press, 1961. ix, 113 p.   MT875.M164 I5

     Focuses on the development of interpretive skills by the choral director.
     Numerous musical examples; no bibliography, although footnotes provide
     some bibliographic information; no index.

262. Moe, Daniel T. *Basic Choral Concepts*. Minneapolis, Minnesota: Augsburg
     Publishing House, 1972. 31 p.   MT85 .M62 1972

     Brief. Part of text in outline form. Divided into three parts: first part gives
     basic guidelines for young conductors in regard to communication via ges-
     ture, developing a concept of the composition, and function and scope of
     prerehearsal analysis; second part devoted to articulation; third part gives
     preconcert remarks to University of Iowa choral ensembles. Many musical
     examples; no bibliography; no index.

263. Moe, Daniel T. *Problems in Conducting*. Rev. ed. Minneapolis, Minnesota:
     Augsburg Publishing House, 1973. 20 p.   MT85 .M52 1973

     Brief, rather unusual compilation. Includes nine one- to two-page excerpts
     from choral compositions by Moe, followed by four pages of analytical
     comments and performance suggestions. Each musical excerpt presents a
     number of "conducting problems" the conductor is to practice and learn to
     execute. Excerpts arranged so that the difficulties steadily increase. Begins
     with a few irregular meters and triplets and progresses through canonic imi-
     tations, mild diatonic dissonances, some problems of diction, balance
     between voices and long lines, handling intonation problems, and sophisti-
     cated meter changes. No bibliography; no index.

264. Ross, Allan A. *Techniques for Beginning Conductors*. Belmont, California:
     Wadsworth Publishing, 1976. 344 p. ISBN 0-534-00403-2   MT85 .R72

     Conducting manual. Emphasizes three areas: conducting techniques, score
     reading, and English, French, German, and Italian music terminology.
     Musical exercises increase in complexity. Some sections specifically
     address issues of choral conducting. Numerous charts, graphs, and musical
     examples; bibliography of 59 books; expansive index.

265. Simons, Harriet. *Choral Conducting: A Leadership Teaching Approach.* Champaign, Illinois: Mark Foster Music Company, 1983. xi, 122 p. ISBN 0-916656-18-7 (pbk)   MT85 .S547 1983

Primary focus is explanation of the psychological principles involved in effective musical leadership. Ideas based on the self-actualization theories of Abraham Maslow and the transactional-analysis concepts of Eric Berne and Thomas Harris. First chapter is on self-actualization. The following six chapters deal with developing group identity, "I'm OK; You're OK," group leadership, leading songs, conducting, and rehearsal techniques. Final chapter answers seven questions about conducting pedagogy. Well organized, perceptive, well written, and useful. Bibliography of over 60 writings; no index.

266. Stanton, Royal. *The Dynamic Choral Conductor.* Delaware Water Gap, Pennsylvania: Shawnee Press, 1971. xi, 205 p.   MT85 .S82

Relationship of the choral conductor with changing conditions of conducting, communicative techniques, choral tone, voice training, group musicianship, the conductor's numerous tasks, attitudes about styles and repertoire, and the impact of the conductor's image. Two appendices present 11 practical projects and provide practical answers to nine recurring problems. Illustrations, charts, and musical examples; classified bibliography of more than 30 books; no index.

267. Thomas, Kurt. *The Choral Conductor: The Technique of Choral Conducting in Theory and Practice.* Translated by Alfred Mann and William H. Reese. New York: Associated Music Publishers, 1971. vi, 91 p. ISBN 0-911320-93-8   MT85 .T513

English adaptation of Thomas's *Lehrbuch der Chorleitung.* Based on the author's conducting classes. Addresses basic conducting technique, chorus formation, vocal training for the chorus, choral diction, problems of intonation, and rehearsal considerations. Includes illustrations, photographs, and musical examples; updated, classified bibliography (conducting technique, vocal technique, and history and literature) of 22 books; expansive index.

PERFORMANCE PRACTICE

268. Phillips, Elizabeth V., and John-Paul Christopher Jackson. *Performing Medieval and Renaissance Music: An Introductory Guide.* New York: Schirmer Books; London: Collier Macmillan, 1986. xiv, 316 p. ISBN 0-02-871790-2   ML430.5 .P52 1986

Deals with performance practice of ensemble music of the Middle Ages and Renaissance (A.D. 700–1650). Organized into 3 parts: (1) constitution of early music ensemble; (2) general guidelines for early music performance; and (3) music repertory of 35 representative works. Several appendices, including pronunciation guides and selected journals dealing with early music. Recommended projects; musical examples, illustrations, and facsimiles; bibliography of nearly 500 writings; expansive index.

269. Poe, Frances R. *Teaching and Performing Renaissance Choral Music: A Guide for Conductors and Performers*. Metuchen, New Jersey: Scarecrow Press, 1994. viii, 227 p. ISBN 0-8108-2778-6, ISBN 0-8108-2886-3 (pbk) MT875 .P55 1994

Provides a sampling of Renaissance choral music along with essential information about performance practice. Two parts: conductor's manual and performer's workbook. Conductor's manual addresses the French chanson, Italian madrigal and balletto, English madrigal and ballett, German lied, Renaissance motet, Mass, anthem, and chorale motet. Brief introduction for each section. Examines 17 compositions, giving information about the title, type of composition, composer, text, background, structural and stylistic elements, other editions, and recordings. An edition of the music follows each analysis. The analysis is not in depth, but beneficial; intended as an aid to conductors to teach musical style and structure through performance. Performer's workbook consists of questions about each of the compositions discussed. Bibliography of 100 writings.

See also: Poe, Frances R. "The Development of Instructional Materials for Teaching and Performing Renaissance Choral Music" (item 228)

VOCAL TECHNIQUE

270. Armstrong, Kerchal, and Donald Hustad. *Choral Musicianship and Voice Training: An Introduction, with Music for Conducting Class*. Carol Stream, Illinois: Somerset Press, 1986. vii, 252 p. ISBN 0-916642-29-1   MT875 .A75 1986

Presents concepts toward developing choral singing. Intended as a textbook; recommended assignments at the ends of chapters. Includes 30 complete choral works to which to apply studied techniques; rehearsal notes provided for each composition. Musical examples and illustrations; selected bibliography of more than 40 writings; index of choral literature.

271. Christensen, Helga. *Better Choir Singing: A Textbook on Choral Work*. Translated by Paulette Moeller. Dallas, Texas: Choristers Guild, 1973. 98 p. MT875 .C5613 1973

English translation of the Danish monograph *Kon Kor Klang*. A textbook designed to assist conductors in teaching voice-production technique. Divided into 10 lessons: basic voice production and use; singing in rhythm; agility; starting tone; breathing techniques; vowel color and relation to articulation; articulation of consonants; staccato, interval leaps, and flexibility and lightness of tone; dynamics; and vocal registers and recapitulation. The lessons are accompanied by compositions that illustrate each vocal production issue. Abundance of musical examples and illustrations; no bibliography; index of musical examples.

272. Darrow, Gerald F. *Four Decades of Choral Training.* Metuchen, New Jersey: Scarecrow Press, 1975. xii, 233 p. ISBN 0-8108-0791-2   MT875 .D23

Limited to writings concerned with the mixed chorus of changed voices. Describes the nature of choral training as evidenced in more than 950 writings on the subject published in English between 1930 and 1970. Demonstrates general patterns of agreement or disagreement among such diverse personalities as John Finley Williamson, F. Melius and Olaf C. Christiansen, Fred Waring, Father William Finn, Robert Shaw, and Peter Wilhousky. Topics include choral tone, breathing, posture, intonation, range, dynamics, and diction. Particularly valuable: an annotated bibliography of 475 titles. Expansive index of terms.

273. Ehmann, Wilhelm, and Frauke Haasemann. *Handbuch der chorischen Stimmbildung* [Handbook of choral voice training]. Kassel, Germany: Bärenreiter, 1984. 188 p. ISBN 3-7618-0691-4   MT875.E33 H23 1984

German only. Addresses posture, breathing, vocal training, and choral vocal training. Applies principles to selected Lieder, motets, oratorios, Requiems, and Masses. Numerous musical examples; glossary of terms; bibliography of 15 writings.

274. Ehmann, Wilhelm, and Frauke Haasemann. *Voice Building for Choirs.* Rev. ed. Translated by Brenda Smith. Chapel Hill, North Carolina: Hinshaw Music, 1982. xiv, 141 p. ISBN 0-937276-02-2   MT875 .E3613 1982

English translation of *Chorische Stimmbildung* (1963). Part I addresses issues of posture, breathing, voice building, and voice training in a choir rehearsal. Part II presents practical exercises in choral voice building. Part III provides warm-up exercises designed to develop various choral sounds indicative of musical style periods and to confront specific problems of individual compositions. Numerous musical examples; glossary of terms; bibliography of 12 writings; no index.

275. Ehmann, Wilhelm. "Voice Training and Sound Ideal as a Means of Musical Interpretation in Choral Music." In *Festschrift, Theodore Hoelty-Nickel: A Collection of Essays on Church Music*, ed. Newman W. Powell, 51–63. Valparaiso, Indiana: Valparaiso University, 1967.   ML3000.1 .F48

Addresses choral singing and employment of varying sound ideals in performance of music compositions from varying style periods.

276. González, Marilyn M. *Choir Care: Building Sound Technique*. New York: American Guild of Organists, 1993. 100 p.   MT875 .G66 1993

Compilation of 13 revised and enlarged articles originally published in *The American Organist* along with 2 new articles. Focuses on developing basic skills, refining tone, and shaping vocal phrasing. Musical examples; no bibliography.

277. Haasemann, Frauke, and James M. Jordan. *Group Vocal Technique*. Chapel Hill, North Carolina: Hinshaw Music, 1991. xx, 196 p. ISBN 0-937276-11-1   MT875 .H12 1991

Haasemann, Frauke, and James M. Jordan. *Group Vocal Technique: The Vocalise Cards*. Chapel Hill, North Carolina: Hinshaw Music, 1992. Looseleaf cards. ISBN 0-937276-13-8

Haasemann, Frauke, and James M. Jordan. *Group Vocal Technique*. Chapel Hill, North Carolina: Hinshaw Music, 1989. Videorecording

Updates *Voice Building for Choirs* (item 274) by Wilhelm Ehmann and Haasemann. Discusses group vocal technique, relaxation and posture, voice building, breathing, anatomy of the sigh, resonance and placement, dynamics, register consistency, range extension, vocal technique, diction, auditioning singers, seating and standing plans, selection of literature, and conducting technique. Addresses music aptitude and music achievement. Musical examples, charts, tables, illustrations; discography of 25 recordings; bibliography of approximately 250 writings; no index. Accompanied by vocalise cards and videorecording.

278. Hofbauer, Kurt. *Praxis der chorischen Stimmbildung* [The practice of choral vocal development]. Mainz, Germany: Schott, 1978. 107 p. ISBN 3-7957-1033-2   MT875 .H65

German only. Primarily consists of 163 lessons, addressing posture, breathing, and vocal production and development. Illustrations and musical examples; bibliography of 20 writings; index. Series: *Bausteine für Musikerziehung und Musikpflege*, Schriftenreihe B 33.

279. Lorenz, Ellen Jane. *The Learning Choir: Lessons and Anthem Arrangements*. Nashville, Tennessee: Abingdon Press, 1968. 96 p.   MT875 .L8

Intended for use by amateur choirs (children's, youth, or adult). Organized into 20 lessons, each coupled with an anthem. Topics include posture and breathing, pronunciation, time signatures, rhythm, key signatures, clefs, musical symbols and terms, singing in parts, and musical expression.

280. May, William V., and Craig Tolin. *Pronunciation Guide for Choral Literature: French, German, Hebrew, Italian, Latin, Spanish*. Reston, Virginia: Music Educator's National Conference, 1987; reprint, Denton, Texas: University of North Texas, 1988. xii, 79 p.   MT883 .M39 1988

Covers phonetics and diction in singing, the international phonetic alphabet, and pronunciation guides for French, German, Hebrew, Italian, Latin, and Spanish.

281. Robinson, Russell L., and Jay Althouse. *The Complete Choral Warm-Up Book: A Sourcebook for Choral Directors*. Van Nuys, California: Alfred, 1995. 128 p. ISBN 0-88284-657-4   MT875.R67 C6 1995

Presents 211 warm-up exercises for children's choirs to adult choirs. Each exercise accompanied by an explanation of its purpose and how to perform the exercise correctly. Index. Series: *Alfred Choral Builders*.

282. Stone, Leonard. *Belwin Chorus Builder*. Long Island, New York: Belwin, 1961–1962. 2 vols. 32 p.; 36 p.   MT875 .S76

Two brief volumes presenting the fundamentals of successful choral singing. Many musical drills and exercises; list of musical terms; no bibliography; no index.

283. Wilson, Harry Robert. *Artistic Choral Singing: Practical Problems in Organization, Technique and Interpretation*. New York: G. Schirmer, 1959. vii, 374 p.   MT875 .W49

Summation of ideas and technique Wilson developed in a long and successful career. Topics include values of choral singing, the art of choral conducting, general considerations for interpretation, basic elements of expression, styles in choral singing, diction, developing choral tone, special vocal problems, blend and balance, types and organization of choral groups, the choral rehearsal, planning choral programs, and the choral performance. Still offers useful ideas and techniques for the choral musician. Four appendices, the first two now quite dated: (1) recordings (about 20); (2) choral collections (about 20). Third and fourth lists still provide some useful titles:

(3) extended works (about 35); (4) miscellaneous brief works (about 490) subdivided by sacred and secular and further subdivided by choral voicing (SATB, SSA, etc.). Entries list composer, publisher, a difficulty rating, accompaniment, and a brief description. Expansive index of terms.

284. Young, Percy M. *A Handbook of Choral Technique*. London: Dennis Dobson, 1953. 72 p.   MT875 .Y7

Brief guide. Musical examples and illustrations; no bibliography; index of works discussed in the text. Series: *The Student's Music Library*.

See also: Heffernan, Charles W. *Choral Music: Technique and Artistry* (item 258); Shewan, Robert. *Voice Training for the High School Chorus* (item 229)

V

Surveys of Choral Music, Sacred and Secular

GENERAL WORKS

285. Anhalt, István. *Alternative Voices: Essays on Contemporary Vocal and Choral Composition.* Toronto: University of Toronto Press, 1984. xi, 336 p. ISBN 0-8020-5531-1   ML 1406 .A53 1984

Western vocal and choral composition since World War II. Chapters 2–4 present model analyses of three selected works: Luciano Berio's *Sequenza III*, György Ligeti's *Nouvelles Aventures*, and Witold Lutoslawski's *Trois Poèmes d'Henri Michaux*. Chapters 5–7 cover a broad range of topics, including blurred boundaries between composer and performer, speech and song, and Western and non-Western music; hallowed and cursed names; repetition as a mythical or mystical technique; magical elements in music and language; hierophany of childhood; hierophany of the victim and the substitute celebration of the absurd; performance of music as a spectacle or celebration; and aspects of the use of voice and language by selected contemporary composers. Chapter 8 is devoted to John Beckwith's *Gas!*, Murray Schafer's *In Search of Zoroaster*, and Berio's *Coro*. Musical examples and charts; list of approximately 300 compositions; bibliography of more than 400 items; two expansive indices: (1) names and titles and (2) subjects.

286. Belan, William Wells, ed. *Choral Essays: A Tribute to Roger Wagner.* San Carlos, California: Thomas House Publications, 1993. ix, 189 p.   ML55 .W145 1993

A collection of eight essays, preceded by an interview with Roger Wagner. The essays are: "Roger Wagner: Composer, Arranger, Musicologist" (Robert Stevenon); "The Male Chorus, Medium of Art and Entertainment: Its History and Literature" (Richard H. Trame); "A Choral Conductor's Preparation for Choral/Orchestra Concerts" (Kerry M. Barnett); "Whither Gregorian Chant?" (Robert M. Fowells); "L'Antienne *Asperges Me* dans la tradition grégorienne" ["The antiphon *Asperges Me* in the Gregorian tradition"] (Dom Jean Claire, translation by Fowells); "Gregorian Musical Words" (M. Clement Morin and Fowells); "Phrasing in Music of the Renaissance Era" (Dennis Shrock); "Essay: Tempo Rubato in the Nineteenth Century" (Belan). Musical examples and bibliographies included with some essays. Index.

287. Garretson, Robert L. *Choral Music: History, Style, and Performance Practice.* Englewood Cliffs, New Jersey: Prentice Hall, 1993. xi, 240 p. ISBN 0-13-137191-6   ML1500 .G37 1993

Intended for choral conductors. Organized into five chapters covering the Renaissance, baroque, classical, romantic, and 20th century. Each surveys social conditions, major choral composers, composition of choirs, musical style and performance practice, and related arts, and concludes with suggested bibliographies for further study. Four appendices: (1) classified list of major composers with nationality and dates; (2) graded bibliography of approximately 750 octavo publications; (3) bibliography of about 500 extended choral works; and (4) list of music publishers and distributors with addresses. Musical examples, illustrations, and photos; bibliographies of nearly 500 writings; expansive index.

288. Jacobs, Arthur, ed. *Choral Music: A Symposium.* Baltimore; Middlesex, England: Penguin Books, 1963 (rep. 1966, 1969, 1978). 448 p. ISBN 0-14-020533-0 (UK)   ML1500 .J3

Twenty-one essays by noted experts: "Choir and People in the Later Middle Ages" (F. Ll. Harrison); "From Ockeghem to Palestrina" (Caldwell Titcomb); "Tudor England and After" (Elizabeth Cole); "Germany and Northern Europe, before Bach" (J. Merrill Knapp); "At the Courts of Italy and France" (Denis Arnold); "Church and State in England" (J. A. Westrup); "Bach and His Time" (Walter Emery); "England in the Age of Handel" (Arthur Jacobs); "The Viennese Classical Period" (Roger Fiske); "After Handel—in Britain and America" (Richard Franko Goldman); "The French Revolution: Beethoven and Berlioz" (J. H. Elliot); "The Oratorio and Cantata Market: Britain, Germany, America" (Theodore M. Finney); "The Mass—from Rossini to Dvořák" (Mosco Carner); "Chorus and Symphony: Liszt, Mahler, and After" (Deryck Cooke); "Britain from Stanford to Vaughan Williams" (Charles Reid); "Slavonic Nationalism from Dvořák to the Soviets" (Gerald Seaman); "Four Revolutionaries" (Dita Newlin); "France from the Age of Fauré and Debussy" (Rollo H. Myers); "Modern British Composers" (Ernest Bradbury); "A Mixed Modern Group" (Peter J. Pirie); and "Twentieth-Century Americans" (Robert Sabin). Two appendices: (1) Latin text with English translation of Mass Ordinary and Requiem

Mass (in part) and (2) information about the continuo. Bibliography of recommended books for each essay.

289. Lowinsky, Edward E. *Music in the Culture of the Renaissance and Other
Essays.* Forewords by Howard Mayer Brown and Ellen T. Harris. Edited
and with introduction by Bonnie J. Blackburn. Chicago: University of
Chicago Press, 1989. 2 vols., xxi, 993 p. ISBN 0-226-49478-0   ML160
.L83 1989

Impressive compilation of 43 articles and essays by Lowinsky; some
reprints, some published for first time. Organized into eight sections: (1)
music and the history of ideas, (2) musical iconography, (3) 16th-century
motet, (4) Josquin des Prez, (5) Cipriano de Rore as court composer at Fer-
rara and Munich, (6) *musica ficta*, (7) the compositional process, and (8)
views and reviews. Articles related to choral music sprinkled throughout.
Musical examples, facsimiles, tables, photos, and illustrations; partially
annotated bibliography of four books, four editions, and 58 articles, forewords, and introductions, and 14 review articles; expansive general index
and index of manuscripts cited.

290. *New Oxford History of Music* (series).

Vol. 3. Hughes, Anselm, and Gerald Abraham, eds. *Ars Nova and the
Renaissance, 1300–1540.* London; Oxford: Oxford University Press, 1960
(rep. 1964, 1969, 1986, 1994, 1998). xix, 565 p. ISBN 0-19-316303-9
(hbk), ISBN 0-19-816450-5 (pbk)   ML160 .N44 vol.3

Vol. 4. Abraham, Gerald, ed. *The Age of Humanism, 1540–1630.* London:
Oxford University Press, 1968 (rep. 1998). xxv, 978 p. ISBN 0-19-316304-7
ML160 .N44 vol.4

Vol. 6. Abraham, Gerald, ed. *Concert Music, 1630–1750.* Oxford: Oxford
University Press, 1986 (rep. 1991, 1994). xx, 786 p. ISBN 0-19-316306-3
(hbk), ISBN 0-19-816453-X (pbk)   ML160 .N44 vol.6

Vol. 8. Abraham, Gerald, ed. *The Age of Beethoven, 1790–1830.* London:
Oxford University Press, 1982 (rep. 1985, 1988, 1994). xix, 747 p. ISBN
0-19-316308-X (hbk), ISBN 0-19-816-455-6 (pbk)   ML160 .N44 vol.8

Vol. 9. Abraham, Gerald, ed. *Romanticism (1830–1890).* Oxford; London:
Oxford University Press, 1990 (rep. 1994). xx, 935 p. ISBN 0-19-316309-8
(hbk), ISBN 0-19-816456-4 (pbk)   ML160 .N44 vol.9

Vol. 10. Cooper, Martin, ed. *The Modern Age, 1890–1960.* London: Oxford
University Press, 1974 (rep. 1994). xix, 764 p. ISBN 0-19-316310-1 (hbk),
ISBN 0-19-816457-2 (pbk)   ML160 .N44 vol.10

291. *Norton Introduction to Music History* (series).

Renaissance:

Atlas, Allan W. *Renaissance Music: Music in Western Europe, 1400–1600.* New York: W. W. Norton, 1998. xxi, 729 p. ISBN 0-393-97169-4   ML172 .A84 1998

Atlas, Allan W., ed. *Anthology of Renaissance Music: Music in Western Europe, 1400–1600.* New York: W. W. Norton, 1998. ix, 496 p. ISBN 0-393-97170-8   MT91 .A58 1998

Classical:

Downs, Philip G. *Classical Music: The Era of Haydn, Mozart, and Beethoven.* New York: W. W. Norton, 1992. xvi, 697 p. ISBN 0-393-95191-X ML195 .D68 1992

Downs, Philip G., ed. *Anthology of Classical Music.* New York: W. W. Norton, 1992. xi, 554 p. ISBN 0-393-95209-6   MT6.5 .A56 1992

Romantic:

Plantinga, Leon. *Romantic Music: A History of Musical Style in Nineteenth-Century Europe.* New York: W. W. Norton, 1984. xiii, 523 p. ISBN 0-393-95196-0   ML196 .P6 1984

Plantinga, Leon, ed. *Anthology of Romantic Music.* New York: W. W. Norton, 1984. ix, 637 p. ISBN 0-393-01811-3, ISBN 0-393-95211-8 (pbk) MT6.5 .A59 1984

Twentieth Century:

Morgan, Robert P. *Twentieth-Century Music: A History of Musical Style in Modern Europe and America.* New York: W. W. Norton, 1991. xvii, 554 p. ISBN 0-393-95272-X   ML197 .M675 1990

Morgan, Robert P., ed. *Anthology of Twentieth-Century Music.* New York: W. W. Norton, 1991. xii, 452 p. ISBN 0-393-95284-3   MT6.5 .A595 1991

292. Poellein, John Alfred. "New Choral Techniques: An Historical-Analytical Study." D.M.A. dissertation. University of Illinois at Urbana-Champaign, 1974. x, 301 p.

Study of 20th-century developments in choral music, namely the use of the speaking voice, innovative "formal" shapes, electronics, and microtonal music. Several appendices, including the international phonetic alphabet, microtonal music glossary of terms, and lists of nearly 100 representative choral works with Sprechstimme and 50 representative choral works with electronic tape. Musical examples (some graphic notation), illustrations, and tables; bibliography of about 70 writings.

293. Poos, Heinrich, ed. *Chormusik und Analyse: Beiträge zur Formanalyse und Interpretation mehrstimmiger Vokalmusik* [Choral music and analysis: Essays on analysis of form and on the interpretation of polyphonic vocal music]. Mainz: Schott, 1983. 2 vols. 281 p.; 170 p. ISBN 3-7957-1783-3 ML1500 .C56 1983

Part I: Two volumes. Vol. 1: collection of articles, mostly in German; two in English. "Eine Motette der ars antiqua: *Quant flourist - Non orphanum - Et gaudebit*" [A motet of the ars antiqua: *Quant flourist - Non orphanum - Et gaudebit*] (Wolfgang Dömling); "Guillaume de Machaut, Motette Nr. 22" [Guillaume de Machaut, motet no. 22] (Hellmut Kühn); "Die Florentiner Domweihmotette Dufays (1436)" [Dufay's motet for the consecration of the Florence cathedral (1436)] (Rolf Dammann); "Josquin Desprez, *Dominus regnavit* (Psalm 92)" (Ludwig Finscher); "Gombert's Motet *Aspice Domine*" (Jerome Roche); "Gesualdos Madrigal *Moro lasso al mio duolo*: Eine Studie zur Formtechnik des musikalischen Manierismus" [Gesualdo's madrigal *Moro, lasso, al mio duolo*: A study of formal technique in musical Mannerism] (Poos); "Die Motette *Exaudi, Domine, vocem meam* von Orlando di Lasso" [The motet *Exaudi, Domine, vocem meam* by Orlando di Lasso] (Martin Ruhnke); "Das *Kyrie I* der Messe *Quem dicunt homines* von Palestrina" [The *Kyrie I* from the Mass *Quem dicunt homines* by Palestrina] (Poos); "*Ecco mormorar l'onde*: Versuch, ein Monteverdi-Madrigal zu interpretieren" [*Ecco mormorar l'onde*: An attempt to interpret a Monteverdi madrigal] (Carl Dahlhaus); "On William Byrd's *Emendemus in melius*" (Joseph Kerman); "Musikalische Gestaltungsprinzipien bei Heinrich Schütz: Eine Analyse der Motette *Die Himmel erzählen die Ehre Gottes* (SWV 386)" [Principles of musical form in Heinrich Schütz: An analysis of the motet *Die Himmel erzählen die Ehre Gottes* (SWV 386)] (Wolfram Steinbeck); "Werkstruktur und Textexegese in Bachs Motette *Fürchte dich nicht, ich bin bei dir* (BWV 228)" [Compositional structure and text exegesis in Bach's motet *Fürchte dich nicht, ich bin bei dir* (BWV 228)] (Friedhelm Krummacher); "Der zweite Psalm op. 78/1 von Felix Mendelssohn Bartholdy" [The second Psalm, op. 78, no. 1 by Felix Mendelssohn-Bartholdy] (Hellmuth Christian Wolff); "Franz Schuberts Vokalquartett für 4 Männerstimmen *Grab und Mond* (D 893)" [Franz Schubert's quartet for four male voices, *Grab und Mond* (D. 893)] (Hans Jaskulsky); "Johannes Brahms, *Nachtwache Nr. 1* op. 104/1" (Hans Michael Beuerle); "Paul Hindemiths Chorsatz *Du mußt dir Alles geben*" [Paul Hindemith's choral work *Du mußt dir Alles geben*] (Winfried Kirsch); "Die Abendmahls-Motette aus dem *Passionsbericht des Matthäus* von Ernst Pepping" [The Communion

motets from the *Passionsbericht des Matthäus* by Ernst Pepping] (Poos);
"Gegenwärtiges und historischer Raum Anmerkungen zu Frank Michael
Beyers *Lavatio*" [Past and present space: Observations on Frank Michael
Beyer's *Lavatio*] (Clemens Kühn). Musical examples, facsimiles, and
tables; bibliographies follow some essays; no index. Vol. 2: complete musi-
cal selections in modern notation of works discussed in Vol. 1.

Poos, Heinrich, ed. *Chormusik und Analyse: Beiträge zur Formanalyse und
Interpretation mehrstimmiger Vokalmusik* [Choral music and analysis:
Essays on analysis of form and on the interpretation of polyphonic vocal
music]. Zweiter Teil [Part II]. Mainz, Germany: Schott, 1997. 2 vols. 291
p.; 180 p. ISBN 3-7957-0299-2   ML1500 .C57 1997

Part II: Two volumes. Vol. 1: collection of articles, mostly in German; one in
English. "Zur Circulatio-Tradition und Josquins *Maria Lactans*" [The circu-
latio tradition and Josquin's *Maria lactans*] (Warren Kirkendale); "Die *Octo
Beatitudines* in der Vertonung von Adrian Willaert und Orlando di Lasso"
[The eight beatitudes as set by Adrian Willaert and Orlando di Lasso] (Bernhard Meier); "*Nun bitten wir den Heiligen Geist*. Hermeneutischer Versuch
über einen Liedsatz Caspar Othmayrs" [*Nun bitten wir den Heiligen Geist*: A
hermeneutic essay of Caspar Othmayr's work for voice] (Poos); "Giaches de
Wert: *Io non son però morto* (8. Madrigalbuch, 1586)" [Giaches de Wert: *Io
non son però morto* (Eighth book of madrigals, 1586)] (Ludwig Finscher);
"Interpretierende Übersetzung. Analytisches zur Motette *Es ist erschienen
die heilsame Gnade Gottes* aus der *Geistlichen Chormusik* von Heinrich
Schütz" [Interpretive transposition: Analytical notes on the motet *Es ist
erschienen die heilsame Gnade Gottes* from the *Geistliche Chormusik* by
Heinrich Schütz] (Lukas Richter); "*Es ist genug*. Versuch über einen Bach-
Choral (BWV 60, 5)" [*Es ist genug*: Essay on a Bach chorale (BWV 60, no.
5)] (Poos); "Anton Bruckners motettisches Graduale *Christus factus est*: Der
musikalische Prozeß als entfaltete Inhaltlichkeit" [Anton Bruckner's motet-
like gradual *Christus factus est*: Musical process as the evolution of content]
(Ellinore Fladt); "Arabeskes und Groteskes. Claude Debussy, *Trois Chan-
sons de Charles d'Orleans*—III: *Yver, vous n'estes qu'un villain*"
[Arabesques and grotesques: Claude Debussy, *Trois chansons de Charles
d'Orleans*—No. 3, *Yver, vous n'estes qu'un villain*] (Ulrich Mahlert); "Max
Regers Chorwerke" [Max Reger's choral works] (Ludwig Ernst
Weinitschke); "Zukunftsverheißung und musikalische Zielgerichtetheit.
Arnold Schönberg: *Friede auf Erden* op. 13" [The promise of the future and
goal orientation in music: Arnold Schoenberg's *Friede auf Erden*, op. 13]
(Christian Martin Schmidt); "Die Motette *Jesus und die Krämer* von Zoltán
Kodály" [Zoltán Kodály's motet *Jesus es a kufarok*] (László Eosze);

"Aneignung und Verfremdung. *A bujdosó* aus Béla Bartóks *Ungarischen Volksliedern* [Appropriation and alienation: *A bujdosó*, from Béla Bartók's *Magyar nepdalok*] (Hartmut Fladt); "Das Madrigal *Eines Narren, eines Künstlers Leben* von Paul Hindemith" [Paul Hindemith's madrigal *Eines Narren, eines Kunstlers Leben*] (Albrecht Rubeli); "Ernst Peppings Chorlied *Anakreons Grab*" [Ernst Pepping's choral song *Anakreons Grab*] (Poos); "Olivier Messiaen: *Cinq Rechants* pour douze voix mixtes" [Olivier Messiaen: *Cinq Rechants* for twelve mixed voices] (Michèle Reverdy); "Benjamin Britten's *Hymn to St. Cecilia*" (Peter Aston); "Hugo Distler: *Um Mitternacht* für gemischten Chor (aus dem *Mörike-Chorliederbuch* op. 19)—Versuch einer praxisorientierten Analyse" [Hugo Distler: *Um Mitternacht* for mixed chorus, from the *Mörike-Chorliederbuch*, op. 19—Towards a performance-oriented analysis] (Winfried Kirsch). Musical examples, tables, and illustrations; documented with footnotes; no index. Vol. 2: complete musical selections in modern notation of works discussed in Vol. 1.

294. *Prentice-Hall History of Music Series*. H. Wiley Hitchcock, ed.

Renaissance:

Brown, Howard Mayer. *Music in the Renaissance*. 2nd ed. Upper Saddle River, New Jersey: Prentice-Hall, 1999. xx, 396 p. ISBN 0-13-400045-5 (pbk)   ML172 .B86 1999

Baroque:

Palisca, Claude V. *Baroque Music*. 3rd ed. Englewood Cliffs, New Jersey: Prentice-Hall, 1991. xi, 356 p. ISBN 0-13-058496-7 (pbk)   ML193 .P34 1991

Classical:

Pauly, Reinhard G. *Music in the Classic Period*. 4th ed. Upper Saddle River, New Jersey: Prentice-Hall, 2000. xvi, 272 p. ISBN 0-13-011502-9 ML195 .P38 2000

Romantic:

Longyear, Rey M. *Nineteenth-Century Romanticism in Music*. 3rd ed. Englewood Cliffs, New Jersey: Prentice-Hall, 1988. xiv, 367 p. ISBN 0-13-622697-3 (pbk)   ML196 .L65 1988

Twentieth Century:

Salzman, Eric. *Twentieth-Century Music: An Introduction*. 3rd ed. Englewood Cliffs, New Jersey: Prentice-Hall, 1988. xvi, 330 p. ISBN 0-13-935057-8 (pbk)   ML197 .S17 1988

United States:

Hitchcock, H. Wiley. *Music in the United States: A Historical Introduction.*
4th ed. Upper Saddle River, New Jersey: Prentice-Hall, 2000. xviii, 413 p.
ISBN 0-13-907643-3 (pbk)   ML200 .H58 2000

Latin American:

Béhague, Gerard. *Music in Latin America, an Introduction.* Englewood
Cliffs, New Jersey: Prentice-Hall, 1979. xiv, 369 p. ISBN 0-13-608919-4,
ISBN 0-13-608901-1 (pbk)   ML199 .B44

295. Robinson, Ray, ed. *Choral Music: A Norton Historical Anthology.* New
York: W. W. Norton, 1978. xvi, 1099 p. ISBN 0-393-02201-3, ISBN 0-393-
9062-0 (pbk.)   M1495 .C54218

Anthology of 111 choral works dating from 1300 to the mid-1970s. Provides biographical sketches of composers, commentary on individual
works, and source list for each work. Glossary of terms; indices for composers, titles, and genres.

296. Young, Percy M. *The Choral Tradition.* Rev. ed. New York: W. W. Norton,
1981. 373 p. ISBN 0-393-00058-3   ML1500 .Y7 1981

Revised edition of original, *The Choral Tradition: An Historical and Analytical Survey from Sixteenth Century to the Present Day* (1962). Approximately 350 works analyzed. Chapters cover the 16th and 17th centuries, the
period of J. S. Bach and G. F. Handel, the period of Joseph Haydn and W. A.
Mozart, and the 19th and 20th centuries. Numerous musical examples; classified bibliography of about 150 writings. Two indices: (1) principal works,
classified by time periods, giving composer, title, vocal/instrumental forces,
and page reference; and (2) expansive general index.

See also: Heintze, James R., ed. *American Musical Life in Context and
Practice to 1865* (item 369)

SACRED CHORAL MUSIC

General Works

297. Blezzard, Judith. *Borrowings in English Church Music, 1550–1950.* London:
Stainer & Bell, 1990. 224 p. ISBN 0-85249-784-9   ML2931 .B54 1990

Three sections: (1) music borrowed from sacred sources, (2) music borrowed from secular sources, and (3) borrowings of musical style. Majority
of works discussed are vocal and choral. Musical examples; bibliography of
almost 200 writings; expansive index.

298. Dakers, Lionel. *Church Music at the Crossroads: A Forward Looking Guide for Today.* London: Marshall, Morgan & Scott, 1970. 160 p. SBN 551-05246-5 MT88 .D26

Discusses the music of the services, introduction of new music to the congregation, choir training, organ playing and accompaniment, recruitment of choir members and organists, and the roles and responsibilities of the clergy, choir, and organist. Numerous appendices, including short, annotated lists of hymn books, collections of hymn tunes with varied harmonizations, modern hymn tunes, Psalters, anthems, chant books, organ music for manuals only, organ voluntaries, settings of the Holy Communion Service, recommended editions of John Merbecke's Communion setting, books on elementary choir training, organ primers and books on technique, books with special reference to organ accompaniment, and handbooks on conducting. Also appended is information about the Royal School of Church Music, including their principles, description of facilities offered, and list of guides issued by the organization. In addition, a short essay entitled "Simplicity in a Modern Idiom" by Alan Gibbs is appended, which recommends several 20th-century musical works performable by the average church choir. Musical examples; no index.

299. Dickinson, Edward. *Music in the History of the Western Church: With an Introduction on Religious Music among Primitive and Ancient Peoples.* New York: Charles Scribner's Sons, 1902 ML3000 .D65; reprint, New York: Greenwood Press, 1969. ISBN 0-837-11062-9 ML3000 .D65 1969; reprint, New York: AMS Press, 1970. ISBN 0-404-02127-1 ML3000 .D65 1970b; reprint, St. Clair Shores, Michigan: Scholarly Press, 1970. viii, 426 p. ISBN 0-837-11062-9 ML3000 .D65 1970

Originally published in 1902. Surveys church music "under the influence of varying ideals of devotion, liturgic usages, national temperaments, and types and methods of expression." Among the topics discussed: the development of medieval chorus music, the modern Mass, the rise of the Lutheran hymnody, the rise of the German cantata and Passion, German Protestant music, and congregational song in England and America. Musical examples; bibliography of more than 80 writings; expansive index.

300. Douglas, Charles Winfred. *Church Music in History and Practice.* Rev. with additional material by Leonard Webster Ellinwood. London: Faber and Faber; New York: Charles Scribner's Sons, 1962. xxii, 266 p. ML2900.D73 C4 1962

Not a history of church music. Survey of "the development of Christian liturgical worship and of Christian hymns . . . in order to arrive at practical and intelligent conclusions regarding the present musical worship of the church." Emphasis on historical and practical matters that relate to the music of the Church of England and the Episcopal Church of the United States. Musical examples; bibliography of more than 50 writings; index. Slight differences between the two editions. The Faber and Faber edition includes a guide for hymns discussed in the text cross-referenced with several hymnals. Bibliography in Scribner edition includes one more writing than Faber and Faber and also includes a dated discography of 25 recordings. Series: *The Hale Memorial Lectures of Seabury-Western Theological Seminary.*

301. Ellinwood, Leonard Webster. *The History of American Church Music.* Rev. ed. New York: Da Capo Press, 1970. xiv, 274 p. ISBN 0-306-71233-4 ML200 .E4 1970

Corrected reprint of the 1953 edition. Discusses American church music from Spanish colonization (1494) to the mid-20th century. Topics include metrical psalmody, hymnody, fuging tunes, singing schools and early choirs, quartet choirs, boy's choirs, significant composers and musicians, and choral repertory. A classified list of approximately 400 church works and brief biographies of around 70 American church musicians appended. Photographs, illustrations, facsimiles, and musical examples; documented with endnotes; expansive index. Series: *Da Capo Press Music Reprint Series.*

302. Fellowes, Edmund Horace. *English Cathedral Music.* New edition revised by J. A. Westrup. London: Methuen, 1973. ISBN 0-416-77640-X ML3131 .F3 1973; reprint, Westport, Connecticut: Greenwood Press, 1981. xi, 283 p. ISBN 0-313-22643-1   ML3131 .F3 1981

First published in 1941 under the title *English Cathedral Music from Edward VI to Edward VII* and revised in 1969 by Westrup. Nineteen chapters survey topics from the Reformation to late Victorian and Edwardian composers, 1509 to the first decade of the 20th century. Numerous musical examples; documented with footnotes; expansive index of music examples and general index.

303. Gatens, William J. *Victorian Cathedral Music in Theory and Practice.* Cambridge, England: Cambridge University Press, 1986. ix, 227 p. ISBN 0-521-26808-7   ML3131.4 .G37 1986

Study of 19th-century English church music. Detailed studies of the music of Thomas Attwood, Thomas Attwood Walmisley, John Goss, Samuel

Sebastian Wesley, Frederick Ouseley, John Stainer, and Joseph Barnby. Musical examples; bibliography of nearly 100 writings; expansive index of compositions and expansive general index.

304. Gelineau, Joseph. *Voices and Instruments in Christian Worship: Principles, Laws, Applications.* Translated by Clifford Howell. Collegeville, Minnesota: Liturgical Press; London: Burns & Oates, 1964. 224 p. ML3003 .G343

English translation of *Chant et Musique dans le Culte Chrétien: Principes, Lois et Applications* (1962). First part "sets out to answer three general questions: Why should there be singing in Christian worship? How should music be coordinated with ritual action? What function does it fulfill therein?" Second part tries to "explain the ritual function of music as deduced from the rite celebrated according to the mind of the Church." Addresses chant, "sacred polyphony," "modern sacred music," psalmody, and hymnody. Few musical examples and illustrations; bibliography of more than 50 writings; expansive index.

305. Halter, Carl, and Carl Schalk, eds. *A Handbook of Church Music.* St. Louis: Concordia Publishing House, 1978. 303 p. ISBN 0-570-01316-X ML3168 .H33

Companion to *Key Words in Church Music: Definition Essays on Concepts, Practices, and Movements of Thought in Church Music* (item 316) also edited by Schalk, though the *Handbook* concerns only Lutheran worship music. Each book is cross-referenced to the other. Introduction, "Music in Lutheran Worship: An Affirmation," by Halter and Schalk, followed by seven chapters by various authors: "The Liturgical Life of the Church" (Eugene L. Brand); "Sketches of Lutheran Worship" (Carl Schalk); "The Music of the Congregation" (Louis G. Nuechterlein); "The Music of the Choir" (Carlos R. Messerli); "The Music of Instruments" (Herbert Gotsch and Edward W. Klammer); "The Pastor and the Church Musician" (Adalbert Raphael Kretzmann); and "Music in the Church Today: An Appraisal" (Richard Hillert). Extensive annotated bibliography of about 200 items: "Resources for the Church Musician," prepared by Messerli; tables of the Church Year, the Mass, and various Lutheran Orders; no index.

306. Hutchings, Arthur. *Church Music in the Nineteenth Century.* London: Jenkins; New York: Oxford University Press, 1967. ML3131 .H88, ML3131 .H88 1967; reprint, Westport, Connecticut: Greenwood Press, 1977. 166 p. ISBN 0-837-19695-7 ML3131 .H88 1977

Surveys choral, congregational, and organ music during the 19th century. Covers the music of many denominations. Musical examples; no bibliography; index. Series: *Studies in Church Music.*

307. Long, Kenneth R. *The Music of the English Church.* New York: St. Martin's Press, 1972   ML3131 .L6 1972b; London: Hodder & Stoughton, 1972 (rep. 1991). 479 p. ISBN 0-340-14962-0   ML3131 .L6

Historical survey of English church music from the English Reformation through the mid-20th century. Musical examples and illustrations; bibliography of approximately 275 writings; index to musical examples and expansive general index.

308. Morehen, John, ed. *English Choral Practice, 1400–1650.* Cambridge, England: Cambridge University Press, 1995. xiii, 246 p. ISBN 0-521-44143-9 ML3031.2 .E54 1995

Collection of articles by various authors: "To Chorus from Quartet: The Performing Resource for English Church Polyphony, c. 1390–1559" (Roger Bowers); "Editing and Performing *musica speculativa*" (Roger Bray); "The Sound of Latin in England before and after the Reformation" and "English Pronunciation, c. 1500-c. 1625" (Alison Wray); "Byrd, Tallis and Ferrabosco" (David Wulstan); "John Baldwin and Changing Concepts of Text Underlay" (David Mateer); "Sacred Songs in the Chamber" (John Milsom); "The Education of Choristers in England during the Sixteenth Century" (Jane Flynn); and "The 'Burden of Proof': The Editor as Detective" (Morehen). Musical examples, facsimiles, and tables; documented with footnotes; three indices: names and places; manuscript and printed music sources; and works cited. Series: *Cambridge Studies in Performance Practice*, no. 5.

309. Phillips, C. Henry. *The Singing Church: An Outline History of the Music Sung by Choir and People.* With new material by Arthur Hutchings and revised by Ivor Keys. London: Mowbrays, 1979. 288 p. ISBN 0-264-66600-3 ML3000 .P48 1979

First published in 1945. Historical survey of sacred choral music and prominent musicians. Six sections: (1) pre-Reformation services and music, (2) 16th century, (3) 17th century, (4) from Croft to Wesley, (5) since 1871, and (6) an essay on principles and practice. Annotated list of recommended books and music at end of most sections. Musical examples and chronology charts; classified general bibliography of about 40 writings; expansive index and index to music examples.

310. Rapp, Robert Maurice. "Stylistic Characteristics of the Short Sacred Choral Composition in the U. S. A., 1945–1960." Ph.D. dissertation. University of Wisconsin, Madison, 1970. ix, 298 p.

Analytical study of the "most frequently performed American sacred choral music for mixed voices" composed between 1945 and 1960. Examines text, arrangement of voices and instrument(s), musical characteristics, and idiomatic choral devices. Tables and musical examples; classified bibliography of about 45 writings; list of publishers with addresses appended.

311. Rice, William C. *A Concise History of Church Music.* New York: Abingdon Press, 1964. 128 p.   ML3000 .R5

Described by the author as "a brief, nontechnical, reliable discussion of the most important persons and the significant events that have brought church music to its present state of enthusiastic experimentation." Covers pre-Christian era through the mid-20th century. Introductory to topics, at best; lacks detailed discussion. Musical examples; bibliography of about 60 writings; no index.

312. Robertson, Alec. *Sacred Music.* London: Parrish; New York: Chanticleer Press, 1950. 70 p.   ML3000 .R6

Brief but worthy survey; emphasizes the music of the Roman liturgy. Topics range from Gregorian chant to Stravinsky's *Mass.* Beautifully illustrated; index. Series: *World of Music*, no. 11.

313. Routley, Erik. *The Church and Music: An Enquiry into the History, the Nature, and the Scope of Christian Judgment on Music.* Rev. ed. London: Duckworth; Boston: Crescendo, 1967; reprint, London: Duckworth, 1978. 262 p. ISBN 0-7156-0062-1   ML3001 .R8

Survey of opinions regarding the role of music in worship from pre-Christian times through the mid-20th century. Three appendices, including a table of hymn tunes and their locations in various sources. Documented with footnotes; bibliography of nearly 20 recommended sources; index.

314. Routley, Erik, and Lionel Dakers. *A Short History of English Church Music.* New ed. London: Mowbrays, 2000. 160 p. ISBN 0-264-67514-2   ML2931 .R68 2000

The 2000 edition not available for examination; annotation based on 1997 editions (London: Mowbrays; Carol Stream, Illinois: Hope Publishing Company). Brief survey of English church music from ca. 1100 to present. Described by the author as "a quick journey, with a broad picture of the country but resisting the temptation to stop and dally in the picturesque places." Economical; the reader should consult other writings on the subject for more detailed discussion. Musical examples; no bibliography; index.

315. Routley, Erik. *Words, Music, and the Church.* London: Jenkins; Nashville, Tennessee: Abingdon Press, 1968. 224 p.   ML3106 .R69

Theological and musical perspective. Discusses the descent from orthodox theology and examines "new" developments in church music. Based on lectures given in the United States in 1966. Musical examples; documented with footnotes; index.

316. Schalk, Carl, ed. *Key Words in Church Music: Definition Essays on Concepts, Practices, and Movements of Thought in Church Music.* St. Louis: Concordia Publishing House, 1978. 365 p. ISBN 0-570-01317-8 ML102.C5 K5

Not a dictionary. Collection of 76 essays by 30 contributors. Grouped into 56 topics, many related to choral music. Each essay concludes with suggested additional readings. Companion to *A Handbook of Church Music,* (item 305), edited by Carl Halter and Schalk. Cross-references between essays as well as between the two companion books. Graphs, illustrations, and musical examples.

317. Somerville, Thomas Charles. "A Study and Performance of Sacred Choral Music by Contemporary Scottish Composers, 1950–1970." D.M.A. dissertation. University of Southern California, Los Angeles, 1972. viii, 207 p.

Presents a brief survey of sacred choral music in Scotland from the Middle Ages to the second half of the 20th century, followed by a discussion of contemporary (1950–1970) Scottish sacred choral music. Focuses on the music and influence of composers at Scottish universities, namely Glasgow, Edinburgh, Aberdeen, and St. Andrews. Includes the music of non-Scottish composers admitted to the Scottish Music Archive. Three appendices: (1) copy of the author's D.M.A. performance program; (2) classified list (anthems and motets, services and Masses, carols and choral hymns, and oratorios and major works) of approximately 100 sacred choral works scored for SATB, SAB, or unison choir, composed between 1950 and 1970, and held at the Scottish Music Archive; lists composer, title, voicing, accompaniment, and publisher, along with a dated list of publishers and addresses; and (3) discography of nine sound discs. Musical examples; bibliography of about 60 books, anthologies, articles, and pamphlets.

318. Temperley, Nicholas. *The Music of the English Parish Church*. Cambridge, England: Cambridge University Press, 1979. 2 vols. xxiv, 447 p.; v, 213 p. ISBN 0-521-22045-9 (Vol. 1), ISBN 0-521-22046-7 (Vol. 2)   ML3131 .T44

Two volumes: Vol. 1 is a survey of the various music and musical practices in English parish churches from the Middle Ages to the present, with primary focus on 1549–1965; Vol. 2 is an anthology of music. Appendices, including a list of collegiate parish churches and others endowed for choral music. Photos, illustrations, facsimiles, tables and music; bibliography of approximately 900 manuscript sources and printed collections of music and nearly 800 writings; expansive index. Series: *Cambridge Studies in Music*.

319. Ulrich, Homer. *A Survey of Choral Music*. New York: Harcourt Brace Jovanovich, 1973. ix, 245 p. ISBN 0-15-584863-1   ML1500 .U44

Survey of the development of choral music, ca. 1250 to the present. Two appendices: (1) glossary of terms and (2) Latin texts with English translations of the Mass Ordinary, Requiem Mass, Te Deum, Stabat Mater, and Magnificat. Musical examples, facsimiles, photos, and illustrations; bibliography of 66 writings; list of "principal sources of the choral compositions mentioned or discussed"; expansive index. Series: *The Harbrace History of Musical Forms*.

320. Wienandt, Elwyn A. *Choral Music of the Church*. New York: The Free Press, 1965   ML3000 .W53; reprint, New York: Da Capo Press, 1980. xi, 494 p. ISBN 0-306-76002-9   ML3000 .W53 1980

Organized into three parts: Catholic contribution, Catholic traditions and Protestant innovation, and the breakdown of denominational distinctions. Chronological coverage of the Catholic Mass, motet, Requiem, and Magnificat, the Anglican service and anthem, and the Lutheran chorale and cantata. Text with English translation of the Mass Ordinary, Requiem, and Magnificat, with an English translation of "Bull of Pope John XXII Issued in the Year 1324–1325 at Avignon" and "Letter of Archbishop Cranmer to King Henry VIII" appended. Numerous musical examples, with facsimiles, tables, and photographs; annotated bibliography/discography of nearly 275 books, music editions, periodicals, articles, and recordings; expansive index. Series: *Da Capo Press Music Reprint Series*.

321. Wienandt, Elwyn A., ed. *Opinions on Church Music: Comments and Reports from Four-and-a-Half Centuries*. Waco, Texas: Baylor University Press, 1974 (rep. 1984). x, 214 p. ISBN 0-918954-30-4 (pbk)   ML3000 .W535

Forty-nine essays, letters, and memoirs in chronological order spanning four and a half centuries (16th through the middle of the 20th century). Ranges from Erasmus's "A Brief Comment about Church Music" to Stephen Koch's "God on Stage," which mentions Bernstein's *Mass* and Lloyd Webber and Rice's *Jesus Christ Superstar*. Noteworthy authors include Martin Luther, J. S. Bach, W. A. Mozart, Charles Burney, Ludwig van Beethoven, and Lowell Mason, to name a few. Bibliography of about 60 entries; expansive index.

See also: Yoder, David Winston. "A Study and Performance of Extended Sacred Choral Works with Brass Instruments by Contemporary American Composers" (item 114)

Jewish Synagogue Music

322. Werner, Eric. *In the Choir Loft: A Manual for Organists and Choir Directors in American Synagogues*. New York: Union of American Hebrew Congregations, 1957. 54 p.   ML3195 .W4

Briefly surveys the development of American synagogue music. Examines tonality, stylistic characteristics, and form and structure of the music. Includes a classified bibliography of then-contemporary compositions and hymn and song collections for the American synagogue; gives composer, title, and indication of easy, medium, and difficult performance levels. Concludes with suggestions for successful programming. Numerous musical examples; no index.

Moravian Church Music

See: White, Arthur Carlton. "Published Moravian Choral Music" (item 176, nos. 135, 136)

Mormon Church Music

323. Hicks, Michael. *Mormonism and Music: A History*. Urbana: University of Illinois Press, 1989. xii, 243 p. ISBN 0-252-01618-1   ML3174 .H5 1989

Historical survey of the music within the Church of Jesus Christ of Latter-Day Saints from the 1830s through the 1970s. Discusses hymnology, the role of choral music, and use of instruments in church. Entire chapter dedicated to the history of the Mormon Tabernacle Choir. Musical examples and photos; documented with endnotes; expansive general index and index of first lines and titles of hymns and songs. Series: *Music in American Life*.

Protestant Church Music

324. Blume, Friedrich, in collaboration with Ludwig Finscher, Georg Feder, Adam Adrio, Walter Blankenburg, Torben Schousboe, Robert Stevenson, and Watkins Shaw. *Protestant Church Music: A History*. Foreword by Paul Henry Lang. New York: W. W. Norton, 1974. ISBN 0-393-02176-9; reprint, London: Gollancz, 1975. xv, 831 p. ISBN 0-575-01996-4 ML3100 .B5193

   English translation of *Geschichte der evangelischen Kirchenmusik* (1965) with revisions and additional sections and chapters. Two-thirds of book deals with history of the Lutheran tradition in Europe. Nine sections: "The Period of the Reformation" and "The Age of Confessionalism" (Blume); "Decline and Restoration" (Feder); "Renewal and Rejuvenation" (Adrio); "Church Music in Reformed Europe" and "The Music of the Bohemian Brethren" (Blankenburg); "Protestant Church Music in Scandinavia" (Schousboe); "Protestant Music in America" (Stevenson); and "Church Music in England from the Reformation to the Present Day" (Shaw). Numerous musical examples, illustrations, facsimiles, and portraits; classified bibliography of about 1,500 entries (general history, church history, and theology; music history and church history; chorales and hymn books; historia and passion; organ music; and monographs on individuals); expansive index.

325. Brown, Bruce Calvin. "The Choral Music of the American Lutheran Church: A Study and Performance of the Music of Daniel Moe, Paul Fetler, and Rolf Espeseth." D.M.A. dissertation. University of Southern California, Los Angeles, 1974. iv, 223 p.

   History of choral composition in the American Lutheran church with focus upon the influence of the F. Melius Christiansen choral tradition and the compositional output of Moe, Fetler, and Espeseth. Several appendices, including catalogs of the choral music of Moe, Fetler, and Espeseth. Concludes with editions of five works by Espeseth. Musical examples; bibliography of 29 writings and interviews.

326. Dean, Talmage W. *A Survey of Twentieth Century Protestant Church Music in America*. Nashville, Tennessee: Broadman Press, 1988. 284 p. ISBN 0-8054-6813-7 ML3111.5 .D4 1988

   Surveys 20th-century music of Protestant churches in the United States within the context of religious, social, economic, and political influences. Bibliography of more than 100 writings; index.

327. Dearnley, Christopher. *English Church Music, 1650–1750: In Royal Chapel, Cathedral and Parish Church.* London: Barrie & Jenkins; New York: Oxford University Press, 1970. xii, 308 p. SBN 257-65787-8 ML3131 .D4

Described by the author as a "series of studies, rather than a comprehensive history, . . . [with each topic] allowed to range freely, darting across chronological divisions." Discusses music of the Church of England (ca. 1650–1750), namely Psalms, anthems, canticles, and hymns. Lengthy final chapter discusses representative composers and their music. Ample musical examples, facsimiles, illustrations, and photos; several appendices, including a list of music repertoire of cathedral choirs and incipits of Psalm chants (1661–1771). Documented with endnotes; expansive index. Series: *Studies in Church Music.*

328. Etherington, Charles L. *Protestant Worship Music: Its History and Practice.* New York: Holt, Rinehart and Winston, 1962   ML3100 .E8; reprint, Westport, Connecticut: Greenwood Press, 1978. x, 278 p. ISBN 0-313-20024-6 ML3100 .E8 1978

Survey of the music of Protestant churches. Includes discussion of Jewish music, music in the early church, the influence of early Greek music and the Celtic church, the Post-Gregorian era, church music in the Middle Ages, ars nova, the age of polyphony, the Reformation, music in the American colonies, the baroque period, the Century of Neglect (1750–1850), the late 19th century, and a forward-looking view of worship music. Bibliography of more than 80 items; expansive index.

329. Le Huray, Peter. *Music and the Reformation in England, 1549–1660.* London: Jenkins; New York: Oxford University Press, 1967. viii, 454 p. ML3131 .L44 1967; reprint with corrections, Cambridge, England: Cambridge University Press, 1978. xv, 454 p.   ML3131 .L44 1978

Historical survey. Complements Frank Ll. Harrison's *Music in Medieval Britain* (item 351), which explores music set to Latin liturgical texts; Le Huray's volume primarily focuses on the music of the Anglican Church. Four appendices: (1) bibliography of approximately 60 books containing devotional music; (2) 10 modern editions of organ music; (3) 6 collected editions and more than 400 separate publications of modern editions containing vocal and choral music; (4) a bibliography of more than 350 writings. Numerous musical examples, facsimiles, tables, and illustrations; expansive index of musical examples and expansive general index. Series: *Studies in Church Music.*

330. Liemohn, Edwin. *The Organ and Choir in Protestant Worship.* Philadelphia: Fortress Press, 1968. x, 178 p.   ML3100 .L54

Historical survey of the use of choirs and organs in Protestant church music from the pre-Reformation through the present. Emphasis upon Lutheran, Anglican, and Reformed (including Presbyterian) music, with frequent mention of Baptist, Methodist, and Moravian music. Concentrates geographically upon Scandinavian countries, Germany, Switzerland, the Netherlands, the British Isles, and the United States. Bibliography of 217 items; expansive index.

331. Lovelace, Austin C., and William C. Rice. *Music and Worship in the Church.* Rev. and enl. Nashville, Tennessee: Abingdon Press, 1976. 256 p. ISBN 0-687-27357-9   ML3100 .L7 1976

Focuses on Protestant church music. Separate chapters discuss the music committee, the director, the organist, the adult choir, children's and youth choirs, the choir's music, the soloist, the congregation, music in Christian education, and contemporary music and worship. Many chapters conclude with annotated lists of recommended music. Classified bibliography of more than 350 writings, music collections, and periodicals; expansive index.

332. Lundberg, John William. "Twentieth Century Male Choral Music Suitable for Protestant Worship." D.M.A. dissertation. University of Southern California, Los Angeles, 1974. iii, 178 p.

Broadly surveys male choral music with primary focus on 20th-century choral compositions for adult male voices suitable for Protestant worship. Discusses representative compositions and presents critical analysis. Provides a list of 85 choral works for male voices. Bibliography of 58 writings.

333. Neve, Paul Edmund. "The Contribution of the Lutheran College Choirs to Music in America." S.M.D. dissertation. Union Theological Seminary, New York, 1967. 227, 4 p.

Historical study of the organizational structure of Lutheran Synods in the United States, of Lutheran educational institutions, and choral traditions within Lutheran institutions. Covers ca. 1875–1963. Special attention given to the influence of F. Melius Christiansen and the St. Olaf choir. Several appendices: programs of Lutheran college choirs, 1924–1962, 1964; programs of state college and university choirs, 1934–1961; programs of private college and university choirs, 1957–1961; programs of the St. Olaf college choir, 1912–1944. Bibliography of approximately 450 writings, most of which are catalogs, bulletins, magazine and newspaper articles, yearbooks, personal letters, and programs; also lists 20 personal interviews. No index.

334. Rainbow, Bernarr. *The Choral Revival in the Anglican Church (1839–1872)*. London: Barrie & Jenkins; New York: Oxford University Press, 1970. xiv, 368 p. SBN 257-65088-1 (Barrie & Jenkins)   ML3131 .R3

Historical study of the Anglican Church choral revival in 19th-century England. Organized into two sections: the birth of the choral movement and the growth of the movement. Illustrations; bibliography of approximately 220 writings; expansive index. Series: *Studies in English Church Music*.

335. Routley, Erik. *Twentieth Century Church Music*. Carol Stream, Illinois: Agape, 1984. 244 p. IBSN 0-916642-23-2   ML3131 .R68

Survey of 20th-century Protestant church music. Primarily devoted to English music, but includes a chapter on American music. Musical examples; index of composers and titles; discography of approximately 50 recordings; index.

336. Seeley, Gilbert Stewart. "German Protestant Choral Music Since 1925." D.M.A. dissertation. University of Southern California, Los Angeles, 1969. viii, 342 p.

Study of German Protestant music of three generations of composers, namely Ernst Pepping, Hugo Distler, and Johann Nepomuk David (first generation), Siegfried Reda (second generation), and Helmut Barbe, Heinz Werner Zimmermann, and Wolfgang Hufschmidt (third generation). Several appendices, including a discography of about 50 recordings and a bibliography of approximately 700 published 20th-century German Protestant choral works. Musical examples; bibliography of about 145 writings, many in German.

337. Spink, Ian. *Restoration Cathedral Music: 1660–1714*. Oxford, England: Clarendon Press, 1995. xvi, 487 p. ISBN 0-19-816149-2   ML3166 .S75 1995

Historical survey of music of the Anglican Church in England, Wales, and Ireland from the restoration of the monarchy in 1660 to the death of the last Stuart monarch in 1714. Addresses the choral service and its music, namely liturgy and chant, services and anthems, choirs and places, organs and organ music, and sources and performances. More than three-quarters of the book devoted to The Chapel Royal and its composers as well as descriptions of the music and musicians of a number of specific cathedrals and collegiate foundations. Various appendices; musical examples and tables; bibliography of approximately 400 writings; expansive index. Series: *Oxford Studies in British Church Music*, no. 3.

338. Steere, Dwight. *Music in Protestant Worship.* Richmond, Virginia: John Knox Press, 1960. 256 p.   ML3100 .S72

Organized into three main sections: (1) description of physical aspects of the church building; (2) the minister and church musicians; and (3) the music, including the hymn, processional and recessional, congregational service music (Gloria Patri, doxology, offertory response, and benediction response), anthem, choral response, organ music, solo song, and occasional service music (communion, funeral service, and wedding). Musical examples; classified bibliography of more than 50 writings; expansive index.

339. Stevenson, Robert Murrell. *Protestant Church Music in America: A Short Survey of Men and Movements from 1564 to the Present.* New York: W. W. Norton, 1966. xiii, 168 p.   ML3111 .S83

Purpose: "to provide a compressed text for use in seminaries, choir schools, and colleges." Topics include early contacts with the aborigines; New England Puritanism (1620–1720); "regular singing" (1720–1775); Pennsylvania Germans; native-born composers in the middle Atlantic colonies; the south before 1800; singing-school masters in the New Republic; the half-century preceding the civil war; Negro spirituals: origins and present-day significance; and diverging currents (1850–present). Musical examples and facsimiles; bibliography of approximately 250 items; expansive index.

340. Valentin, Erich, and Friedrich Hofmann, eds. *Die evangelische Kirchenmusik: Handbuch für Studium und Praxis* [Protestant church music: Handbook for study and practice]. Regensburg: Gustav Bosse, 1967. 533 p. ML3100 .V34

German only. Sixteen essays about church music by various authors and an extensive bibliography: "Wesen und Aufrag der Evangelischen Kirchenmusik"[The nature and mission of Prostestant church music] and "Die Organisation der Evangelischen Kirchenmusik" [The organization of Protestant church music] (Friedrich Hofmann); "Die Geschichte der Evangelischen Kirchenmusik" [The history of Protestant church music] (Walter Blankenburg); "Das Amt des Kirchenmusikers" [The duties of the church musician] (Karl Ferdinand Müller); "Hymnologie" [Hymnology] and "Evangelische Choralkunde" [Prostestant chorale] (Otto Brodde); "Der Evangelische Gottesdienst" [The Protestant church service] (Friedrich Kalb); "Das Orgelspiel im Gottesdienst" [Organ playing in the church service] (Friedrich Högner); "Choralbegleitung und Choralbearbeitung" [Chorale accompaniment and chorale arrangement] (Ewald Weiß); "Kirchenmusikalische Bläserpraxis" [Wind instruments in church music] (Johannes E. Koch); "Der Kinderchor in der Kirche" [The children's choir in the church] (Klaus Linkenbach); "Im Vorhof des Tempels—Das 'geistliche' Lied" [In the forecourt of the temple: The 'religious' song] (Erich Valentin); "Die Ausbildung des Kirchenmusikers" [The education of the church musician] (Joachim Widmann); "Orgelbau" [Organ building] (Walter Supper); "Über Glocken" [Concerning bells] (Otto Meyer); "Die Rechtsverhältnisse" [Circumstances of law] (Margarethe Schwarze); and "Die Bibliothek des Kirchenmusikers" [The library of the church musician] (Gerhard Littmann). The latter is a classified, annotated bibliography of nearly 700 writings, primarily in German with a few English titles. Musical examples, illustrations, and tables; no index.

341. Wilhite, Charles Stanford. "Eucharistic Music for the Anglican Church in England and the United States at Mid-Twentieth Century (1950–1965): A Stylistic Study with Historical Introduction." Ph.D. dissertation. University of Iowa, Iowa City, 1968. x, 307 p.

Selective study of the Anglican Eucharist, variously referred to as the Lord's Supper, the Holy Communion, and the Mass. Discusses the nature and purpose of corporate worship and describes the development of the *Book of Common Prayer*; provides a historical survey of Anglican church music in England and United States; presents a historical, sociological, theological, and musical basis for critical evaluation of Eucharistic music. Chapters IV and V discuss Anglican Eucharistic music in England and the United States, including a classified bibliography with analysis of about 55 works. Four appendices: (1) classified bibliography of about 40 additional musical works not discussed in detail in the text; (2) classified list of 25 canticles and 80 anthems; (3) annotated bibliography of 19 historical writings and 21 historical collections and editions of music concerning Anglican church music; (4) discography of 7 works discussed in Chapters IV and V. Musical examples; bibliography of about 200 writings; index of works discussed in Chapters IV and V.

342. Wohlgemuth, Paul W. *Rethinking Church Music*. With a Foreword by Don G. Fontana. Rev. ed. Carol Stream, Illinois: Hope Publishing Company, 1981. x, 101 p. ISBN 0-916642-15-1   ML3000 .W7

Meditation on church music, primarily drawing upon the author's extensive experience as a music minister and church music academician. No attempt to place trends in contemporary church music in historical perspective. Makes the point that church music has repeatedly adapted to change in church and society and that tension between the traditional and the new has been a constant in church history. Approaches the question of "contemporary gospel" and "Christian rock" from a conservative Evangelical viewpoint. Briefly considers issues and concerns that impinge on church music programs. Contains little that would be new to an experienced church musician, but could serve to educate pastors and laymen to the problems, contradictions, and pressures facing church music programs. No bibliography; no index.

343. Wolf, Edward. "Lutheran Church Music in America during the Eighteenth and Early Nineteenth Centuries." Ph.D. dissertation. University of Illinois, Urbana 1960. xviii, 454 p.

Three aims: (1) to record and evaluate information regarding the position music held in Lutheran life in America before ca. 1825; (2) to assess the relation of Lutheran musical activities to the history of American church music in general; and (3) to provide examples that would be applicable to church music today. Numerous appendices, which include musical texts, excerpts of writings, and music. Musical examples; bibliography of approximately 185 writings and music; no index.

See also: Hooper, William L. *Church Music in Transition* (item 393)

Roman Catholic Church Music

344. Arnold, Denis. *Monteverdi Church Music*. London: British Broadcasting Corporation, 1982. 64 p. ISBN 0-563-12884-4   ML410.M77 A815 1982

Concise study of Monteverdi's career and compositional output in the area of church music from his early motets of 1582 to his *Selva morale* published in 1640. Musical examples; no bibliography; expansive index of works discussed within the text. Series: *BBC Music Guides*.

345. Bowers, Roger. "Choral Institutions within the English Church: Their Constitution and Development, 1340–1500." Ph.D. dissertation. University of East Anglia, Norwich, England, 1975. Various pagination.

Historical survey of English liturgical choirs from 1340 to 1500. Traces the growth of choral institutions in the later Middle Ages, the rise of polyphonic music in the liturgy, and influences of composers, choirs, and liturgical ideals. Tables; 25 appendices; bibliography of numerous manuscript sources and approximately 260 printed sources; no index.

346. Bowers, Roger. *English Church Polyphony: Singers and Sources from the 14th to the 17th Century*. Aldershot, England; Brookfield, Massachusetts: Ashgate/Variorum, 1999. Various pagination. ISBN 0-86078-778-8 ML2931.1 .B69 1999

Collection of 10 articles, each previously published, with the purpose of identifying "the resources which between c. 1340 and 1642 the English church saw fit to direct towards the performance of its liturgical music." Organized into three sections: first section addresses performing ensembles, vocal scoring, choral balance, and performing pitch; second section discusses individual choral establishments, namely Canterbury Cathedral, Lady Chapel of Winchester, Lincoln Cathedral, and Thomas Wolsey's household chapel; third section surveys composers and their music. Musical examples and tables. Four indices: (1) choral institutions, (2) names, (3) music manuscripts and topics, and (4) compositions. Series: *Variorum Collected Studies Series*.

347. Brough, Delma. *Polish Seventeenth-Century Church Music: With Reference to the Influence of Historical, Political, and Social Conditions*. New York: Garland, 1989. viii, 387 p. ISBN 0-8240-0187-7 ML2951.P6 B76 1989

Historical survey of sacred choral music, primarily of the Jesuit and Piarist orders, in 17th-century Poland. First portion of the book presents social, political, religious, and cultural background; second portion examines dramatic religious music, the Mass, the a cappella and polychoral motets, small ensemble concertato motets, and large-scale concertato motets for voices and instruments. Numerous musical examples; several appendices; bibliography of about 180 writings (many in Polish) and 45 individual musical works and collected editions; no index. Series: *Outstanding Dissertations in Music from British Universities*.

348. Carver, Anthony F. *Cori spezzati*. Cambridge, England: Cambridge University Press, 1988. 2 vols. xv, 282 p.; vi, 162 p. ISBN 0-521-36172-9 ML2902 .C37 1988

Vol. 1, *The Development of Sacred Polychoral Music to the Time of Schütz*, examines polychoral music of such representative composers as Orlando di Lasso, Giovanni Pierluigi da Palestrina, Tomás Luis de Victoria, Andrea and

Giovanni Gabrieli, Michael Praetorius, Johann Hermann Schein, Samuel Scheidt, and Heinrich Schütz. Vol. 2, *An Anthology of Sacred Polychoral Music*, provides a representative collection of the literature. Musical examples and tables; bibliography of about 275 musical manuscripts, early prints, and modern editions, and approximately 170 writings; expansive index.

349. Fellerer, Karl Gustav. *The History of Catholic Church Music*. Translated by Francis A. Brunner. 2nd ed. Baltimore: Helicon Press, 1961   ML3002 .F32 1961; reprint, Westport, Connecticut: Greenwood Press, 1979. 235 p. ISBN 0-313-21147-7   ML3002 .F32 1979

English translation of 2nd edition of Fellerer's *Geschichte der katholischen Kirchenmusik* (1949) with additional notes and corrections supplied by Fellerer and new information on church music in America supplied by Joan Boucher. Three main divisions: (1) "Music of Worship" surveys the development of liturgical chant, liturgical song, the Gregorian tradition, new forms, and tonal expansion; (2) "Music for Worship" discusses regulation and restriction of church music, conservative forms, origin and development of polyphony, homophony, polyphony and polychoral writing, and the ideal style of ecclesiastical polyphony; and (3) "Music at Worship" examines baroque art, *stile moderno* and *stile antico*, church music shaped by the emotions, symphonic church music, romantic expression, efforts at reform, and contemporary church music. Classified bibliography of 40 items; composer and general indices.

350. Göllner, Theodor. *Die mehrstimmigen liturgischen Lesungen* [Polyphonic liturgical recitation]. Tutzing, Germany: Hans Schneider, 1969. 2 vols. xxx, 359 p.; 200 p.   ML3003 .G63

German only. Two volumes respectively entitled: *I: Edition* [Edition]; *II: Studie: Untersuchungen zur Lektionsvertonung von der fruhen Mehrstimmigkeit bis zu Heinrich Schütz* [Commentary: An examination of recitation practices from early polyphony to Heinrich Schütz]. Vol. 1 contains transcriptions in original notation of approximately 100 polyphonic scripture readings, epistles, and Gospels taken from 12th- through 17th-century sources. Vol. 2 presents an historical perspective, discussing individual works, including falsobordone settings of Psalms and Passions, and compares recitation practices with the works of Schütz. Facsimiles, transcriptions, musical examples, tables, and illustrations; bibliography of more than 50 writings; expansive index. Series: *Münchner Veröffentlichungen zur Musikgeschichte*, Bd. 15.

351. Harrison, Frank Llewellyn. *Music in Medieval Britain*. 4th ed. Buren, the Netherlands: Frits Knuf, 1980. xix, 491 p.   ML285.2 .H3 1980

     Historical survey of British music before the Reformation. Topics: institutions and their choirs, liturgy and its plainsong, polyphony of the liturgy from 1100 to 1400, institutions and the cultivation of polyphony from 1400 to the Reformation, Mass and motet, votive antiphon and Magnificat, other ritual forms, and the carol. Musical examples, facsimiles, tables, and illustrations; bibliography of about 350 writings; register and index of musicians, index of titles, and general index.

352. Hofman, May, and John Morehen. *Latin Music in British Sources, c.1485-c.1610*. London: Stainer and Bell, 1987. xiv, 176 p. ISBN 0-85249-673-7 ML120.G7 H63 1987

     Not examined. Index of church music with Latin texts found in English sources between late 15th and early 17th centuries. Companion volume to Ralph T. Daniel's and Peter le Huray's *Sources of English Church Music 1549–1660* (1972). For each entry, provides composer, title or text incipit, voicing, liturgical function, cantus firmus source, modern editions, clefs, and manuscript and printed sources. Primary focus on English and other British composers; contributions by foreign composers included in separate listing with fewer annotative details. Index to first lines of all works; thematic catalog of anonymous compositions. Series: *Early English Church Music*, supplementary vol. 2.

353. Hughes, Andrew. "English Sacred Music (Excluding Carols) in Insular Sources, 1400-c. 1450." Ph.D. dissertation. University of Oxford, Oxford, England, 1963. xvi, 454 p.

     Analytical study of early 15th-century English sacred music based on the examination of a number of manuscript sources. Discusses descant, chanson style, cantus firmus treatment, isorhythm, unification of the Mass, imitation and canon, and variation. Demonstrates presence of French and Italian influence on sacred English music. Numerous musical examples.

354. Hume, Paul. *Catholic Church Music*. Preface by Francis J. Guentner, S. J. New York: Dodd, Mead & Company, 1956. xiv, 259 p.   MT88 .H8

     The author's views concerning music in the Catholic Church. Topics include adult and boys choirs, congregational singing, problems of Catholic hymnody, wedding music, and the church organist. Selected church documents appended. Article by Juan Navarro, "Is the Motu Proprio of Blessed Pius Tenth on Sacred Music Binding in Conscience?" appended. Classified bibliography of 17 writings; classified and graded listing of approximately 60 Masses, about 20 organ works or collections, and a handful of recommended hymnals; classified discography of nearly 250 recordings; expansive index.

355. Robertson, Alec. *Music of the Catholic Church*. London: Burns & Oates, 1961. 157 p. ML3002 .R72

Concise overview of Catholic Church music from pre-Christian sacred music to the mid-20th century. Focus on "plainsong and polyphony," the latter exemplified by the music of Giovanni Pierluigi da Palestrina. Bibliography of 17 writings; no index. Series: *Faith and Fact Books*, no. 117; *Catholicism and the Arts*, no. 75.

356. Roche, Jerome. *North Italian Church Music in the Age of Monteverdi*. Oxford: Clarendon Press, 1984. xii, 177 p. ISBN 0-19-316118-4   ML2933 .R6 1984

Study of church music in 17th-century northern Italy within a social, geographical, and liturgical context. Discusses Mass, motet, and Psalm settings. Musical examples; bibliography of about 130 writings and a list of approximately 170 compositions in original printed sources; expansive general index and index of music examples.

357. Stevenson, Robert Murrell. *Spanish Cathedral Music in the Golden Age*. Berkeley: University of California Press, 1961.   ML3047 .S83; reprint, Westport, Connecticut: Greenwood Press, 1976. 523 p. ISBN 0-8371-8744-3 ML31047 .S83 1976

Stevenson, Robert Murrell. *La Música en las Catedrales Españolas del Siglo de Oro* [Spanish cathedral music in the Golden Age]. Madrid: Alianza, 1993. 600 p. ISBN 84-20-68562-3   ML3047 .S8318 1993

Surveys sacred and secular music in Spain during the 16th and early 17th centuries with emphasis on the music of Cristóbal de Morales, Francisco Guerrero, and Tomás Luis de Victoria. Musical examples; bibliography of approximately 365 writings; expansive index. Alianza edition in Spanish. Series: *Alianza Música*, vol. 62.

358. Tittel, Ernst. *Österreichische Kirchenmusik: Werden, Wachsen, Wirken* [Austrian church music: Development, growth, influence]. Vienna: Herder, 1961. xii, 394 p. MT3022 .T6

German only. Discusses musical culture of the monasteries, sacred music at the Imperial Court, music of the Viennese baroque and classical periods, and music in the Austro-Viennese bourgeoisie from the romantic period through the present. Musical examples; bibliography of nearly 60 writings; expansive index. Series: *Allgemeiner Cäcilien-Verband für die Länder der Deutschen Sprache. Schriftenreihe*, Bd. 2.

359. Ward, Tom R. "The Polyphonic Office Hymn from the Late Fourteenth Century until the Early Sixteenth Century." Ph.D. dissertation. University of Pittsburgh, Pennsylvania, 1969. 2 vols. v, 612 p.

Study of preexistent material in polyphonic office hymn settings. Concentrates on Italian and Germanic archetypes. Examines feasts receiving polyphonic hymns, text chosen for those feasts, and melody associated with each text. Two appendices: (1) extensive thematic index of nearly 600 hymns, providing title, incipit, source, remarks, and modern editions; (2) 41 hymn transcriptions. Numerous tables; bibliography of about 90 writings, 50 manuscripts, and 5 early prints.

Russian Orthodox Church Music

360. Reid, Robert Addison. "Russian Sacred Choral Music and Its Assimilation into and Impact on the American A Cappella Choir Movement." D.M.A dissertation. University of Texas, Austin, 1983. xvii, 264 p.

Traces the development of unaccompanied choral music of the Russian Orthodox church between 1650 and 1917 and its influence upon the American a cappella movements of the first half of the 20th century. Bibliography of about 120 items (majority in English).

CHORAL MUSIC IN SPECIFIC COUNTRIES AND REGIONS

Africa

361. Ekwueme, Lazarus Edward Nnanyelu. "Ibo Choral Music: Its Theory and Practice." Ph.D. dissertation: Yale University, New Haven, Connecticut 1972. 459 p.

Study of the choral music of the Ibo people (also spelled Igbo), inhabitants of the inland areas around the Bight of Biafra on the west coast of Africa. Discusses anthropological and sociological background, as well as musical form, melody, harmony, rhythm, instrumental accompaniment, and contemporary trends. Bibliography of nearly 100 writings.

Denmark

362. Docter, David Reinhardt. "Choral Music in Denmark, 1900–1960: Repertory and Stylistic Trends." Ph.D. dissertation. University of Minnesota, Minneapolis, 1976. iv, 238 p.

Introductory chapter briefly surveys 18th- and 19th-century Danish choral music. Remainder of study focuses upon Danish choral music traditions from 1900 through the 1960s. Special emphasis on the works of Carl Nielsen. Musical examples; bibliography of more than 100 writings and 80 musical works and collections.

England

363. Hogwood, Christopher, and Richard Luckett, eds. *Music in Eighteenth-Century England: Essays in Memory of Charles Cudworth.* Foreword by Stanley Sadie. Cambridge, England: Cambridge University Press, 1983. xviii, 265 p. ISBN 0-521-23525-1   ML55 .C85 1983

Collection of 14 essays. Those dealing with choral music are as follows: "Thomas Tudway's History of Music" (Hogwood) examines unpublished prefaces to a manuscript collection of services and anthems compiled between 1715 and 1720; "Purcellian Passages in the Compositions of G. F. Handel" (Franklin Zimmerman) discusses similarities between the musical style of Henry Purcell and Handel; " 'Or Rather Our Musical Shakspeare': Charles Burney's Purcell" (Luckett) focuses on Burney's view of the composer's work; "Intellectual Contexts of Handel's English Oratorios" (Ruth Smith) reexamines the libretti in relation to literary, religious, and political establishments of mid-18th century society; "The Late Additions to Handel's Oratorios and the Role of the Younger Smith" (Anthony Hicks); and "New Light on the Libretto of *The Creation*" (Nicholas Temperley). Musical examples, tables, and illustrations; bibliography of the writings of Cudworth prepared by Richard Andrewes; expansive index.

See also: Blezzard, Judith. *Borrowings in English Church Music, 1550–1950* (item 297); Bowers, Roger. "Choral Institutions within the English Church: Their Constitution and Development, 1340–1500" (item 345); Bowers, Roger. *English Church Polyphony: Singers and Sources from the 14th to the 17th Century* (item 346); Dearnley, Christopher. *English Church Music, 1650–1750: In Royal Chapel, Cathedral and Parish Church* (item 327); Fellowes, Edmund Horace. *English Cathedral Music* (item 302); Gatens, William J. *Victorian Cathedral Music in Theory and Practice* (item 303); Harrison, Frank Llewellyn. *Music in Medieval Britain* (item 351); Hofman, May, and John Morehen. *Latin Music in British Sources, c.1485–c.1610* (item 352); Hughes, Andrew. "English Sacred Music (Excluding Carols) in Insular Sources, 1400-c. 1450" (item 353); Le Huray, Peter. *Music and the Reformation in England, 1549–1660* (item 329); Long, Kenneth R. *The Music of the English Church* (item 307); Morehen, John, ed. *English Choral Practice, 1400–1650* (item 308); Routley, Erik. *A Short History of English Church Music* (item 314); Routley,

Erik. *Twentieth Century Church Music* (item 335); Spink, Ian. *Restoration Cathedral Music: 1660–1714* (item 337); Temperley, Nicholas. *The Music of the English Parish Church* (item 318); Wilhite, Charles Stanford. "Eucharistic Music for the Anglican Church in England and the United States at Mid-Twentieth Century (1950–1965): A Stylistic Study with Historical Introduction" (item 341)

Germany and Austria

See: Göllner, Theodor. *Die mehrstimmigen liturgischen Lesungen* (item 350); Seeley, Gilbert Stewart. "German Protestant Choral Music Since 1925" (item 336); Tittel, Ernst. *Österreichische Kirchenmusik: Werden, Wachsen, Wirken* (item 358); Valentin, Erich, and Friedrich Hofmann, eds. *Die evangelische Kirchenmusik: Handbuch für Studium und Praxis* (item 340)

Russia

364. Morosan, Vladimir. *Choral Performance in Pre-Revolutionary Russia.* Rev. and corrected. Madison, Connecticut: Musica Russica, 1994. xx, 376 p. ISBN 0962946028   ML1537 .M67 1994

Historical development and performance practices of the Russian choral tradition up to 1917. Emphasis on 19th-century music. Numerous tables and musical examples; bibliography of over 200 writings; expansive index. Series: *Russian Music Studies*, no. 17.

See also: Brough, Delma. *Polish Seventeenth-Century Church Music: With Reference to the Influence of Historical, Political, and Social Conditions* (item 347); Reid, Robert Addison. "Russian Sacred Choral Music and Its Assimilation into and Impact on the American A Cappella Choir Movement" (item 360)

Scotland

See: Somerville, Thomas Charles. "A Study and Performance of Sacred Choral Music by Contemporary Scottish Composers, 1950–1970" (item 317)

United States

365. Carroll, Lucy E. "Three Centuries of Song: Pennsylvania's Choral Composers, 1681–1981." D.M.A. dissertation. Combs College of Music, Philadelphia, 1982. xvi, 335 p.

Study of the choral music of Pennsylvania composers from 1681 to 1981, including the works of Francis Hopkinson, Benjamin Carr, Benjamin Cross, William Henry Fry, Stephen Foster, Henry Thacker Burleigh, Charles Wakefield Cadman, Samuel Barber, Vincent Persichetti, and Peter Mennin. Musical examples, facsimiles, and photos; chronology; bibliography of around 180 writings, 40 hymnals and choral collections, and 110 scores and recordings; no index.

366. DeVenney, David P. *Source Readings in American Choral Music: Com-posers' Writings, Interviews & Reviews.* Missoula, Montana: College Music Society, 1995. xiii, 258 p. ISBN 0-9650647-0-0, ISBN 0-9650647-1-9 (pbk) ML1511 .D48 1995

Purpose: "to present important documents relating to the history and perfor-mance of choral literature written in the United States." Prefaced with a seven-page chronology of American choral music. Main body organized into three parts: (1) music before 1830; (2) music from 1830–1920; and (3) music since 1920. In all, 30 reprinted essays and articles by 28 composers with annotations and comments. Attributes of documents chosen: "reflec-tions on the nature and purposes of choral music by major contributors to the repertory, critical responses to landmark works, and instruction on per-formance practice." Classified bibliography of approximately 270 writings; expansive index. Series: *Monographs and Bibliographies in American Music*, no. 15.

367. DeVenney, David P. *Varied Carols: A Survey of American Choral Litera-ture.* Westport, Connecticut: Greenwood Press, 1999. xi, 315 p. ISBN 0-313-31051-3   ML1511 .D48 1999

An historical survey of American choral literature, based on examination of almost 3,000 choral works by nearly 300 composers active in the United States between 1760 and the 1990s. DeVenney has attempted to keep the text narrowly focused on the literature of American choral music, not on its creators, performers, or conductors. Provides brief descriptive analyses for some works. Bibliography of nearly 300 writings. Index.

368. Harris, Carl Gordon. "A Study of Characteristic Stylistic Trends Found in the Choral Works of a Selected Group of Afro-American Composers and Arrangers." D.M.A. dissertation. University of Missouri-Kansas City, 1972. viii, 178 p.

The development of choral music by selected late 19th-century and 20th-century African-American composers and arrangers. Identifies three groups of musicians: African-American trailblazers, nationalists, and innovators. Biographical sketch of each composer, analyses of works, and brief history of performances of African-American spirituals. Includes selected list of approximately 200 choral works by 25 African-American composers, giving composer with dates, title, publisher and music number. Musical examples; bibliography of about 120 writings.

369. Heintze, James R., ed. *American Musical Life in Context and Practice to 1865*. New York: Garland, 1994. x, 366 p. ISBN 0-8153-0816-7   ML200.4 .A4 1994

A collection of 10 articles about American musical life prior to 1865. Of special interest are "Peter Erben and America's First Lutheran Tunebook in English" (Edward C. Wolf); "The Anthem in Southern Four-Shape Shape-Note Tunebooks, 1816–1860" (David W. Music); "Catholic Church Music in the Midwest before the Civil War: The Firm of W. C. Peters & Sons" (Richard D. Wetzel); "An American Muse Learns to Walk: The First American-Music Group" (Richard Jackson). Other articles include: "Music and Dance in Philadelphia's City Tavern, 1773–1790" (Sterling E. Murray); "Gaetano Carusi: From Sicily to the Halls of Congress" (James R. Heintze); "Edward Little White, Professor of Music" (Barbara Owen); "The 1838–40 American Concert Tours of Jane Shirreff and John Wilson, British Vocal Stars" (Katherine K. Preston); "The Origins of Music Journalism in Chicago: Criticism as a Reflection of Musical Life" (James A. Deaville); "The Beginnings of Bach in America" (J. Bunker Clark). Index of names and titles. Series: *Essays in American Music*, vol. 1; *Garland Reference Library of the Humanities*, vol. 1583.

See also: Brown, Bruce Calvin. "The Choral Music of the American Lutheran Church: A Study and Performance of the Music of Daniel Moe, Paul Fetler, and Rolf Espeseth" (item 325); Dean, Talmage W. *A Survey of Twentieth Century Protestant Church Music in America* (item 326); Ellinwood, Leonard Webster. *The History of American Church Music* (item 301); Hitchcock, H. Wiley. *Music in the United States: A Historical Introduction* (item 294); MacNeill, Roger. "Secular Choral Chamber Music in America since 1950, as Represented by the Music for this Genre by Samuel Adler, Jean Berger, Eugene Butler, and Kirke Mechem" (item 454); Neve, Paul Edmund. "The Contribution of the Lutheran College Choirs to Music in America" (item 333); Rapp, Robert Maurice. "Stylistic Characteristics of the Short Sacred Choral Composition in the U. S. A., 1945–1960" (item 310); Stevenson, Robert Murrell. *Protestant Church Music in America: A Short Survey of Men and Movements from 1564 to the Present* (item 339); Werner, Eric. *In the Choir Loft: A Manual for Organists and Choir*

Directors in American Synagogues (item 322); Wilhite, Charles Stanford. "Eucharistic Music for the Anglican Church in England and the United States at Mid-Twentieth Century (1950–1965): A Stylistic Study with Historical Introduction" (item 341); Wolf, Edward. "Lutheran Church Music in America during the Eighteenth and Early Nineteenth Centuries" (item 343); Yoder, David Winston. "A Study and Performance of Extended Sacred Choral Works with Brass Instruments by Contemporary American Composers" (item 114)

VI

Studies of Choral Genres

ANTHEM

370. Cook, Warren Edward. "The Anthem in the Twentieth-Century English Renaissance." D.M.A. dissertation. University of South Carolina, Columbia, 1993. viii, 113 p.

Study of selective 20th-century anthems, focusing on the music of 31 English composers from C. Hubert H. Parry to John Rutter. Musical examples; bibliography of approximately 50 writings and 50 musical sources.

371. Dakers, Lionel. *The Church Anthem Handbook: A Companion to the One Hundred Anthems in "The New Church Anthem Book."* Oxford: Oxford University Press, 1994. vii, 67 p. ISBN 0-19-353108-9   M2060 .N54 1992 Suppl.

Provides general and performance notes for each anthem contained in *The New Church Anthem Book: One Hundred Anthems* (1992) compiled and edited by Dakers. Liturgical index.

372. Daniel, Ralph T. *The Anthem in New England before 1800.* With a Foreword by George Howerton. Evanston, Illinois: Northwestern University Press, 1966   ML2911 .D35; reprint, New York: Da Capo Press, 1979. xvi, 282 p. ISBN 0-306-79511-6   ML2911 .D35 1979

Study of the primitive multisectional New England anthem, ca. 1760–1800. Considers 118 indigenous American anthems with comparisons to more than 70 anthems by 18th-century English composers. Confirms the influence of an English singing-school movement on the New England movement. Works of 21 American composers, including William Billings and such lesser known figures as Jacob French, Daniel Read, Samuel Holyoke, William Cooper, Supply Belcher, and Oliver Holden. Two appendices: anthems by non-American composers published in New England before

1800; anthems by native composers published in New England before 1800. Many musical examples throughout the text; lengthy bibliography lists not only books, articles, and manuscripts, but some 125 scores and collections of anthems; expansive index.

373. Fansler, Terry Lee. "The Anthem in America, 1900–1950." Ph.D. dissertation. University of North Texas, Denton 1982. xvii, 230 p.

Study of anthem literature published and performed in the United States during the first part of the 20th century. Focuses on the quartet anthem, anthems in the Anglican tradition, prominent choral ensembles, dissemination of the anthem, anthems by prominent music educators, anthems in the Russian style, and the Negro spiritual. Biographical sketches of major composers and detailed analyses of selected anthems. Musical examples; bibliography of over 150 writings, editions of music, and recordings.

374. Foster, Myles Birket. *Anthems and Anthem Composers: An Essay upon the Development of the Anthem from the Time of the Reformation to the End of the Nineteenth Century.* London: Novello, 1901. ML3260 .F75; reprint, New York: Da Capo Press, 1970. SBN 306-70012-3 ML3260 .F75 1970; reprint, Hildesheim: G. Olms, 1980. 225 p. ISBN 3-487-06952-0 ML3260 .F75 1980

Of historical interest; reprint of Foster's pioneering, though inaccurate, study of the history and development of the anthem in England. Quite out of date. Brief narrative chapters trace the form from the Reformation to the end of the 19th century. Includes a "complete" list of anthems and composers for all four centuries. Many incorrect attributions. Seventeen portraits and photographs of anthem composers. Index of composers subdivided by century; index of anthem titles. Series: *Da Capo Press Music Reprint Series.*

375. Gerlach, Bruce A. "A Critical Study of Selected Anthems, Published 1961–1991, by Twentieth-Century American and British Composers." D.M.A. dissertation. Southern Baptist Theological Seminary, Louisville, Kentucky, 1992. ix, 275 p.

Examines 42 selected 20th-century anthems with regard to textual considerations and rehearsal and performance considerations, and presents descriptive and critical analysis of each work. Musical examples; bibliography of nearly 100 writings and 19 additional compositions cited in the text. Separate indices for compositions by title and performances.

376. King, William Joseph. "The English Anthem from the Early Tudor Period through the Restoration Era." Ph.D. dissertation. Boston University, 1962. 2 vols. xvii, 362; v, 192 p.

Survey of the 16th- and 17th-century English anthem. Emphasis placed upon the music of Christopher Tye, Thomas Tallis, William Byrd, Orlando Gibbons, Thomas Weelkes, Thomas Tomkins, Pelham Humphrey, Michael Wise, John Blow, and Henry Purcell. "Account for Liveries for the Household for the Burial of Henry VIII" appended. Second, supplement volume contains 22 unpublished anthems by Tye, Tallis, and Weelkes. Musical examples and facsimiles; classified bibliography of over 80 books and scores.

377. Price, Shelby Milburn. "The Restoration Verse Anthem." D.M.A. dissertation. University of Southern California, Los Angeles, 1967. vi, 208 p.

Study of the English verse anthem stylized during the reign of Charles II (1660–1685), commonly known as the *Restoration era*. Focuses on the anthems of Henry Purcell, along with the works of Michael Wise, Pelham Humfrey, John Blow, and William Turner. Two appendices: (1) bibliography of approximately 280 Restoration anthems with reference to printed and manuscript sources; (2) list of 22 Restoration anthems available in performing editions. Musical examples; bibliography of about 70 writings and 11 musical works and collections.

378. Turner, Ronald A. *A Study Guide to Anthem Literature: History and Performance Practice.* 4th ed. Louisville, Kentucky: Southern Baptist Theological Seminary, 1989. 296 p.

Revision of the "textbook" originally compiled in 1979 by students at the School of Church Music of Southern Seminary. Three units: anthem in England, European schools of church music composition, and the anthem in America. Musical examples and charts; documented with footnotes; expansive index.

379. Wienandt, Elwyn A., and Robert H. Young. *The Anthem in England and America.* New York: The Free Press, 1970. xiii, 495 p.   ML3265 .W53

First comprehensive study of the anthem since Myles B. Foster's long-outdated *Anthems and Anthem Composers* (item 374). Major addition to the literature on church music when originally published. Remains fine study of the anthem from the Reformation to the 1960s. First four chapters provide a concise description of the origin and development of the anthem in England from the Reformation to 1825. Fifth and sixth chapters concern decorative church music in America, early 18th to mid-19th century. In the rest of the book, alternate chapters trace developments in England and America through the 1960s. Significant Canadian contributions included. Numerous musical examples; valuable extensive bibliography; expansive index.

See also: Dykes Bower, John, and Allan Wicks. *A Repertory of English Cathedral Anthems* (item 133); Zimmerman, Franklin B. *The Anthems of Henry Purcell* (item 486)

CANTATA

380. Bolton, Jacklin Talmage. "Religious Influences on American Secular Cantatas, 1850–1930." Ph.D. dissertation. University of Michigan, Ann Arbor, 1964. xvii, 483 p.

Religious influences on secular cantatas written by U. S. composers published between 1850 and 1930. Limited to works for adult choral groups and works with librettos "pertaining to American life and heritage." Two parts. Part I: discussion; Part II: a bio-bibliography of the cantatas, arranged alphabetically by composer, providing title of composition, classification, librettist, scoring, publisher, date of initial publication, estimation of performance time, with annotations and summary of libretto. Traces secular and sacred chronology of composers and librettists. Provides index of librettists, index of cantatas with location of scores, and topical index. Three appendices: (1) list of Roman Catholic liturgical materials identified in selected works, (2) list of Native American music identified in selected works, and (3) list of cantatas "of possible value for contemporary performance." Musical examples; bibliography of over 250 writings and scores (Part I) and a special, classified bibliography of about 80 writings (Part II); no index.

381. Holst, Robert Inar. "Toward a Stylistic History of the North German 'Cantata' in the Second Half of the Seventeenth Century." Ph.D. dissertation. University of Chicago, 1995. xxii, 970 p.

Not examined. Analytical study focusing on harmony of 70 selected north German cantatas composed in the latter half of the 17th century.

382. Jones, Maurice Allen. "American Theater Cantatas: 1852–1907." D.M.A. dissertation. University of Illinois at Urbana-Champaign, 1975. iii, 162 p.

Historical survey of American theater cantatas of the latter half of the 19th century and beginning of the 20th century. Theater cantata defined as "extended vocal compositions for solo voices, chorus, and (often) orchestra" which are considered "stageworthy." Not to be confused with "dramatic cantatas" which, although dramatic in nature, are not "stageworthy." Three appendices: (1) annotated list of 18 American cantatas of the pageant or floral concert type composed between 1852 and 1922; (2) annotated list of 17 American cantatas of the dramatic cantata, sacred cantata, scripture cantata, and undesignated cantata types composed between 1860 and 1907; (3) alphabetical listing by composer of almost 200 American cantatas by nearly 80 composers composed between 1850 and 1927. Each appendix provides title, composer, source of text, publishing information, and performing forces. First two appendices are briefly to moderately annotated; third is not annotated. Musical examples; bibliography of about 240 writings; no index.

383. Konold, Wulf. *Weltliche Kantaten im 20. Jahrhundert: Beiträge zu einer Theorie der funktionalen Musik* [Secular cantatas in the 20th century: Contributions on a theory of functional music]. Wolfenbüttel: Möseler, 1975. 254 p. ML2400 .K66

German only. Study of the 20th-century secular cantata, spanning the years 1900–1972, with specific focus on the genre in Germany. Provides descriptions and analysis of musical works. Includes a bibliography of 1,541 published secular cantatas. Discussion preceded by a brief history of the cantata before 1900. Musical examples and tables; bibliography of about 75 writings; index of names.

384. Ryder, Georgia Atkins. "Melodic and Rhythmic Elements of American Negro Folk Songs as Employed in Cantatas by Selected American Composers between 1932 and 1967." Ph.D. dissertation. New York University, 1970. xiii, 264 p.

Identifies African-American folk music idioms and their use in cantatas by Robert Nathaniel Dett, Earl Robinson, William Grant Still, Roy Ringwald, Charles Haubiel, Wynn York, and Elie Siegmeister. Two appendices: (1) classified listing of more than 100 songs, giving transcription source, song number, and recorded source; and (2) bibliography of 12 cantatas discussed in the text, listing general bibliographic information with date of composition, source of text, and significant performances. Bibliography of approximately 150 writings.

See also: Bach, Johann Sebastian. *Cantata No. 4: Christ lag in Todesbanden: An Authoritative Score, Backgrounds, Analysis, Views and Comments* (item 458); Bach, Johann Sebastian. *Cantata No. 140: Wachet auf, ruft uns die Stimme: The Score of the New Bach Edition, Backgrounds, Analysis, Views and Comments* (item 459); Day, James. *The Literary Background to Bach's Cantatas* (item 462); Dox, Thurston J. *American Oratorios and Cantatas: A Catalog of Works Written in the United States from Colonial Times to 1985* (item 147); Dürr, Alfred. *Die Kantaten von Johann Sebastian*

Bach mit ihren Texten (item 463); Dürr, Alfred. *Studien über die frühen Kantaten Johann Sebastian Bachs* (item 464); Neumann, Werner. *Handbuch der Kantaten Johann Sebastian Bachs* (item 466); Pahlen, Kurt. *The World of the Oratorio: Oratorio, Mass, Requiem, Te Deum, Stabat Mater and Large Cantatas* (item 433); Robertson, Alec. *The Church Cantatas of J. S. Bach* (item 468); Terry, Charles Sanford. *Bach: The Cantatas and Oratorios; The Passions; The Magnificat, Lutheran Masses and Motets* (item 470); Vollen, Gene E. *The French Cantata: A Survey and Thematic Catalog* (item 51); Young, W. Murray. *The Cantatas of J. S. Bach: An Analytical Guide* (item 472)

CAROL

385. Brice, Douglas. *The Folk-Carol of England.* London: Jenkins, 1967. xviii, 174 p. M3652 .B75

    Survey of the English carol from a historical, musical, literary, and liturgical perspective. Musical examples; documented with endnotes; expansive index.

386. Nettel, Reginald. *Christmas and Its Carols.* London: Faith Press, 1960. 144 p. ML2880 .N48

    Discusses historical and analytical aspects of the carols, including possible theory of origins, polyphonic carols, the wassail, and the carol revival. Illustrations and musical examples; no bibliography; expansive index.

387. Routley, Erik. *The English Carol.* London: Jenkins, 1958   ML2881.E5 R7; New York: Oxford University Press, 1959   ML2881.E5 .R7 1959; reprint, Westport, Connecticut: Greenwood Press, 1973. 272 p. ISBN 0-8371-6989-5 ML2881.E5 R7 1973

    Historical study of the English carol from the 16th century to the mid-20th century. Emphasis on carol texts; a companion to carol literature, specifically *The Oxford Book of Carols* (London: Oxford University Press, 1956), to which numerous references are made. Documented with endnotes; musical examples, facsimile, and photos; general index and index to carols in *The Oxford Book of Carols*.

388. Studwell, William E. *Christmas Carols: A Reference Guide.* Indices by David A. Hamilton. New York: Garland Publishing, 1985. xxxiii, 278 p. ISBN 0-8240-8899-9   ML102.C3 S9 1985

    Excellent guide to nearly 800 sacred and secular Christmas carols and songs. Three main sections: historical background of the carol, bibliography, and historical dictionary. Three-page chronology traces the development of the carol from the 12th century through the early 1960s. Extensive historical dictionary lists lyricists and composers, places and dates of origin for text and music, variant titles, tunes, and first lines, and published source(s) of the carols. Bibliography lists carol sources cited in the historical dictionary, reference sources, and other information. Three indices: title, person and group, and place.

CHORALE

389. Riedel, Johannes. *The Lutheran Chorale: Its Basic Traditions.* Minneapolis, Minnesota: Augsburg Publishing House, 1967. 120 p.   ML3184 .R53

Historical survey of the development of the chorale. Surveys four main chorale traditions: medieval tradition, Martin Luther tradition (1483–1608), Johann Crüger tradition (1600–1660), and Johann Anastasius Freylinghausen tradition (ca. 1644–1756). Musical examples; bibliography of approximately 75 writings; index of first line of chorales.

HYMN

390. Benson, Louis F. *The English Hymn: Its Development and Use in Worship.* New York: Hodder & Stoughton, George H. Doran, 1915 BV312 .B4; reprint, Richmond, Virginia: John Knox Press, 1962. xvii, 19–624 p.   BV312 .B4 1962

Based on lectures given by the author between 1907 and 1914. Historical study of the English hymn, tracing the origins and development and the decline of the practice of singing metrical Psalm versions. Spans 16th century to the early 20th century. Topics: evolution and liturgical use of the English hymn; Isaac Watts' "Renovation of Psalmody"; hymnody of the Methodist revival, Evangelical revival, Oxford revival, and romantic movement; Evangelical hymnody in America; and 20th-century hymnody. Documented with footnotes; expansive index.

391. Christ-Janer, Albert, Charles W. Hughes, and Carleton Sprague Smith. *American Hymns Old and New.* New York: Columbia University Press, 1980. xv, 838 p. ISBN 0-231-03458-X   M2117 .A573

Hughes, Charles W. *American Hymns Old and New: Notes on the Hymns and Biographies of the Authors and Composers.* New York: Columbia University Press, 1980. x, 621 p. ISBN 0-231-04934-X   ML3270 .H8

First volume is a collection of American hymns dating as far back as the 17th century and 60 American hymns commissioned from contemporary poets and composers. Organized by centuries; each set of hymns briefly introduced with a historical perspective. Most of the newly commissioned works written in the late 1950s. Described as a "historical singing book" by Hughes. Not intended for use in the modern church service. Concludes with five helpful indices: first lines/titles, authors and composers, tunes, meters, and Bible verses. Second volume is organized into two sections: (1) hymns presented in the first volume are discussed, and (2) brief biographical sketches for each author and composer are given. Concludes with a bibliography of over 150 items.

392. Frost, Maurice, ed. *Historical Companion to Hymns Ancient & Modern.* London: William Clowes & Sons, 1962. xvi, 716 p.   ML3166 .H58

Revision of W. H. Frere's *Historical Edition of Hymns Ancient and Modern* (1909). Original edition comments on hymns included in 1904 edition of the hymnal *Hymns Ancient and Modern*; revised edition enlarged to cover all editions from 1860 to the 1960s. Consists of various indices, chronologies, and information about composers, authors of hymns, the music, and texts. Facsimiles, musical examples, illustrations, and portraits.

393. Hooper, William L. *Church Music in Transition.* Foreword by Loren R. Williams. Nashville, Tennessee: Broadman Press, 1963. vi, 208 p. ML3111 .H66

History of church music with emphasis on hymnody of evangelical denominations in the United States, namely the Baptists, Methodists, Presbyterians, and Disciples. Musical examples and facsimiles; bibliography of about 160 writings; expansive general index and expansive index of hymnals.

394. Patrick, Millar. *The Story of the Church's Song.* Rev. for American use by James Rawlings Sydnor. Richmond, Virginia: John Knox Press, 1962. 208 p.   ML3186 .P35

Historical survey of Christian hymnody, including discussion of metrical Psalms and the Scottish paraphrases. First published in 1927; Sydnor's revision adds descriptive footnotes to the original text and includes an appendix, "American Hymnody 1927–61." No musical examples; the reader is referred to selected hymnals. Original classified bibliography (1927) of nearly 40 writings; revised classified bibliography of about 80 writings; expansive general index and index of titles.

MADRIGAL

395. Arnold, Denis. *Monteverdi Madrigals*. London: British Broadcasting Corporation, 1967. 61 p. MT115.M7 A7; reprint, Seattle: University of Washington Press, 1969. 61 p. MT115.M7 A7 1969; reprint, London: Ariel Music, BBC Books, 1987. 59 p. ISBN 0-563-20555-5 MT115.M7 A7 1987

Chronological treatment, not only of Claudio Monteverdi's madrigals, but also the canzonette, scherzi musicali, and other genres. Musical examples; no bibliography; index. Series: *BBC Music Guides*.

396. Einstein, Alfred. *The Italian Madrigal*. Translated by Alexander H. Krappe, Roger H. Sessions, and Oliver Strunk. Contributions by Joel Newman, Antonio Illiano, and Howard E. Smither. Princeton, New Jersey: Princeton University Press, 1949 ML2633 .E32; reprint, Princeton, New Jersey: Princeton University Press, 1971. 3 vols. ISBN 0-691-09112-9 ML2633 .E32 1971

Originally published in 1949. Historical survey of the Italian madrigal from early antecedents through the 17th century. Musical examples, facsimiles, and illustrations. Separate indices for names, places, and capoversi and titles, the latter compiled by Joel Newman. Volume 3 contains madrigal texts revised and translated by Antonio Illiano and Howard E. Smither and scores of 97 madrigals in modern notation.

397. Fabbri, Paolo, ed. *Il madrigale tra Cinque e Seicento* [The madrigal between the 16th and 17th centuries]. Bologna: Società editrice il Mulino, 1988. 372 p. ISBN 88-15-01992-8 ML2602 .M32

In Italian. Eleven essays devoted to the madrigal. All previously published between 1962 and 1981 in English, German, or Italian. Essays: "Ripercorrendo gli esordi del madrigale" [The early madrigal: A reappraisal of its beginnings], "Giuochi musicali del Cinquecento" [Musical games in the 16th century], and "'Pace non trovo': Una parodia letteraria e musicale" [Pace non trovo: A literary and musical parody] (James Haar); "Pietro Bembo e le origini letteraire del madrigale italiano" [Pietro Bembo and the literary origins of the Italian madrigal] (Dean T. Mace); "Tipologie metriche e formali del madrigale ai suoi esordi" [Typologies of meter and form in early madrigal] (Don Harrán); "Circolazione letteraria e circolazione musicale del madrigale: Il caso G. B. Strozzi" [The literary and musical dissemination of the madrigal: the case of G. B. Strozzi] (Lorenzo Bianconi, Antonio Vassalli); "Gli esordi della 'canzone villanesca alla napolitana'"

[The debut of the "canzone villanesca alla napolitana"] (Donna G. Cardamone); "La modalità di 'Vestiva i colli' " [The modality of *Vestiva i colli*] (Harold S. Powers); "Il cromatismo di Gesualdo" [Gesualdo's chromatic technique] (Carl Dahlhaus); "La Franceschina, la Girometta e soci in un madrigale 'a diversi linguaggi' di L. Marenzio e O. Vecchi" [Franceschina, Girometta and their companions in a madrigal "a diversi linguaggi" by Luca Marenzio and Orazio Vecchi] (Warren Kirkendale); "Questioni formali nei madrigali di Monteverdi" [Problems of form in Monteverdi's madrigals] (Reinhold Hammerstein). Classified bibliography of over 100 items; no index.

398. Fellowes, Edmund Horace. *The English Madrigal.* London: Oxford University Press, H. Milford, 1925   ML2631 .F45 (rep. 1935, 1947, 1952); reprint, Freeport, New York: Books for Libraries Press, 1972. ISBN 0-8369-6929-4   ML2631 .F45 1972; reprint, Salem, New Hampshire: Ayer, 1984. 111 p. ISBN 0-8369-6929-4   ML2631 .F45 1984

Surveys the music, text, and composers of the 16th-century English madrigal. Musical examples, facsimiles, and illustrations; no bibliography; no index.

399. Fellowes, Edmund Horace. *The English Madrigal Composers.* 2nd ed. London: Oxford University Press, 1948 (rep. 1958, 1963, 1967, 1972, 1975). ISBN 0-19-315102-2 (1972)   ML2631 .F46 1948; reprint, New York: J. & J. Harper Editions; Harper & Row, 1969. 364 p.   ML2631 .F46 1969

Two parts: (1) history and meaning of English madrigal; (2) life and works of more than 30 English madrigal composers, along with about 20 English lutenist composers. Musical examples and table; documented with footnotes; index of first lines and expansive general index.

400. Fenlon, Iain, and James Haar. *The Italian Madrigal in the Early Sixteenth Century: Sources and Interpretation.* Cambridge, England: Cambridge University Press, 1988. x, 369 p. ISBN 0-521-25228-8   ML2633 .F46 1988

Organized into two parts. Part I: Traces the origins of the madrigal in relation to the frottola, concluding that the madrigal was not derived from the frottola. Part II: Presents and describes inventories and concordances of manuscript and printed sources. Facsimiles and illustrations; a listing of approximately 160 manuscripts and music printed before 1601, and a bibliography of more than 300 modern writings; index of capoversi and expansive general index.

401. Kerman, Joseph. *The Elizabethan Madrigal: A Comparative Study.* S.l.: American Musicological Society, 1962. xxii, 318 p.   ML2631 .K47

Comparative study of the origins and early development of the English madrigal and its Italian influences. No attempt to address the late English madrigal. Emphasis on the music of Alfonso Ferrabosco, William Byrd, Orlando Gibbons, Thomas Morely, Thomas Weelkes, and John Wilbye. Tables and musical examples; classified bibliography (bibliographical works, music, historical and critical works) of approximately 125 items; expansive index. Series: *American Musicological Society: Studies and Documents,* no. 4.

402. Myers, Patricia Ann. "An Analytical Study of the Italian Cyclic Madrigals Published by Composers Working in Rome ca. 1540–1614." Ph.D. dissertation. University of Illinois at Urbana-Champaign, 1971. xii, 414 p.

Study of multimovement settings of Italian strophic texts. General survey, as well as discussion of Roman institutions and patrons, verse types employed in the cyclic madrigals, musical treatment of the poetic form, and descriptions of groups for which the cycles were specifically written. Two appendices: (1) collections and anthologies containing cyclic madrigals, supplying composer, title of collection, publisher, city and date of publication, dedication, and list of the cycles; (2) index of the 523 cyclic madrigals listed in first appendix, giving text incipit for first movement, author and poetic source, list of composers who set that particular text, number of movements, number of voices, and dates of publication. Musical examples; bibliography of approximately 225 writings.

403. Opheim, Vernon Holman. "The English Romantic Madrigal." D.M.A. dissertation. University of Illinois at Urbana-Champaign, 1971. v, 392 p.

Assesses general characteristics of the English Romantic madrigal, 1741–ca. 1910. Limited to examination of approximately 90 works labeled "madrigal" by the composer. Musical examples and facsimiles; bibliography of about 70 writings.

404. Roche, Jerome. *The Madrigal.* 2nd ed. Oxford: Oxford University Press, 1990. vi, 184 p. ISBN 0-19-313131-5   ML2600 .R63 1990

Development of the madrigal. Emphasizes Italian madrigals, but discusses English madrigals and madrigals north of the Alps. Musical examples; complete alphabetical listing of all madrigals discussed in the text (approximately 200) with title, composer, and published source; classified bibliography of about 50 items; expansive index. Series: *Early Music Series,* vol. 11.

405. Slim, H. Colin. *A Gift of Madrigals and Motets*. Chicago: University of Chicago Press, 1972. 2 vols. xiii, 306 p.; vii, 451 p. ISBN 0-226-76271-8 M2 .N5

Vol. 1, subtitled "Description and Analysis," examines the manuscript collection of 30 Latin motets and 30 Italian madrigals as part of the Newberry Library, Case MS.-VM 1578.M91 (olim Ry 14), dated approximately 1528. Representative composers include Philippe Verdelot, Adrian Willaert, and Claude de Sermisy. Concludes that Florence is the birthplace of the madrigal and Verdelot the creator of the genre. Vol. 2 presents transcriptions of all 60 works in modern notation with texts and translations. Author composed missing altus parts when necessary. Musical examples, illustrations, facsimiles, tables; sources for the Newberry manuscript; bibliography of approximately 170 manuscripts and 775 writings; expansive index.

Slim, H. Colin, ed. *Ten Altus Parts at Oscott College Sutton Coldfield*. S.l.: s.p., n.d. 28 p.   M2 .N5 Suppl.

Ten Altus Parts at Oscott College Sutton Coldfield serves as a supplement to *A Gift of Madrigals and Motets*, supplying missing altus parts once thought to be irrevocably lost.

MAGNIFICAT

406. Bloesch, Richard J. "The Eighteenth-Century Italian Magnificat: A Survey of Representative Settings (ca. 1700–ca. 1750) with an Analysis and Edition of Six Works." D.M.A. dissertation. University of Illinois at Urbana-Champaign, 1971. xiii, 492 p.

Study of polyphonic settings of the Magnificat up to 1700, including descriptions of 43 representative settings by prominent composers. Six works, by Alessandro Scarlatti, Giacomo Antonio Perti, Antonio Lotti, Leonardo Leo, Giovanni Battista Martini, and Nicolò Jommelli, analyzed in greater detail; modern editions provided for each. Musical examples and analysis; bibliography of 105 writings.

407. Grigsby, John Roland. "A Study of the Magnificat and an Analysis and Performance of Selected Settings." Ed.D. dissertation. Teachers College, Columbia University, New York, 1972. vii, 262 p.

General overview of the Magnificat. Presents analysis of six selected Magnificats: Tomás Luis de Victoria's *Magnificat Primi Toni*, Michael Praetorius's *Meine Seel Erhebt den Herren*, Antonio Vivaldi's *Magnificat in G minor*, W. A. Mozart's *Magnificat: Vesperae Solennes de Confessore*, K. 339, Gerald Finzi's *Magnificat: My Soul Doth Magnify the Lord*, and

Halsey Stevens's *My Soul Doth Magnify the Lord*. Musical examples and tables; bibliography of nearly 100 writings and approximately 90 editions of music; also, 100 performance editions of selected settings of the Magnificat. No index.

408. Illing, Carl-Heinz. *Zur Technik der Magnificat-Komposition des 16. Jahrhunderts*. Wolfenbüttel: George Kallmeyer, 1936. x, 57 p. ML3093 .I29 Z9

German only. Major study of the 16th-century Magnificat with emphasis on the works of Giovanni Pierluigi da Palestrina. Updated in part by Winfried Kirsch's *Die Quellen der mehrstimmigen Magnificat- und Te Deum-Vertonungen bis zur Mitte des 16. Jahrhunderts* (item 140). Includes a lengthy, chronological bibliography of Magnificats from 1440 to 1628. Tables and musical examples; dated bibliography of about 60 writings and music manuscripts; expansive index. Series: *Kieler Beiträge zur Musikwissenschaft*, Heft 3.

409. Johnson, Axie Allen. "Choral Settings of the Magnificat by Selected Twentieth Century American Composers." D.M.A. dissertation. University of Southern California, Los Angeles 1968. iv, 166 p.

Chapter V, "Contributions of Selected Twentieth Century American Composers to Magnificat Settings," lists 37 Magnificat and Nunc dimittis settings appropriate for liturgical use. Entries include title, composer, voicing, publisher, and date of publication. Remainder of the study examines three choral settings of the Magnificat by Jean Berger, Alan Hovhaness, and Halsey Stevens. Provides biographical data, discusses general stylistic characteristics, assesses the composers's contribution to modern music with a classified list of choral works, presents an analysis of the selected Magnificats, and summarizes the composers's style. Chapter IV compares the styles of the composers. Musical examples; bibliography of almost 100 books, articles, scores, and interview.

410. McCray, James Elwin. "The British Magnificat in the Twentieth Century." Ph.D. dissertation. University of Iowa, Iowa City, 1968. xxxi, 273 p.

Magnificats by British composers published since 1900, with emphasis on works published after 1945. Initial chapter presents historic background on British Magnificat from 1400–1900. Following chapters examine 20th-century Magnificats, presenting detailed analysis of 22 selected works. Five appendices: (1) classified bibliography of Magnificats available to performers; (2) classified bibliography of Magnificats out-of-print; (3) non-British composers of Magnificats; (4) 19th-century British composers of Magnificats; and (5) text used by Ralph Vaughan Williams in *Magnificat*. Bibliography of about 100 writings.

411. McCray, James Elwin. "A Survey of Published Magnificats for Treble Voices." *Choral Journal*, 28–8 (March 1988), 5–11

Brief, historical survey of the Magnificat for treble voices. Musical examples; documented with endnotes. Concludes with classified list of about 60 published Magnificats for treble voices. Classifications: unison choir accompanied by organ or piano; SA, SSA, SSAA choir accompanied by organ or piano; treble voices unaccompanied; and treble voices with instruments.

See also: Terry, Charles Sanford. *Bach: The Cantatas and Oratorios; The Passions; The Magnificat, Lutheran Masses and Motets* (item 470)

MASS

412. Brothers, Lester Dwayne. "The Hexachord Mass: 1600–1720." Ph.D. dissertation. University of California, Los Angeles, 1973. 2 vols. ix, 378 p.; ii, 266 p.

Study of the hexachord Mass, namely the works of Francesco Soriano, Paolo Agostini, Antonio Cifra, Lorenzo Ratti, Giacomo Carissimi, Stefano Pasini, Giovanni Angelo Capponi, Tommaso Bai, Juan del Vado, Francisco López Capillas, and Francisco Valls. Introduced by a brief history of the use of hexachord in theory from the 11th to the 18th centuries and a survey of its employment in musical composition to the 18th century. Volume 2: transcriptions of nine Masses in modern notation. Musical examples and charts; bibliography of approximately 70 treatises, 40 scores, and 250 books and articles; no index.

413. Cavanaugh, Philip Stephen. "A Liturgico-Musical Study of German Polyphonic Mass Propers, 1490–1520." Ph.D. dissertation. University of Pittsburgh, Pennsylvania, 1972. iv, 375 p.

Study of liturgical reform and its effect on polyphonic settings of the Mass Proper in 15th- and 16th-century German church music. Focuses on the following manuscripts: Annaberg 1248 and 1126, Jena manuscripts nos. 30, 33, 34, 35, and Weimar A. Examines compositional techniques, performance practice, and the treatment of pre-existent material. Includes thematic indices for the Annaberg 1248 and 1126 manuscripts with musical incipits. Tables and musical examples; transcriptions of selected manuscripts (167 pages of music); bibliography of nearly 100 items.

414. Georgiades, Thrasybulos Georgos. *Musik und Sprache: das Werden der abendländischen Musik dargestellt an der Vertonung der Messe* [Music and language: The rise of Western music as exemplified in settings of the Mass]. 2nd ed. Berlin: Springer-Verlag, 1974 (rep. 1984). 142 p. ISBN 3-540-65342-2   ML3849 .G43 1974

Georgiades, Thrasybulos Georgos. *Music and Language: The Rise of Western Music as Exemplified in Settings of the Mass.* Translated by Marie Louise Göllner. Cambridge, England: Cambridge University Press, 1982. x, 139 p. ISBN 0-521-23309-7, ISBN 0-521-29902-0 (pbk)   ML3849 .G43 1982

Originally published in 1954 (rev. 2nd ed., 1974). Contrary to the author's intentions as revealed in the preface, this study is "a speculative treatment on the theme of music and language," specifically contrasting Latin and German settings of the Mass Ordinary. It is not, however, a historical survey of the Mass. Musical examples; documented with endnotes; no index. Series: German edition: *Verständliche Wissenschaft*, Bd. 50.

415. Igoe, James Thomas. "Performance Practices in the Polyphonic Mass of the Early Fifteenth Century." Ph.D. dissertation. University of North Carolina at Chapel Hill, 1971. v, 169 p.

Investigates the lack of text in the tenor and contratenor parts of the polyphonic Mass during the early 15th century. Researches use of organ, choir practice, and scribal customs of notating text. Concludes that lack of text is graphological abbreviation and does not indicate use of instruments. Tables and facsimiles; bibliography of about 140 items; brief subject index.

416. Josephson, Nors Sigurd. "The Missa De Beata Virgine of the Sixteenth Century." Ph.D. dissertation. University of California, Berkeley, 1970. iii, 288 p.

Traces the development of the 15th- and early 16th-century Marian Mass *Missa De Beata Virgine* and its forerunners. Emphasis on variety of chants used, cyclic design, and the stylistic interrelationships between individual works. Examines the works of Pierre de La Rue, Josquin des Prez, Antoine Brumel, Adam Rener, and others. Bibliography of Masses and Mass sections appended. Musical examples and tables; bibliography of about 135 writings.

417. Lütolf, Max. *Die mehrstimmigen Ordinarium Missae-Sätze vom ausgehenden 11. bis zur Wende des 13. zum 14. Jahrhundert* [Polyphonic movements

of the *Ordinarium Missae* from the end of the 11th century to the beginning of the 14th]. Bern, Germany: Haupt, 1970. 2 vols.   ML3088 .L84

Text in German. Evaluation of 83 polyphonic pieces for the Mass Ordinary drawn from 22 sources. Volume 1 is a study of each source with descriptions of the pieces; Volume 2 provides transcriptions. Discusses tropes, dispersion of the repertory, development of the polyphonic Ordinary, and problems of notation. Tables, facsimiles, and music transcriptions; bibliography of more than 250 items; no index.

418. Mac Intyre, Bruce C. *The Viennese Concerted Mass of the Early Classic Period.* With a Foreword by Jens Peter Larsen. Ann Arbor, Michigan: UMI Research Press, 1986. xxi, 764 p. ISBN 0-8357-1673-2   ML3088 .M24 1986

The concerted Mass in Vienna between 1741 and 1783. Two parts: (1) historical background and (2) style. Analyses of 72 Masses by 28 composers. Three appendices: liturgical year in Vienna; choirmasters of Vienna during the 18th century; and thematic catalog of the 72 selected Masses, which gives title, date, scoring, thematic incipit, location of manuscript and printed editions when known, and general comments. Charts, illustrations, and numerous examples; bibliography of approximately 250 books, dissertations, and articles and 26 editions of music; expansive index. Series: *Studies in Musicology,* no. 89.

419. Schmidt-Görg, Joseph. *Geschichte der Messe.* Köln, Germany: Arno Volk Verlag, 1967. 118 p.   M2 .M945 Heft 30

Schmidt-Görg, Joseph. *History of the Mass.* Translated by Robert Kolben. Köln, Germany: Arno Volk Verlag; sole distributors for United States: MCA Music, New York, 1968. 118 p.   M2 .M94512 no. 30

Brief historical survey of the Mass from its beginning to the mid-20th century. Includes a collection of 30 complete musical examples. Series: *Das Musikwerk,* Heft 30; *Anthology of Music,* vol. 30.

420. Sparks, Edgar H. *Cantus Firmus in Mass and Motet, 1420–1520.* Berkeley: University of California Press, 1963   ML174 .S7; reprint, New York: Da Capo Press, 1975. xi, 504 p. ISBN 0-306-70720-9   ML174 .S7 1975

Three parts: (1) development of cantus firmus procedures (1420–1450); (2) cantus firmus technique in Mass and motet (1450–1485), primarily focusing on the music of Guillaume Dufay, Johannes Ockeghem, and their contemporaries; and (3) study of the Masses and motets of Jacob Obrecht and Josquin des Prez. A reworking of the author's dissertation (1950), this study has been criticized for its lack of discussion of post-Dunstable English music, brief mention or lack of inclusion of important contemporaries of Obrecht and Josquin (such as Alexander Agricola, Loyset Compère, Pierre de La Rue, Antoine Brumel, Heinrich Isaac, and Antoine de Févin), and the omission of important manuscripts, recent critical editions of music, and significant, recent studies. Despite criticism, valuable study of those composers and musical works chosen. Appended essay, "Some Theories of Cantus Firmus Usage," discusses the theories of Rudolf von Ficker and Jacques Handschin. Musical examples; documented with endnotes; expansive index. Series: *Da Capo Press Music Reprint Series.*

421. Stäblein-Harder, Hanna, ed. *Fourteenth-Century Mass Music in France.* S.l.: American Institute of Musicology, 1962. 144 p.   M2 .S76

Stäblein-Harder, Hanna, ed. *Fourteenth-Century Mass Music in France: Critical Text.* S.l.: American Institute of Musicology, 1962. 182 p.   M2 .S76

Two parts: modern transcriptions of 78 Mass movements and critical text. Critical text addresses categories of 14th-century Masses, paraphrasing of liturgical melodies, harmonic analysis, parodistet procedure, the interrelationship of the manuscripts, the Apt manuscript, and provides detailed annotations about the transcriptions. Musical examples and charts; bibliography of about 60 writings; index. Series: *Corpus Mensurabilis Musicae*, 29 (transcriptions); *Musicological Studies and Documents*, 7 (critical text).

422. Tortolano, William. "The Mass and the Twentieth Century Composer: A Study of Musical Techniques and Style, Together with the Interpretive Problems of the Performer." D.M. dissertation. University of Montreal, Canada, 1964. 2 vols. xxv, 164 p.

Study of Masses composed between 1903 and 1963 in relationship to church music legislation. Examines compositional techniques, musical style, and practicality for use in church services. Presents detailed analyses of significant 20th-century Masses, including the works of Roy Harris, Lou Harrison, Vincent Persichetti, Benjamin Britten, Ralph Vaughan Williams, Francis Poulenc, Ernst Krenek, and Igor Stravinsky. Separate chapters on texts and formal structure, rhythm, melody, and harmony and polyphony. Bibliography of approximately 100 books and periodical articles; discography of 11 then-available long-playing recordings; list of 65 20th-century Masses, not all discussed in the text. Volume 2 includes musical examples.

See also: Fiske, Roger. *Beethoven's Missa Solemnis* (item 473); Kerman, Joseph. *The Masses and Motets of William Byrd* (item 476); Pahlen, Kurt. *The World of the Oratorio: Oratorio, Mass, Requiem, Te Deum, Stabat*

Mater and Large Cantatas (item 433); Palestrina, Giovanni Pierluigi da. *Pope Marcellus Mass: An Authoritative Score, Backgrounds and Sources, History and Analysis, Views and Comments* (item 485); Terry, Charles Sanford. *Bach: The Cantatas and Oratorios; The Passions; The Magnificat, Lutheran Masses and Motets* (item 470)

MOTET

423. Apfel, Ernst. *Anlage und Struktur der Motetten im Codex Montpellier.* Heidelberg, Germany: Carl Winter, 1970. 117 p.   ML178 .A6

German only. Survey of selective aspects of the 13th-century motet found in the Montpellier Codex. Two parts: first part discusses structure, formal design, and phrasing of the tenors; second part examines elements of counterpoint. Rich in statistical data. Musical examples; documented with footnotes; index of the Montpellier motets. Series: *Annales Universitatis Saraviensis: Philosophische Fakultät*, Bd. 10.

424. Banks, Jon. *The Motet as a Formal Type in Northern Italy, ca. 1500.* New York: Garland, 1993. 2 vols. xv, 356 p.; xiii, 215 p. ISBN 0-8153-0950-3 ML2933.2 .B3 1993

Vol. 1: Examines compositions generally classified as motets in writings on Renaissance music with intent to "define specific sub-genres" and to "identify various styles and formal procedures associated with them." Studies single-movement free motets, *cantus firmus* and paraphrase motets, Psalm motets, Latin *Laude* motets, and textless motets. Vol. 2: Transcriptions of 112 works in modern notation. Musical examples; bibliography of about 62 manuscript and printed music sources and approximately 360 writings. Series: *Outstanding Dissertations in Music from British Universities.*

425. Clarkson, G. Austin Elliott. "On the Nature of Medieval Song: The Declamation of Plainchant and the Lyric Structure of the Fourteenth-Century Motet." Ph.D. dissertation. Columbia University, New York, 1970. x, 450 p.

Study of lyric structure of monophonic and polyphonic Medieval songs. Includes analysis of texts of 141 French 14th-century motets with detailed description of the *Roman de Fauvel* collection. Traces development of motet from 13th through 14th centuries. Five appendices: (1) 6 chants on *Diffusa est gratia*; (2) declamation diagrams of 54 iambic hymns; (3) annotated list of 35 manuscripts containing motets; (4) annotated list of the 141 motets considered for study; (5) transcriptions of and critical notes for 3 motets from Brussels, Bibliothèque Royale, 19606 (Br). Musical examples, tables, and figures; documented with footnotes.

426. Dunning, Albert. *Die Staatsmotette 1480–1555*. Utrecht, the Netherlands: A. Oosthoek's Uitgeversmaatschappij, 1970. xxiv, 361 p. ML190 .D85

German only. Study of the Staatsmotette (literally, "state motet") which is any vocal composition with Latin text intended for a political, ceremonial function. Covers the years 1480 (emergence of the Habsburg empire in Europe and beginning of the "Netherlandish" style) to 1555 (close of Charles V's reign and appearance of a new compositional style exemplified by Orlando di Lasso). Chronological listing of over 100 "state motets" and their occasions and a list of sources and editions appended. Musical examples, facsimiles, and illustrations; bibliography of more than 250 items; expansive index.

427. Lefferts, Peter. *The Motet in England in the Fourteenth Century*. Ann Arbor, Michigan: UMI Research Press, 1986. xvi, 371 p. ISBN 0-8357-1722-4 ML2931.2 .L44 1986

Discussion of the development of motet in England during the 14th century with comparison to French and Italian counterparts. Examines approximately 130 motets, 60 of which are complete, from about 35 sources. Three appendices: list of manuscripts cited, critical reports, and 13th-century English motet repertoire. Highly specialized, yet of interest to the choral conductor. Of particular value are the critical reports of Appendix 2, which gives the source for each motet, origin of the cantus firmus when known, current literature about the work, recordings, and discussion of form, notation, and text. Illustrations, tables, figures, but few musical examples; complete works are accessible in *Polyphonic Music of the Fourteenth Century* (Monaco: Editions de l'Oiseau-Lyre, 1956–1991) and fragments are accessible in an appendix of the author's dissertation by the same title. Bibliography of about 250 items; expansive index. Series: *Studies in Musicology*, no. 94.

428. Mathiassen, Finn. *The Style of the Early Motet (c. 1200–1250): An Investigation of the Old Corpus of the Montpellier Manuscript*. Translated by Johanne M. Stochholm. Copenhagen, Denmark: Dan Fog Musikforlag, 1966. 212 p.   ML178 .M19

Manuscript contains approximately 230 motets. Analytical study based upon Yvonne Rokseth's transcriptions which, unfortunately, are not always accurate, rather than an examination of the original source. Discussion limited to stylistic characteristics of the upper voice, linear aspects of counterpoint, and two-, three-, and four-part harmony. No special consideration of the tenors and their treatment. Numerous musical examples and tables, with facsimiles; bibliography of about 150 writings; two indices: (1) theorists and (2) motets in the "Old Corpus of the Montpellier." Series: *Aarhus universitet. Musikvidenskabeligt institut. Studier og Publikationer*, no. 1.

429. Pesce, Dolores, ed. *Hearing the Motet: Essays on the Motet of the Middle Ages and Renaissance*. New York: Oxford University Press, 1997. xi, 380 p. ISBN 0-19-509709-2   ML3275 .H4 1997

Collection of 16 essays: "The Polyphonic Progeny of an *Et gaudebit*: Assessing Family Relations in the Thirteenth-Century Motet" (Rebecca A. Baltzer); "Beyond Glossing: The Old Made New in *Mout me fu grief/Robin m'aime/Portare*" (Pesce); "Which Vitry? The Witness of the Trinity Motet from the *Roman de Fauvel*" (Anne Walters Robertson); "Polyphony of Texts and Music in the Fourteenth-Century Motet: *Tribum que non abhorruit/Quoniam secta latronum/Merito hec patimur* and Its 'Quotations' " (Margaret Bent); "Du Fay and the Cultures of Renaissance Florence" (Robert Nosow); "For Whom the Bell Tolls: Reading and Hearing Busnoys's *Anthoni usque limina*" (Rob C. Wegman); "Love and Death in the Fifteenth-Century Motet: A Reading of Busnoys's *Anima mea liquefacta est/Stirps Jesse*" (Paula Higgins); "Obrecht as Exegete: Reading *Factor orbis* as a Christmas Sermon" (M. Jennifer Bloxam); "Conflicting Levels of Meaning and Understanding in Josquin's *O admirabile commercium* Motet Cycle" (Richard Sherr); "Josquin, Good King René, and *O bone et dulcissime Jesu*" (Patrick Macey); "Miracles, Motivicity, and Mannerism: Adrian Willaert's Videns *Dominus flentes sorores Lazari* and Some Aspects of Motet Composition in the 1520s" (Joshua Rifkin); "Lasso as Historicist: The Cantus-Firmus Motets" (James Haar); "Tonal Compass in the Motets of Orlando di Lasso" (David Crook); "Palestrina as Reader: Motets from the Song of Songs" (Jessie Ann Owens); "On William Byrd's *Emendemus in melius*" (Joseph Kerman); and "Byrd, the Catholics, and the Motet: The Hearing Reopened" (Craig Monson). Musical examples, facsimiles, graphic analyses, and tables; documented with endnotes; index of names.

See also: Kerman, Joseph. *The Masses and Motets of William Byrd* (item 476); Slim, H. Colin. *A Gift of Madrigals and Motets* (item 405); Sparks, Edgar H. *Cantus Firmus in Mass and Motet, 1420–1520* (item 420); Terry, Charles Sanford. *Bach: The Cantatas and Oratorios; The Passions; The Magnificat, Lutheran Masses and Motets* (item 470)

ORATORIO

430. American Academy of Teachers of Singing. *The Sacred Oratorio: A Pronouncement of the American Academy of Teachers of Singing*. Bryn Mawr, Pennsylvania: Theodore Presser, 1950. 19 p.   ML3201 .A5

Designed as a "source of preparation for young singers through the channels of practical advice, suggestion and encouragement of teacher and student alike." Brief historical outline of the sacred oratorio; recommended procedure for the study and performance of the oratorio; comments on tempi, the appoggiatura, and translations; list of about 110 18th-, 19th-, and a few early 20th-century sacred oratorios, listing composer, title, year composed, language of text, editor and/or translator, and publisher; list of over 500 principal recitatives, arias, duets, trios, and quartets from 18th-, 19th-, and a few 20th-century oratorios, including composer, title, required voices, and recitative and aria title. No bibliography; no index.

431. Arnold, Denis, and Elsie Arnold. *The Oratorio in Venice.* London: Royal Musical Association, 1986. vii, 117 p. ISBN 0-947854-01-0   ML3233 .A85 1986

History of the late 17th-century through early 19th-century oratorio in Venice, Italy. Lists nearly 600 performances of oratorios in Venice between 1662 and 1809, classified by places of performance (Fava, Incurabili, Mendicanti, Ospedaletto, Pietà, and miscellaneous). Documented with footnotes; three indices: singers, oratorios, and general index. Series: *Royal Musical Association Monographs*, no. 2.

432. Johnson, Joyce L. *Roman Oratorio, 1770–1800: The Repertory at Santa Maria in Vallicella.* Ann Arbor, Michigan: UMI Research Press, 1987. xvii, 328 p. ISBN 0-8357-1692-9   ML3233.8.R62 S24 1987

Examines texts, performance practice, and stylistic development of the oratorio at the Vallicella Oratory in Rome, Italy at the close of the 18th century. Includes transcriptions of various significant documents. Musical examples and tables; bibliography of approximately 100 writings; expansive index. Series: *Studies in Musicology*, no. 91.

433. Pahlen, Kurt. *The World of the Oratorio: Oratorio, Mass, Requiem, Te Deum, Stabat Mater and Large Cantatas.* With the collaboration of Werner Pfister and Rosemarie König. Translated by Judith Schaefer. Additional material for the English language edition by Thurston Dox. Aldershot: Scolar Press; Portland, Oregon: Amadeus Press, 1990. 357 p. ISBN 0-85967-866-0 (UK), ISBN 0-931340-11-X (U.S.)   MT110 .P3313 1990

English translation of Pahlen's *Oratorien der Welt: Oratorium, Messe, Requiem, Te Deum, Stabat Mater und grosse Kantate* (1985). Also includes Passion, Magnificat, and ode. Brief introductory chapter entitled "Historical and Other Observations on the Oratorio." Presents 119 composers in alphabetical order, including 17 entries on 19th- and 20th-century American composers contributed by Dox. Brief biographical information and discussion of repertoire. Very selective; no attempt to be comprehensive. For each work, gives origin of text, language, dates of composition and first performance, form, scoring and cast, history of work, and analysis. Three appendices: (1) Latin texts with English translations of the Mass Ordinary, Requiem Mass, Te Deum, and Stabat Mater; (2) glossary of terms; and (3) sources of illustrations found throughout the book. Numerous musical examples, illustrations, photos, and facsimiles; few footnotes; no bibliography; no index.

434. Smither, Howard E. *A History of the Oratorio: The Oratorio in the Baroque Era: Italy, Vienna, Paris.* Vol. 1. Chapel Hill: University of North Carolina Press, 1977. xxvii, 480 p. ISBN 0-8078-1274-9   ML3201. S6

In three parts: (1) antecedents and origins of the oratorio; (2) oratorio in Italy, ca. 1640–1720; and (3) Italian oratorio outside Italy, namely Vienna and Paris. Discusses oratorio within social context. Examines libretto and music and includes brief analyses of selected works. Musical examples, facsimiles, and illustrations; bibliography of about 430 writings; expansive index.

Smither, Howard E. *A History of the Oratorio: The Oratorio in the Baroque Era: Protestant Germany and England.* Vol. 2. Chapel Hill: University of North Carolina Press, 1977. xxii, 393 p. ISBN 0-8078-1294-3 ML3201. S6

In three parts: (1) 17th-century antecedents and origins of the oratorio in Protestant Germany; (2) the early 18th-century oratorio in Protestant Germany; and (3) G. F. Handel and the English oratorio. Includes brief analyses of selected works. Part 3 focuses upon historical and analytical discussion of each of Handel's oratorios. Musical examples, facsimiles, and illustrations; bibliography of about 280 writings; expansive index.

Smither, Howard E. *A History of the Oratorio: The Oratorio in the Classical Era.* Vol. 3. Chapel Hill: University of North Carolina Press, 1987. xxiv, 711 p.   ML3201. S6

In four parts: (1) Italian oratorio; (2) English oratorio after Handel; (3) German oratorio; and (4) oratorio in French and other languages. Includes brief analyses of selected works. Two appendices: (1) nearly 140 title pages of Italian and Latin printed librettos; and (2) a checklist of 213 composers of Italian and Latin oratorios, ca. 1720–1820. Musical examples, facsimiles, tables, and illustrations; bibliography of about 350 writings; expansive index.

Smither, Howard E. *A History of the Oratorio: The Oratorio in the Nineteenth and Twentieth Centuries.* Vol. 4. Chapel Hill: University of North Carolina Press, 2000. xxiv, 829 p. ISBN 0-8078-2511-5   ML3201. S6

Not available for examination.

See also: Brown, A. Peter. *Performing Haydn's The Creation: Reconstructing the Earliest Renditions* (item 482); Dean, Winton. *Handel's Dramatic Oratorios and Masques* (item 477); Larsen, Jens Peter. *Handel's Messiah: Origins, Composition, Sources* (item 478); Myers, Robert Manson. *Handel's Messiah: A Touchstone of Taste* (item 479); Shaw, Watkins. *A Textual and Historical Companion to Handel's Messiah* (item 480); Terry, Charles Sanford. *Bach: The Cantatas and Oratorios; The Passions; The Magnificat, Lutheran Masses and Motets* (item 470); Werner, Jack. *Mendelssohn's "Elijah": A Historical and Analytical Guide to the Oratorio* (item 484); Young, Percy M. *The Oratorios of Handel* (item 481)

PART-SONG

435. Silantien, John Joseph. "The Part-Song in England, 1837–1914." D.M.A. dissertation. University of Illinois at Urbana-Champaign, 1980. vi, 363 p.

Traces the evolution of the English part-song composed between the accession of Queen Victoria and the beginning of World War I. Identifies various types and styles, shows its relation to earlier forms of English part-music (namely, the madrigal, lute ayre, ballett, glee, and harmonized air), discusses the influence of foreign vocal forms, and notes choirs, conductors, and composers who significantly contributed to the development of the genre. Musical examples and illustrations; bibliography of approximately 160 writings and 50 collections of part-music.

PASSION

436. Braun, Werner. *Die mitteldeutsche Choralpassion im achtzehnten Jahrhundert* [The "high" German choral Passion during the eighteenth century]. Berlin: Evangelische Verlagsanstalt, 1960. 228 p.   ML2929 .B73 1960

German only. Historical study of the German choral Passion of the 18th century. In three parts: (1) music denkmäler, surveying the Passion from 1530 through the 18th century; (2) text denkmäler, discussing the origin and development of the Passion text; and (3) the Passion in the divine service. Musical examples, facsimiles, and tables; documented with footnotes; glossary of terms; index.

437. Davidson, Audrey Ekdahl. *The Quasi-Dramatic St. John Passions from Scandinavia and Their Medieval Background.* Foreword by Richard Rastall. Kalamazoo, Michigan: Medieval Institute Publications, Western Michigan University, 1981. viii, 135 p. ISBN 0-918720-13-3, ISBN 0-918720-14-1 (pbk)   ML3188 .D38

Explores the Roskilde Passion in relationship to the Swedish St. John Passion tradition. Includes a prepared edition of the Roskilde Passion. Musical examples, facsimiles, and illustrations; no bibliography; index. Series: *Early Drama, Art, and Music Monograph Series*, vol. 3.

438. Malinowski, Stanley Anthony. "The Baroque Oratorio Passion. Part II: An Edition of the St. Matthew Passion of Johann Valentin Meder." Ph.D. dissertation. Cornell University, Ithaca, New York, 1978. 2 vols. 595 p.

Part I traces the development of the Passion from the monophonic Passions in the Catholic Liturgy through the late 18th century. Five appendices: (1) chronological list of German oratorio Passions; (2) surviving Telemann oratorio Passions; (3) surviving C. P. E. Bach oratorio Passions; (4) other manuscript sources used in the study; and (5) tables of contents of selected oratorio Passions. Musical examples and facsimiles; bibliography of 220 books, dissertations, and articles and 45 scores. Part II presents discussion and a critical edition of Johann Valentin Meder's *Passions oratorium*.

439. Smallman, Basil. *The Background of Passion Music: J. S. Bach and His Predecessors*. 2nd rev. and enlarged ed. New York: Dover, 1970. 180 p. ISBN 0-486-22250-0   ML3260 .S6 1970

Examination of Bach's *St. John Passion* and *St. Matthew Passion* "in relation to their historical context and to show their position as the culmination of a musical and liturgical tradition of great antiquity." Presents brief background of the Passion, followed by a discussion of Bach's treatment of drama, *dramatis personae*, the crowd, lyrical elements in the chorales, arias, and choruses, and the role of the orchestra. First published in 1957; revised edition alters little of the original text; new material in form of ten added appendices, expanded bibliography, and expanded list of available modern editions of Passions. Appendices present discussions of (1) letter-symbols in Passion music, (2) earliest polyphonic Passions, (3) dramatic and motet Passion, (4) authorship of the Obrecht/Longaval Passion, (5) Augenmusik (eye-music), (6) *St. Matthew Passion* attributed to Friedrich Funcke, (7) Johann Meder's *St. Matthew Passion*, (8) chromaticism and word-painting, (9) J. S. Bach's *St. Mark Passion*, and (10) Passions of G. P. Telemann. Musical examples and facsimiles; bibliography of 50 writings; list of 43 Passions available in modern editions; expansive index.

See also: Chailley, Jacques. *Les "Passions" de J.-S. Bach* (item 460); Steinitz, Paul. *Bach's Passions* (item 469); Terry, Charles Sanford. *Bach: The Cantatas and Oratorios; The Passions; The Magnificat, Lutheran Masses and Motets* (item 470)

REQUIEM

440. Kovalenko, Susan Chaffins. "The Twentieth Century Requiem: An Emerging Concept." Ph.D. dissertation. Washington University, St. Louis, Missouri, 1971. vii, 329 p.

Traces the origins of the secular Requiem, with focus on its evolution since World War I. Also examines other large-scale works that may be considered counterparts of the Roman Catholic Requiem. Numerous musical examples and graphic analyses; texts of several of the works appended; annotated bibliography of 15 works for soloist(s) and/or chorus with orchestra, 6 vocal chamber works, and 11 instrumental works; bibliography of about 100 writings.

441. Matonti, Charles J. "Discovering Principles for the Composition and Use of Contemporary Liturgical Music through the Study of Selected Requiem Masses." Ed.D. dissertation. Columbia University, New York, 1972. 3, iii, 291 p.

Study of the evolution of liturgical music through examination of the Requiem Mass. Addresses the early Requiem Mass in chant and its relevance to the Western world, the influence of the Councils of Trent and Vatican II, and selected Requiems, discussing the relevance of Tomás Luis de Victoria's *Officium defunctorum* (1603) to the Renaissance, Jean Gilles's *Messe des morts* (ca. 1696) to the baroque era, W. A. Mozart's *Requiem*, K. 626 (1791) to the classical period, Hector Berlioz's *Grande Messe des morts* (1837) to early 19th-century France, Gabriel Fauré's *Requiem*, op. 48 (1887) to late 19th-century France, Giuseppe Verdi's *Requiem* (1874) to 19th-century Italy, and Benjamin Britten's *War Requiem* (1961) to 20th-century England. Latin text of Requiem Mass and English translation appended. Few musical examples; classified bibliography of approximately 140 writings and scores; no index.

442. Robertson, Alec. *Requiem: Music of Mourning and Consolation.* London: Cassell; New York: Frederick A. Praeger, 1967   ML3088 .R62, ML3088 .R62 1967; reprint, Westport, Connecticut: Greenwood Press, 1976. xii, 300 p. ISBN 0-8371-8552-1   ML3088 .R62 1976

Two sections: (1) settings of the Latin Requiem Mass dealt with chronologically, following a discussion of liturgical origins and Requiem plainsong; and (2) other Requiem music, including Holy Week music, Lutheran and Anglican funeral music, memorial music and laments, and modern elegiac works. Numerous musical examples; no bibliography; expansive general index.

443. Roeckle, Charles Albert. "Eighteenth-Century Neapolitan Settings of the Requiem Mass: Structure and Style." Ph.D. dissertation. University of Texas, Austin, 1978. 2 vols. xxxiii, 624 p.

Examines structural and stylistic tendencies in Requiem Masses by 10 significant 18th-century Neapolitan composers: Francesco Provenzale, Nicola Fago, Domenico Sarro, Francesco Feo, Francesco Durante, Nicolò Jommelli, Pasquale Cafaro, Fedele Fenaroli, Domenico Cimarosa, and Giovanni Paisiello. Musical examples, analyses, and tables; bibliography of around 120 writings and 30 manuscripts and editions.

See also: Pahlen, Kurt. *The World of the Oratorio: Oratorio, Mass, Requiem, Te Deum, Stabat Mater and Large Cantatas* (item 433)

STABAT MATER

444. Blume, Jürgen. *Geschichte der mehrstimmigen Stabat-mater-Vertonungen* [A history of polyphonic Stabat Mater settings]. München, Germany: Katzbichler, 1992. 2 vols. 284 p.; 164 p. ISBN 3-87397-122-4   ML3090 .B6 1992

German only. Originally published as the author's dissertation. Vol. 1 surveys polyphonic settings of the Stabat Mater; Vol. 2 provides musical examples. Text of Stabat Mater translated into German; bibliography of approximately 280 writings; index of composers and works. Series: *Musikwissenschaftliche Schriften*, Bd. 23.

445. Sharp, Avery T. "A Descriptive Catalog of Selected, Published Eighteenth-through Twentieth-Century Stabat Mater Settings for Mixed Voices with a Discussion of the History of the Text." Ph.D. dissertation. University of Iowa, Iowa City, 1978. viii, 286 p.

Historical overview of the Stabat Mater dolorosa followed by annotated bibliography of some 35 settings for mixed chorus from the 18th- through the 20th-centuries. List of 300 additional musical settings of the Stabat Mater cited in more than 200 library catalogs. Facsimiles; bibliography of nearly 50 writings.

See also: Pahlen, Kurt. *The World of the Oratorio: Oratorio, Mass, Requiem, Te Deum, Stabat Mater and Large Cantatas* (item 433)

TE DEUM

446. Davis, Oma Grier. "A Selected, Annotated Bibliography of Te Deums in the Library of Congress, and a History of This Hymn in Ceremonial Music since 1600." Ph.D. dissertation. University of Iowa, Iowa City, 1967. xvi, 199 p.

Presents a historical view of the Te Deum from 1600 to the present, analysis of the treatment of the text by selected composers, and an annotated bibliography of almost 120 Te Deums in the Library of Congress. Seven appendices: (1) text of Te Deum in Latin, English, and German; (2) chronological list of almost 150 major Te Deums; (3)–(7) lists of Te Deums in the Library of Congress: 15 for unaccompanied mixed choir, 29 for male chorus or for choir of men and boys, 46 for unison choir or congregation, 18 for treble voices and organ or piano, and nearly 750 for mixed choir and organ or piano. Bibliography of more than 100 writings.

447. McGowan, John Bailey. "Sixteenth-Century Polyphonic Settings of the Latin Hymn *Te Deum Laudamus.*" Ph.D. dissertation. University of Iowa, Iowa City, 1967. x, 218 p.

Surveys the 16th-century Te Deum in regard to authorship of the hymn, performance practices of the monophonic hymn, extant organ settings, liturgical and other uses, and polyphonic settings. Studies the text and chant of the hymn. Examines works by Hugh Aston, Jacobus Vaet, Jakob Gallus (Handl), Constanzo Festa, Tomás Luis de Victoria, Jacobus de Kerle, John Taverner, Johann Walter, Arnold von Bruck, Girolamo Vespa, and Paolo Aretino. Numerous musical examples; bibliography of almost 100 items; no index.

448. Stein, David Bruce. "The French Te Deum from 1677–1744: Its Esthetic, Style and Development." D.M.A. dissertation. University of Illinois at Urbana-Champaign, 1974. iv, 416 p.

Surveys composers and performances of the French Te Deum between 1677 and 1744. Includes settings by Jean Baptiste Lully, Michel Richard de Lalande, Marc Antoine Charpentier, Henri Desmarets, André Campra, Claude Gervais, François Collin de Blamont, Esprit Joseph Antoine Blanchard, Ohilidor, and Madin. Includes a 202-page transcription of Blamont's *Te Deum* with critical commentary. Five appendices: (1) list of performances of 12 French Te Deums by 10 composers, giving composer, date of composition, date and place of documented performances, and occasion for performance; (2) Te Deum text with English translation; (3) structural analysis of Te Deums; (4) critical commentary on 9 Te Deum settings by 7 composers transcribed by the author but not included in the study; and (5) "The Character of the Modes" drawn from the writings of Charpentier. Bibliography of more than 100 items.

See also: Pahlen, Kurt. *The World of the Oratorio: Oratorio, Mass, Requiem, Te Deum, Stabat Mater and Large Cantatas* (item 433)

VII

Studies of Individual Composers and Works

GENERAL WORKS

449. Dailey, William Albert. "Techniques of Composition Used in Contemporary Works for Chorus and Orchestra on Religious Texts—As Important Representative Works of the Period from 1952 through 1962 the Following Works Will Be Considered: 'Canticum Sacrum'—Stravinsky, 'Prayers of Kierkegaard'—Barber, 'Magnificat'—Hovhaness." Ph.D. dissertation. The Catholic University of America, Washington, DC, 1965. viii, 334 p.

Title self-explanatory. Three works representing widely divergent styles are presented in detailed analysis with regard to text, structural design, tonal and modal organization, harmony, counterpoint, rhythm and meter, melodic line, idiomatic choral practices, voice grouping, and accompaniment. Author considers the chosen works "representative of the individualism of contemporary music in general." Numerous musical examples and charts; bibliography of about 65 writings.

450. *Garland Composer Resource Manuals* series/*Routledge Composer Resource Manuals* series. New York; London, 1981–.

Bio-bibliographies. Subjects represent "Western musical tradition from the Renaissance to the present century." Often consists of brief biographical information, catalog of works unless available elsewhere (some including significant performances and citing principal and/or modern editions), annotated bibliography of selected writings, discography or discographies noted in bibliography of writings, and videographies in some cases. Cross-references. Additional sections and various appendices appropriate for each subject. Indices, some expansive. Bio-bibliographies omitted from the listing below contain little or no information about choral music or are not published volumes as of 2001. Series: *Garland Composer Resource Manuals*; *Routledge Composer Resource Manuals*.

1. Skei, Allen B. *Heinrich Schütz: A Guide to Research*. 1981. xxxi, 186 p. ISBN 0-8240-9310-0   ML134.S412 S5 1981

2. Charles, Sydney Robinson. *Josquin des Prez: A Guide to Research*. 1983. xi, 235 p. ISBN 0-8240-9387-9   ML134.J773 C5 1983

3. Palmieri, Robert. *Sergei Vasil'evich Rachmaninoff: A Guide to Research*. 1985. xvii, 335 p. ISBN 0-8240-8996-0   ML134.R12 P3 1985

5. Studwell, William E. *Adolphe Adam and Léo Delibes: A Guide to Research*. 1987. x, 248 p. ISBN 0-8240-9011-X   ML134.A34 S8 1987

6. Miller, Mina F. *Carl Nielsen: A Guide to Research*. 1987. xvi, 245 p. ISBN 0-8240-8569-8   ML134.N42 M5 1987

7. Turbet, Richard. *William Byrd: A Guide to Research*. 1987. xix, 342 p. ISBN 0-8240-8388-1   ML134.B96 T9 1987

Discography intended as a supplement to and continuation of the author's "Byrd on Record." *BRIO*, 20 (1983), 41–45.

8. Howard, Patricia. *Christoph Willibald Gluck: A Guide to Research*. 1987. xix, 178 p. ISBN 0-8240-8451-9   ML134.G56 H7 1987

9. Hammond, Frederick. *Girolamo Frescobaldi: A Guide to Research*. 1988. xiii, 412 p. ISBN 0-8240-8555-8   ML410.F85 H37 1988

Intended as a companion to the author's biography *Girolamo Frescobaldi* (1983), with corrections and additions.

12. Talbot, Michael. *Antonio Vivaldi: A Guide to Research*. 1988. xlv, 197 p. ISBN 0-8240-8386-5   ML134.V7 T34 1988

13. Picker, Martin. *Johannes Ockeghem and Jacob Obrecht: A Guide to Research*. 1988. xi, 203 p. ISBN 0-8240-8381-4   ML134.O3 P5 1988

Lacks subject and title indices. "Index of Names" excludes authors listed in the bibliography of writings.

14. Kushner, David Z. *Ernest Bloch: A Guide to Research*. 1988. xiii, 345 p. ISBN 0-8240-7789-X   ML134.B623 K9 1988

15. Ossenkop, David. *Hugo Wolf: A Guide to Research*. 1988. xxxii, 329 p. ISBN 0-8240-8474-8   ML134.W75 O87 1988

16. Hastings, Baird. *Wolfgang Amadeus Mozart: A Guide to Research*. 1989. xx, 411 p. ISBN 0-8240-8347-4   ML134.M9 H34 1989

Lacks subject index.

17. Seaman, Gerald R. *Nikolai Andreevich Rimsky-Korsakov: A Guide to Research*. 1988. xxxi, 377 p. ISBN 0-8240-8466-7   ML134.R57 S4 1988

18. Zimmerman, Franklin B. *Henry Purcell: A Guide to Research.* 1989. xi, 333 p. ISBN 0-8240-7786-5   ML134.P95 Z55 1989

Biographical sketch is condensation of the author's *Henry Purcell, 1659–1695: His Life and Times* with additions.

19. Parker-Hale, Mary Ann. *G. F. Handel: A Guide to Research.* 1988. xvii, 294 p. ISBN 0-8240-8452-7   ML134.H16 P37 1988

20. Foster, Donald H. *Jean-Philippe Rameau: A Guide to Research.* 1989. xiii, 292 p. ISBN 0-8240-5645-0   ML134.R14 F7 1989

21. Butterworth, Neil. *Ralph Vaughan Williams: A Guide to Research.* 1990. x, 382 p. ISBN 0-8240-7746-6   ML134.V3 B9 1990

22. Langford, Jeffrey, and Jane Denker Graves. *Hector Berlioz: A Guide to Research.* 1989. xxi, 307 p. ISBN 0-8240-4635-8   ML134.B5 L3 1989

23. Adams, K. Gary, and Dyke Kiel. *Claudio Monteverdi: A Guide to Research.* 1989. xviii, 273 p. ISBN 0-8240-7743-1   ML134.M66 A5 1989

24. Henderson, Donald G., and Alice H. Henderson. *Carl Maria von Weber: A Guide to Research.* 1990. xxii, 385 p. ISBN 0-8240-4118-6 ML134.W39 H4 1990

25. Erb, James. *Orlando di Lasso: A Guide to Research.* 1990. xxxiv, 357 p. ISBN 0-8240-0947-9   ML134.L3 E7 1990

26. Paymer, Marvin E., and Hermine W. Williams. *Giovanni Battista Pergolesi: A Guide to Research.* 1989. xvi, 190 p. ISBN 0-8240-4595-5 ML143.P613 P4 1989

27. Briscoe, James R. *Claude Debussy: A Guide to Research.* 1990. xxi, 504 p. ISBN 0-8240-5795-3   ML134.D26 B7 1990

28. Filler, Susan Melanie. *Gustav and Alma Mahler: A Guide to Research.* 1989. li, 336 p. ISBN 0-8240-8483-7   ML134.M34 F54 1989

29. Saffle, Michael Benton. *Franz Liszt: A Guide to Research.* Discographical contributions by Ben Arnold, Keith Fagan, and Artis Wodehouse. 1991. xviii, 407 p. ISBN 0-8240-8382-2   ML134.L7 S2 1991

31. Grave, Floyd K., and Margaret G. Grave. *Franz Joseph Haydn: A Guide to Research.* 1990. xi, 451 p. ISBN 0-8240-8487-X   ML134.H272 G74 1990

34. Vidali, Carole Franklin. *Alessandro and Domenico Scarlatti: A Guide to Research.* 1993. xxi, 253, xi, 132 p. ISBN 0-8240-5942-5   ML134.S218 V5 1993

35. Picker, Martin. *Henricus Isaac: A Guide to Research.* 1991. xi, 308 p. ISBN 0-8240-5617-5   ML134.I8 P5 1991

37. Kent, Christopher. *Edward Elgar: A Guide to Research.* 1993. xvii, 523 p. ISBN 0-8240-8445-4   ML134.E613 K46 1993

39. Hodgson, Peter J. *Benjamin Britten: A Guide to Research.* 1996. 245 p. ISBN 0-8153-1795-6   ML134.B85 H63 1996

40. Antokoletz, Elliott. *Béla Bartók: A Guide to Research.* 2nd ed. 1997. xxxvii, 489 p. ISBN 0-8153-2088-4   ML134.B18 A7 1997

41. Goss, Glenda Dawn. *Jean Sibelius: A Guide to Research.* 1998. xxi, 298 p. ISBN 0-8153-1171-0   ML134.S49 G67 1998

42. Harwood, Gregory W. *Giuseppe Verdi: A Guide to Research.* 1998. xxx, 396 p. ISBN 0-8240-4117-8   ML134.V47 H37 1998

43. Cramer, Eugene. *Tomás Luis de Victoria: A Guide to Research.* 1998. xv, 403 p. ISBN 0-8153-2096-5   ML134.V6 C73 1998

44. Houlahan, Mícheál, and Philip Tacka. *Zoltán Kodály: A Guide to Research.* 1998. xiv, 611 p. ISBN 0-8153-2853-2   ML134.K64 H68 1998

46. Parker, Robert. *Carlos Chávez: A Guide to Research.* 1998. x, 180 p. ISBN 0-8153-2087-6   ML134.C43 P37 1998

48. Fairtile, Linda B. *Giacomo Puccini: A Guide to Research.* 1999. xvi, 381 p. ISBN 0-8153-2033-7   ML134.P94 F35 1999

Puccini's choral output were opera choruses.

49. Phillips, Edward R. *Gabriel Fauré: A Guide to Research.* 2000. xv, 429 p. ISBN 0-8240-7073-9   ML134.F29 P55 2000

Lacks subject index.

51. Cassaro, James P. *Gaetano Donizetti: A Guide to Research.* 2000. xv, 229 p. ISBN 0-8153-2350-6   ML134.D66 C37 2000

52. Link, John F. *Elliott Carter: A Guide to Research.* 2000. xiv, 331 p. ISBN 0-8153-2432-4   ML134.C19 L56 2000

53. Robertson, Marta, and Robin Armstrong. *Aaron Copland: A Guide to Research.* 2001. xii, 216 p. ISBN 0-8153-2178-3   ML134.C66 R63 2001

451. *Greenwood Press, Bio-Bibliographies in Music* series. Westport, Connecticut; New York, 1984–.

Bio-bibliographies. Usual arrangement: brief biography (occasionally includes an interview with the composer), list of works and significant performances, discography, and annotated bibliography of selected writings. Annotated bibliography often a compilation of significant writings about and by the composer. Cross references throughout. Various appendices appropriate for each subject, such as alphabetical and/or chronological listings of compositions, list of archival materials, source of texts of vocal works, awards and honors, etc. Indices, some expansive. Bio-bibliographies omitted from the listing below contain little or no information about choral music or are not published volumes as of 2000. Series: *Greenwood Press, Bio-Bibliographies in Music.*

1. Hixon, Donald L. *Thea Musgrave: A Bio-Bibliography.* 1984. viii, 187 p. ISBN 0-313-23708-5   ML134.M967 H6 1984

2. Skowronski, JoAnn. *Aaron Copland: A Bio-Bibliography.* 1985. x, 273 p. ISBN 0-313-24091-4   ML134.C66 S55 1985

3. Hennessee, Don A. *Samuel Barber: A Bio-Bibliography.* 1985. xii, 404 p. ISBN 0-313-24026-4   ML134.B175 H4 1985

4. Meckna, Michael. *Virgil Thomson: A Bio-Bibliography.* 1986. xiv, 203 p. ISBN 0-313-25010-3   ML134.T43 M4 1986

5. Heintze, James R. *Esther Williamson Ballou: A Bio-Bibliography.* 1987. xii, 125 p. ISBN 0-313-25069-3   ML134.B16 H4 1987

6. Carnovale, Norbert. *Gunther Schuller: A Bio-Bibliography.* 1987. xii, 338 p. ISBN 0-313-25084-7   ML134.S398 C4 1987

7. Grim, William E. *Max Reger: A Bio-Bibliography.* 1988. 270 p. ISBN 0-313-25311-0   ML134.R33 G7 1988

8. Arias, Enrique Alberto. *Alexander Tcherepnin: A Bio-Bibliography.* 1989. xii, 264 p. ISBN 0-313-25318-8   ML134.T28 A9 1989

9. Appleby, David P. *Heitor Villa-Lobos: A Bio-Bibliography.* 1988. xiv, 358 p. ISBN 0-313-25346-3   ML134.V65 A7 1988

Partially annotated bibliography of writings: about 70 briefly annotated books and 150 nonannotated articles. Many are not in English.

10. Thomerson, Kathleen. *Jean Langlais: A Bio-Bibliography.* 1988. ix. 191 p. ISBN 0-313-25547-4   ML134.L18 T5 1988

11. Pemberton, Carol A. *Lowell Mason: A Bio-Bibliography.* 1988. xiii, 206 p. ISBN 0-313-25881-3   ML134.M46 P4 1988

Lacks information about significant performances and a discography. Cross references rare.

12. DeBoer, Kee, and John B. Ahouse. *Daniel Pinkham: A Bio-Bibliography.* 1988. viii, 238 p. ISBN 0-313-25503-2   ML134.P667 D4 1988

13. Craggs, Stewart R. *Arthur Bliss: A Bio-Bibliography.* 1988. 183 p. ISBN 0-313-25739-6   ML134.B62 C7 1988

14. Block, Geoffrey Holden. *Charles Ives: A Bio-Bibliography.* Foreword by J. Peter Burkholder. 1988. xviii, 422 p. ISBN 0-313-25404-4 ML134.I9 B6 1988

16. Patterson, Donald L., and Janet L. Patterson. *Vincent Persichetti: A Bio-Bibliography.* 1988. xiv, 336 p. ISBN 0-313-25335-8   ML134.P6135 P4 1988

17. Kreitner, Kenneth. *Robert Ward: A Bio-Bibliography.* 1988. ix, 173 p. ISBN 0-313-25701-9   ML134.W28 K7 1988

18. Smith, Carolyn J. *William Walton: A Bio-Bibliography.* 1988. x, 246 p. ISBN 0-313-25391-9   ML134.W25 S6 1988

19. Follet, Robert. *Albert Roussel: A Bio-Bibliography.* 1988. x, 134 p. ISBN 0-313-25558-X   ML134.R7 F6 1988

20. Siddons, James. *Anthony Milner: A Bio-Bibliography.* Foreword by David Matthews. 1989. xix, 161 p. ISBN 0-313-25732-9   ML134.M555 S5 1989

21. Tyler, Linda L. *Edward Burlingame Hill: A Bio-Bibliography.* 1989. x, 168 p. ISBN 0-313-25525-3   ML134.H46 T9 1989

22. Bowles, Garrett H. *Ernst Krenek: A Bio-Bibliography.* 1989. xiv, 428 p. ISBN 0-313-25250-5   ML134.K79 B7 1989

23. McDonald, Arlys L. *Ned Rorem: A Bio-Bibliography.* 1989. x, 284 p. ISBN 0-313-25565-2   ML134.R674 M3 1989

24. Craggs, Stewart R. *Richard Rodney Bennett: A Bio-Bibliography.* 1990. xiii, 249 p. ISBN 0-313-26179-2   ML134.B4425 C7 1990

25. Bailey, Walter B., and Nancy Gisbrecht Bailey. *Radie Britain: A Bio-Bibliography.* 1990. xv, 158 p. ISBN 0-313-26277-2   ML134.B845 B3 1990

26. King, Charles W. *Frank Martin: A Bio-Bibliography.* 1990. xii, 251 p. ISBN 0-313-25418-4   ML134.M436 K5 1990

27. Hayes, Deborah. *Peggy Glanville-Hicks: A Bio-Bibliography.* 1990. x, 274 p. ISBN 0-313-26422-8   ML134.G52 H4 1990

28. Keck, George Russell. *Francis Poulenc: A Bio-Bibliography.* 1990. xi, 304 p. ISBN 0-313-25562-8   ML134.P87 K3 1990

29. Ferencz, George Joseph. *Robert Russell Bennett: A Bio-Bibliography.* 1990. xiv, 215 p. ISBN 0-313-26472-4   ML134.B4227 F4 1990

30. Richart, Robert W. *György Ligeti: A Bio-Bibliography.* 1990. xii, 188 p. ISBN 0-313-25174-6   ML134.L57 R5 1990

31. Hitchens, Susan Hayes. *Karel Husa: A Bio-Bibliography.* 1991. x, 162 p. ISBN 0-313-25585-7   ML134.H93 H57 1991

32. Craggs, Stewart R. *John McCabe: A Bio-Bibliography.* 1991. xii, 276 p. ISBN 0-313-26445-7   ML134.M48 C7 1991

Items in bibliography about the composer are annotated; items written by the composer are not.

34. Roberge, Marc-André. *Ferruccio Busoni: A Bio-Bibliography.* 1991. xxix, 400 p. ISBN 0-313-25587-3   ML134.B94 R6 1991

35. Hartsock, Ralph. *Otto Luening: A Bio-Bibliography.* 1991. xiii, 272 p. ISBN 0-313-24320-4   ML134.L86 H4 1991

36. Little, Karen R. *Frank Bridge: A Bio-Bibliography.* 1991. xii, 263 p. ISBN 0-313-26232-2   ML134.B84 L5 1991

37. Perone, Karen L. *Lukas Foss: A Bio-Bibliography.* 1991. viii, 282 p. ISBN 0-313-26811-8   ML134.F59 P47 1991

38. Benser, Caroline Cepin, and David Francis Urrows. *Randall Thompson: A Bio-Bibliography.* 1991. x, 230 p. ISBN 0-313-25521-0 ML134.T42 B46 1991

39. Austin, David L. *Henri Sauguet: A Bio-Bibliography.* 1991. xiv, 271 p. ISBN 0-313-26564-X   ML134.S215 A95 1991

40. Stehman, Dan. *Roy Harris: A Bio-Bibliography.* 1991. xii, 475 p. ISBN 0-313-25079-0   ML134.H175 S7 1991

41. Hartig, Linda Bishop. *Violet Archer: A Bio-Bibliography.* 1991. viii, 153 p. ISBN 0-313-26408-2   ML134.A68 H3 1991

42. Hess, Carol A. *Enrique Granados: A Bio-Bibliography.* 1991. 192 p. ISBN 0-313-27384-7   ML134.G79 H5 1991

43. Evans, Joan. *Hans Rosbaud: A Bio-Bibliography.* Foreword by Pierre Boulez. 1992. xxii, 298 p. ISBN 0-313-27413-4   ML134.5.R68 E9 1992

44. Craggs, Stewart R. *Alun Hoddinott: A Bio-Bibliography.* 1993. x, 237 p. ISBN 0-313-27321-9   ML134.H54 C7 1993

45. Demsey, David, and Ronald Prather. *Alec Wilder: A Bio-Bibliography.* With the assistance of Judith Bell. 1993. xii, 274 p. ISBN 0-313-27820-2 ML134.W638 D4 1993

46. Bortin, Virginia. *Elinor Remick Warren: A Bio-Bibliography.* 1993. viii, 285 p. ISBN 0-313-25879-1   ML134.W32 B7 1993

47. Perone, James E. *Howard Hanson: A Bio-Bibliography.* 1993. viii, 327 p. ISBN 0-313-28644-2   ML134.H173 P47 1993

48. Shapiro, Robert. *Germaine Tailleferre: A Bio-Bibliography.* 1994. xiv, 280 p. ISBN 0-313-28642-6   ML134.T18 S5 1994

49. Burbank, Richard D. *Charles Wuorinen: A Bio-Bibliography.* 1994. xv, 330 p. ISBN 0-313-25399-4   ML134.W86 B87 1994

50. Hayes, Deborah. *Peter Sculthorpe: A Bio-Bibliography*. 1993. xvi, 305 p. ISBN 0-313-27742-7   ML134.S415 H4 1993

51. Doering, William T. *Elliott Carter: A Bio-Bibliography*. 1993. x. 190 p. ISBN 0-313-26864-9   ML134.C19 D6 1993

52. Johnson, Ellen S. *Leslie Bassett: A Bio-Bibliography*. 1994. xvi, 171 p. ISBN 0-313-25851-1   ML134.B185 J6 1994

53. Hobson, Constance Tibbs, and Deborra A. Richardson. *Ulysses Kay: A Bio-Bibliography*. 1994. xv, 196 p. ISBN 0-313-25546-6   ML134.K3 H6 1994

54. O'Connor, Joan. *John Alden Carpenter: A Bio-Bibliography*. 1994. 248 p. ISBN 0-313-26430-9   ML134.C18 O25 1994

Choruses are found in Carpenter's plays.

55. Slomski, Monica J. *Paul Creston: A Bio-Bibliography*. 1994. x, 205 p. ISBN 0-313-25336-6   ML134.C73 S6 1994

56. Sposato, Jeffrey S. *William Thomas McKinley: A Bio-Bibliography*. 1995. xx, 303 p. ISBN 0-313-28923-9   ML134.M485 S66 1995

Bibliographic entries not annotated.

57. Smith, Carolyn J. *Peter Maxwell Davies: A Bio-Bibliography*. 1995. xii, 343 p. ISBN 0-313-26831-2   ML134.D25 S65 1995

58. Craggs, Stewart R. *William Mathias: A Bio-Bibliography*. 1995. xii, 246 p. ISBN 0-313-27865-2   ML134.M468 C7 1995

60. Dodd, Mary Ann, and Jayson Rod Engquist. *Gardner Read: A Bio-Bibliography*. 1996. xv, 270 p. ISBN 0-313-29384-8   ML134.R28 D6 1996

61. Still, Judith Anne, Michael J. Dabrishus, and Carolyn L. Quin. *William Grant Still: A Bio-Bibliography*. 1996. xii, 331 p. ISBN 0-313-25255-6 ML134.S8 S75 1996

62. Green, Alan. *Allen Sapp: A Bio-Bibliography*. Foreword by Jonathan D. Kramer. 1996. xiv, 239 p. ISBN 0-313-28983-2   ML134.S17 G74 1996

63. Hitchens, Susan Hayes. *Ross Lee Finney: A Bio-Bibliography*. 1996. x, 191 p. ISBN 0-313-28671-X   ML134.F49 H58 1996

64. Dressler, John C. *Gerald Finzi: A Bio-Bibliography*. 1997. xiii, 200 p. ISBN 0-313-28693-0   ML134.F495 D74 1997

65. Holmes, Robyn, Patricia Shaw, and Peter Campbell. *Larry Sitsky: A Bio-Bibliography*. 1997. xiv, 207 p. ISBN 0-313-29020-2   ML134.S53 H65 1997

66. Faucett, Bill F. *George Whitefield Chadwick: A Bio-Bibliography*. 1998. xv, 304 p. ISBN 0-313-30067-4   ML134.C413 F38 1998

67. Adams, K. Gary. *William Schuman: A Bio-Bibliography*. 1998. x, 269 p. ISBN 0-313-27359-6   ML134.S3986 A33 1998

69. Craggs, Stewart R. *Malcolm Arnold: A Bio-Bibliography*. 1998. x, 216 p. ISBN 0-313-29254-X   ML134.A77 C73 1998

72. Jordan, Douglas M. *Alfred Reed: A Bio-Bibliography*. 1999. xiv, 282 p. ISBN 0-313-30333-9   ML134.R29 J67 1999

75. Hartsock, Ralph, and Carl Rahkonen. *Vladimir Ussachevsky: A Bio-Bibliography*. 2000. xii, 254 p. ISBN 0-313-29852-1   ML134.U87 H37 2000

77. Hixon, Donald L. *Gian Carlo Menotti: A Bio-Bibliography*. 2000. xii, 339 p. ISBN 0-313-26139-3   ML134.M533 H59 2000

79. Sampsel, Laurie J. *Cyril Scott: A Bio-Bibliography*. 2000. xiv, 337. ISBN 0-313-29347-3   ML134.S414 S36 2000

81. Cunningham, Robert E. *Sergei Rachmaninoff: A Bio-Bibliography*. 2001. xi, 349 p. ISBN 0-313-30907-8   ML134.R12 C86 2001

83. Będkowski, Stanisław, and Stanisław Hrabia. *Witold Lutosławski: A Bio-Bibliography*. 2001. ix, 323 p. ISBN 0-313-25962-3   ML134.L93 B43 2001

452. Hines, Robert Stephan, ed. *The Composer's Point of View: Essays on Twentieth-Century Choral Music by Those Who Wrote It*. Norman: University of Oklahoma Press, 1963. 342 p.   ML1506 .H55; reprint, Westport, Connecticut: Greenwood Press, 1980. xiv, 342 p. ISBN 0-313-22461-7   ML1506 .H55 1980

"A collection of [18] essays by 20th-century composers in which each composer discusses a large choral work or works he has written, along with the principles that guided the composition." Composers organized into three geographical groups: (1) United States: Lukas Foss, Howard Hanson, Ernst Krenek, Peter Mennin, Vincent Persichetti, Bernard Rogers, and Leo Sowerby; (2) English: Peter Racine Fricker, Anthony Milner, Edmund Rubbra, and Michael Tippett; and (3) Continental European: Conrad Beck, Karl-Birger Blomdahl, Luigi Dallapiccola, Jean Françaix, Jean Langlais, Frank Martin, and Hermann Reutter. Numerous musical examples; catalogs of composers's choral works, giving title, voicing/instrumentation, and publication information; expansive index.

453. Jacobson, Joshua R. "Choral Compositions in the 'Eastern Mediterranean' Style: An Analysis of Nationalistic Elements in Selected Works by Israeli Composers." D.M.A. dissertation. University of Cincinnati, 1984. iii, 258 p.

Examines stylistic elements (texts, scales, motives, texture, harmonic structure, rhythm, form, and timbre) found within selected choral compositions by Israeli composers. Presents analyses of four representative works: Tsvi Anvi's *Mizmorei Tehilim*, Yehezkel Braun's *Shlosha Pirkei Hallel*, Paul Ben-Haim's *Roni Akara*, and Mordecai Seter's *Moadim*. Numerous musical examples; bibliography of approximately 50 writings and 30 scores.

454. MacNeill, Roger. "Secular Choral Chamber Music in America since 1950, as Represented by the Music for this Genre by Samuel Adler, Jean Berger, Eugene Butler, and Kirke Mechem." D.A. dissertation. University of Northern Colorado, Greeley, 1986. xiii, 314 p.

History of chamber choirs in America from 1950 to 1984. Analyses of the music of four representative composers: Samuel Adler, Jean Berger, Eugene Butler, and Kirke Mechem. Musical examples; bibliography of about 130 writings and unpublished materials, and 60 musical scores.

455. Manzo, Ralph Dan. "A Study of Selected Choral Works by American Contemporary Composers." Ed.D. dissertation. University of Northern Colorado, Greeley, 1961. xi, 270 p.

Study of "compositional and interpretive techniques employed in selected contemporary American [choral works]." The music of 10 composers was examined: Ernst Bacon, Samuel Barber, Jean Berger, Aaron Copland, Norman Dello Joio, Roy Harris, Paul Hindemith, Normand Lockwood, William Schuman, and Randall Thompson. Addresses basic conducting techniques, interpretation, and theory requisite to cope with contemporary choral music. Tables and musical examples; annotated bibliography of about 60 writings; dated list of publishers with addresses.

456. Minear, Paul Sevier. *Death Set to Music: Masterworks by Bach, Brahms, Penderecki, Bernstein*. Atlanta, Georgia: John Knox Press, 1987. 173 p. ISBN 0-8042-1874-9   ML2900 .M5 1987

Discusses biblical attitudes toward death as found in four musical works: J. S. Bach's *St. Matthew Passion*, Johannes Brahms's *A German Requiem*, Krzysztof Penderecki's *St. Luke Passion*, and Leonard Bernstein's *Mass*. Documented with footnotes; no index.

457. Pisciotta, Louis Vincent. "Texture in the Choral Works of Selected Contemporary American Composers." Ph.D. dissertation. Indiana University, Bloomington, 1967. v, 411 p.

Individual chapters examine texture in the choral works of Samuel Barber, Jean Berger, Elliott Carter, Aaron Copland, Norman Dello Joio, Lukas Foss, Roy Harris, Alan Hovhaness, William Schuman, and Randall Thompson. Numerous musical examples and tables; bibliography of 44 writings; glossary of about 60 terms appended.

See also: Blyth, Alan, ed. *Choral Music on Record* (item 159); Yoder, David Winston. "A Study and Performance of Extended Sacred Choral Works with Brass Instruments by Contemporary American Composers" (item 114)

JOHANN SEBASTIAN BACH (1685–1750)

458. Bach, Johann Sebastian. *Cantata No. 4: Christ lag in Todesbanden: An Authoritative Score, Backgrounds, Analysis, Views and Comments.* Ed. by Gerhard Herz. New York: W. W. Norton, 1967. 138 p. ISBN 0-393-09761-7 M2020 .B16 S.4 1967

Critical edition of score consisting of four main sections: historical background; score of the cantata edited by Arnold Schering; analysis; and views and comments of the writers Philipp Spitta, Albert Schweitzer, André Pirro, W. G. Whittaker, Arnold Schering, Friedrich Smend, Alfred Dürr, and Karl Geiringer. Partially annotated classified bibliography of about 35 writings; no index. Series: *A Norton Critical Score.*

459. Bach, Johann Sebastian. *Cantata No. 140: Wachet auf, ruft uns die Stimme: The Score of the New Bach Edition, Backgrounds, Analysis, Views and Comments.* Ed. by Gerhard Herz. New York: W. W. Norton, 1972. viii, 180 p. ISBN 0-393-02154-8, ISBN 0-393-09555-X (pbk) M2020 .B16 S.140 1972

Critical edition of score consisting of four main sections: historical background; score of the cantata taken from *Johann Sebastian Bach, Neue Ausgabe sämtlicher Werke*; analysis; and views and comments of the writers Carl von Winterfeld, Karl Hermann Bitter, Philipp Spitta, Albert Schweitzer, André Pirro, C. Hubert H. Parry, W. G. Whittaker, Friedrich Smend, Karl Geiringer, and Alfred Dürr. Partially annotated classified bibliography of about 50 writings; index by genre and BWV numbers. Series: *A Norton Critical Score.*

460. Chailley, Jacques. *Les "Passions" de J.-S. Bach* [The "Passions" of J. S. Bach]. Discography prepared by Gilles Cantagrel. 2nd ed. Paris: Presses Universitaires de France, 1984. 460 p. ISBN 2-13-038311-4 MT115.B2 C5 1984

French only. Reprint of the 1963 edition with an updated discography. Following an overview of various types of Passions, discusses Bach's contribution to the genre. Provides detailed analysis of the *St. John* and *St. Matthew Passion.* Documented with footnotes; index.

461. Daw, Stephen. *The Music of Johann Sebastian Bach: The Choral Works.* Rutherford, New Jersey: Fairleigh Dickinson University Press, 1981. 240 p. ISBN 0-8386-1682-8 ML410.B1 D27

Chronological survey of selected cantatas, motets, and large choral works by Bach. Appendices include discussion of recommended books, editions and scores, musical resources of Bach's time, annotated listing of approximately 180 recommended recordings classified by genre, and a chronology of known performances of Bach's choral works. Numerous illustrations and musical examples. Two indices: (1) Bach's works classified by genre and (2) general index of proper names.

462. Day, James. *The Literary Background to Bach's Cantatas.* London: Dobson Books, 1961   ML410.B13 D35; reprint, New York: Dover Publications, 1966. 115 p.   ML410.B13 D35 1966

Discussion of the libretti of J. S. Bach's sacred and secular cantatas. Overview of social conditions in 17th-century Germany and the development of German baroque literature. Illustrations and musical examples; bibliography of 40 books and articles; expansive index.

463. Dürr, Alfred. *Die Kantaten von Johann Sebastian Bach mit ihren Texten* [The cantatas of Johann Sebastian Bach]. 6th ed. München, Germany: Deutscher Taschenbuch Verlag; Kassel, Germany: Bärenreiter, 1995. 1037 p. ISBN 3-423-04431-4 (DTV), ISBN 3-7618-4431-X (Bärenreiter) MT115.B2 D9 1995

German only. Chronological survey of Bach's cantatas. Cantata text, only in German, provided for each. Musical examples; bibliography of approximately 180 writings; glossary of terms; three indices: (1) index of personal names, (2) index to Bach's cantatas listed in alphabetical order, and (3) listed in BWV number order.

464. Dürr, Alfred. *Studien über die frühen Kantaten Johann Sebastian Bachs* [Studies on the early cantatas of Johann Sebastian Bach]. 2nd ed. Wiesbaden, Germany: Breitkopf & Härtel, 1977. 264 p. ISBN 3-7651-0130-3 ML410.B13 D83 1977

German only. Examines the manuscripts, libretti, and formal and melodic structures of Bach's early cantatas (1703–1717). Discusses authenticity and presents chronological list of cantatas, altering accepted dates of some. Several appendices provide information on watermarks, copyists, vocal ranges, texts, and analyses of selected works. Musical examples, graphs, and tables; bibliography of approximately 110 writings; no index.

465. Mann, Alfred. *Bach and Handel: Choral Performance Practice.* Chapel Hill, North Carolina: Hinshaw Music, 1992. 119 p. ISBN 0-937276-12-X MT875 .M36 1992

Addresses the issue of performance practice in the choral music of J. S. Bach and G. F. Handel. Musical examples and illustrations; bibliography of 36 writings; index of works by Bach and Handel and general index.

466. Neumann, Werner. *Handbuch der Kantaten Johann Sebastian Bachs*. 5th ed. Leipzig, Germany: Breitkopf & Härtel, 1984. 323 p.   ML410.B1 N4 1984

German text. Detailed, annotated bibliography of Bach's cantatas. Includes chronology. Various indices, including title, occasion, librettist, scoring, chorale tune, arias, sources, and parodies and parallels between cantatas and between cantatas and Bach's Masses, Passions, and Magnificat.

467. Pelikan, Jaroslav Jan. *Bach among the Theologians*. Philadelphia: Fortress Press, 1986. xiv, 158 p. ISBN 0-8006-0792-9   ML410.B1 P37 1986

Study of J. S. Bach's compositions in the context of the four seasons of the liturgical year. Organized into two parts: (1) theological context of Bach's church music and (2) theological themes. Addresses Bach's cantatas, Passions, and Masses. Documented with endnotes. Two indices: contemporaries of Bach and works of Bach.

468. Robertson, Alec. *The Church Cantatas of J. S. Bach*. London: Cassell; New York: Praeger, 1972. xvi, 356 p.   ML410.B13 R58

Annotated bibliography of Bach's sacred cantatas organized according to the Lutheran church calendar. Provides librettist, opening lines for each number with English translation, and first performances. Discusses scoring and source of chorale employed. Bibliography of 17 writings; indices of cantata titles in numerical and alphabetical order.

469. Steinitz, Paul. *Bach's Passions*. New York: Charles Scribner's Sons, 1978. ISBN 0-684-16229-6   MT115.B2 S73 1978; London: Paul Elek, 1979. ix, 137 p. ISBN 0-236-40132-7   MT115.B2 S73

Discussion of J. S. Bach's Passions with historical perspective. Does not present structural analysis of works. "Origins of Words and Melodies of the Chorales in Bach's Passions" appended. Musical examples; bibliography of approximately 40 writings and critical editions of music; discography of 11 recordings; expansive index. Series: *Masterworks of Choral Music*.

470. Terry, Charles Sanford. *Bach: The Cantatas and Oratorios; The Passions; The Magnificat, Lutheran Masses and Motets*. New York: Johnson Reprint Corp., 1972. 5 vols. bound as 1. 52 p.; 38 p.; 56 p.; 80 p.; 60 p. ML115.B2 T3

Reprint of the 1925, 1928, and 1929 editions. *Bach: The Cantatas and Oratorios* addresses cantata form, church cantatas (including a list of cantatas in numerical order), cantatas in relationship to the Lutheran service, libretti and the chorales (including a list of chorales used in cantatas), secular cantatas (including a list of titles), orchestration, and accompaniment. *Bach: The Passions* discusses the *St. John, Picander's, St. Matthew, St. Mark*, and *St. Luke Passion*. *Bach: The Magnificat, Lutheran Masses and Motets* briefly surveys Bach's contribution to these genres. Musical examples and tables; no index. Series: *The Musical Pilgrim*.

471. Whittaker, W. Gillies. *The Cantatas of Johann Sebastian Bach: Sacred and Secular*. London: Oxford University Press, 1959 (rep. 1964, 1978, 1981). 2 vols. xiv, 717 p.; 754 p.   MT115.B2 W5

Study of Bach's sacred and secular cantatas. Some information outdated by more recent scholarship in the field, especially dating of the cantatas. Three appendices: (1) biblical and apocryphal texts set in the sacred cantatas, motets, and Christmas oratorio; (2) alphabetical listing of church cantatas; and (3) dated list of cantatas published in English and Welsh. Numerous musical examples (approximately 2,500); no bibliography; expansive index.

472. Young, W. Murray. *The Cantatas of J. S. Bach: An Analytical Guide*. Jefferson, North Carolina: MacFarland, 1989. xvi, 307 p. ISBN 0-89950-394-2 MT115.B2 Y7 1989

Guide to Bach's 245 extant sacred and secular cantatas. Presents brief historical information for each cantata. Focus on text and musical treatment. Two appendices: (1) sacred cantatas by type and (2) cantatas arranged by BWV number. Bibliography of 20 writings about Bach's cantatas; expansive index.

See also: Bullock, William J. *Bach Cantatas Requiring Limited Resources: A Guide to Editions* (item 132); Terry, Charles Sanford. *Joh. Seb. Bach: Cantata Texts, Sacred and Secular: With a Reconstruction of the Leipzig Liturgy of His Period* (item 165)

LUDWIG VAN BEETHOVEN (1770–1827)

473. Fiske, Roger. *Beethoven's Missa Solemnis*. London: Paul Elek, 1979. 123 p. ISBN 0-236-40146-7   MT115.B4 F6; New York: Charles Scribner's Sons, 1979. 123 p. ISBN 0-684-16228-8   MT115.B4 F6 1979b

Descriptive account of the Mass with historical perspective. Musical examples; bibliography of 19 items; discography of 12 recordings; expansive index. Series: *Masterworks of Choral Music*.

JOHANNES BRAHMS (1833–1897)

474. Bell, A. Craig. *Brahms: The Vocal Music*. Madison, New Jersey: Fairleigh Dickinson University Press; London: Associated University Presses, 1996. 262 p. ISBN 0-8386-3597-0   ML410.B8 B38 1996

Chapters 9 and 10 survey Brahms's minor and major choral works, respectively. Musical examples; bibliography of selected writings; indices of (1) Brahms's songs and choral works, (2) works other than songs, and (3) general index.

475. Hancock, Virginia. *Brahms's Choral Compositions and His Library of Early Music*. Ann Arbor, Michigan: UMI Research Press, 1983. vi, 229 p. ISBN 0-8357-1496-9   ML410.B8 H19 1983

Documents Brahms's study of early music (Middle Renaissance through high baroque) and its relationship to his own choral compositions. Four appendices: (1) list of performances of early vocal music conducted by Brahms; (2) bibliography of Brahms's copies/transcriptions of early music scores; (3) catalog of Brahms's printed library of early music; and (4) list of Brahms's choral works cross-referenced with main body of text. Musical examples; bibliography of approximately 100 correspondences, books, articles, and dissertations and about 35 scores and collections; expansive index. Series: *Studies in Musicology*, no. 76.

WILLIAM BYRD (1542/3–1623)

476. Kerman, Joseph. *The Masses and Motets of William Byrd*. Berkeley, California: University of California Press; London: Faber and Faber, 1981. 360 p. ISBN 0-520-04033-3 (U.S.)/ ISBN 0-571-11643-4 (UK)   ML410.B996 M9 1978 vol. 1

Volume 1 of a three-volume set (Volume 2, *The Songs, Services and Anthems of William Byrd*, by Philip Brett, "in preparation"; Volume 3, *The Consort and Keyboard Music of William Byrd*, by Oliver Neighbour, published in 1978). Detailed examination of all known motets and three settings of the Ordinary of the Mass to show the composer's creative process and stylistic development. Documented with footnotes; musical examples and tables; two indices: Byrd's works and proper names. Series: *The Music of William Byrd*, vol. 1.

GEORGE FRIDERIC HANDEL (1685–1759)

477. Dean, Winton. *Handel's Dramatic Oratorios and Masques*. London: Oxford University Press, 1959 (rep. 1966, 1972, 1979). ISBN 0-19-315203-7 (1979)   ML410.H13 D35; reprint, Oxford: Clarendon Press, 1990. xii, 694 p. ISBN 0-19-816184-0   ML410.H13 D35 1989

In two parts: (1) historical survey of oratorio before Handel, Handel's style, and background and performance of Handel's oratorios; (2) critical analysis of 18 works: *Acis and Galatea, Esther, Deborah, Athalia, Saul, Samson, Semele, Joseph and His Brethren, Hercules, Belshazzar, Judas Maccabaeus, Alexander Balus, Joshua, Solomon, Susanna, Theodora, The Choice of Hercules*, and *Jephtha*. Several appendices, including a bibliography of approximately 80 writings. Musical examples, tables, illustrations, and facsimiles; expansive index of Handel's works and expansive general index.

478. Larsen, Jens Peter. *Handel's Messiah: Origins, Composition, Sources*. 2nd ed. New York: W. W. Norton, 1972. 337 p. ISBN 0-393-00657-3 ML410.H13 L2 1972; reprint, Westport, Connecticut: Greenwood Press, 1990. 337 p. ISBN 0-313-24426-X   ML410.H13 L2 1990

Purpose: to examine "the idea, the plan and construction of the *Messiah*." Presents historical overview of Handelian oratorio, tackles the problem of the numerous versions of *Messiah*, and investigates the sources (copyists, paper sizes, and watermarks). Numerous musical examples, facsimiles, and tables; bibliography of about 50 writings. Three indices: (1) classified index of Handel's works mentioned in the text; (2) index to individual numbers in *Messiah*; (3) index of names. Series: *Norton Library*, N657.

479. Myers, Robert Manson. *Handel's Messiah: A Touchstone of Taste*. New York: Macmillan, 1948   ML410.H13 M97; reprint, New York: Octagon Books, 1971. xxii, 338 p. ISBN 0-374-96035-6   ML410.H13 M97 1971

Study of *Messiah* within perspective of social conditions and in relation to Handel's other works, as well as works by his contemporaries. Concludes with examination of how the art has been received since Handel's time and the neglect of Handel's other works. Two appendices: (1) text of *Messiah*; (2) list of subscribers to the original full-score edition (1767). Musical examples and illustrations; bibliography of about 325 writings; expansive index.

480. Shaw, Watkins. *A Textual and Historical Companion to Handel's Messiah.* London: Novello, 1982. 217 p.   MT115.H133 S56 1982

Originally published in 1965; 1982 printing with corrections. Textual and historical information about Handel's *Messiah.* Description of the two principal sources (R.M.20.f.2 and Tenbury MSS 346–7); a chronological survey of Handel's singers; and an account of the secondary manuscript sources, namely the Foundling Hospital materials. Numerous music examples, facsimiles, and charts; 16 pages of music appended; bibliography of about 40 items; index.

481. Young, Percy M. *The Oratorios of Handel.* London: Dennis Dobson, 1949 ML410.H13 Y63; reprint, Wilmington, Delaware: International Academic Publishing, 1979. 244 p. ISBN 0-89765-471-4   ML410.H13 Y63 1979

Surveys Handel's sacred oratorios in chronological order. Discusses Italian origins, oratorio singers, and conditions of performance. Numerous musical examples, with illustrations, photos, and facsimiles. No bibliography; expansive index.

See also: Mann, Alfred. *Bach and Handel: Choral Performance Practice* (item 465)

JOSEPH HAYDN (1732–1809)

482. Brown, A. Peter. *Performing Haydn's The Creation: Reconstructing the Earliest Renditions.* Bloomington: Indiana University Press, 1986. xiv, 123 p. ISBN 0-253-38820-1   MT115.H28 B8 1986

Six main divisions: (1) sources; (2) forces, scoring, and dynamics; (3) embellishment and ornamentation; (4) bowing and articulation; (5) tempo; and (6) conclusion. Questions first edition of *Die Schöpfung* [The Creation] as authoritative score. Takes into account early performances and source materials to which Haydn made editorial changes for performance. Five appendices: (1) contents of the numbers; (2) comparison of sources for important variants; (3) solo/tutti indications in *Tonkünstler Parts*; (4) *Ossia* for solo voices in no. 19 from *Tonkünstler Parts*; and (5) original contrabassoon and bass trombone parts. Bibliography of 70-plus items; numerous facsimiles and musical examples; expansive general index and a separate index for individual numbers from *Die Schöpfung.* Series: *Music—Scholarship and Performance.*

483. Schenbeck, Lawrence. *Joseph Haydn and the Classical Choral Tradition.* Chapel Hill, North Carolina: Hinshaw Music, 1996. xi, 513 p. ISBN 0-937276-17-0   ML410.H4 S18 1996

Surveys Haydn's choral output. Includes a classified, annotated catalog (Masses; oratorios and cantatas; smaller sacred works; secular works), listing published editions and a bibliography of writings about each work. Separate listing of his works classified as follows: equal voices and/or younger choirs; changing voices; high school choirs; college and professional choirs; women's choirs; men's choirs; seasons, services, or occasions in the church year; choral music in volumes of the Cologne Haydn Institute. Musical examples and analyses; bibliography of more than 600 writings; expansive index of works by Haydn and expansive general index.

FELIX MENDELSSOHN-BARTHOLDY (1809–1847)

484. Werner, Jack. *Mendelssohn's "Elijah": A Historical and Analytical Guide to the Oratorio*. Foreword by Sir Malcolm Sargent. London: Chappell, 1965. xiii, 109 p.   MT115.M53 W5

An account of the genesis of *Elijah*, the first performance, and later revisions. Analyses of each movement. Two appendices: (1) reprint of "The 'Mendelssohnian Cadence' " (originally appeared in *Musical Times*, January 1956) and (2) dated discography of recordings of *Elijah*. Musical examples, illustrations, and facsimiles; documented with footnotes; expansive index.

GIOVANNI PIERLUIGI DA PALESTRINA (1525?–1594)

485. Palestrina, Giovanni Pierluigi da. *Pope Marcellus Mass: An Authoritative Score, Backgrounds and Sources, History and Analysis, Views and Comments*. Ed. by Lewis Lockwood. New York: W. W. Norton, 1975. ix, 142 p. ISBN 0-393-02185-8   M2011.P25 M38 1975

Critical score consisting of four main sections: background and source material; score of the Mass taken from the *Opere Complete di Giovanni Pierluigi da Palestrina* edited by Raffaele Casimiri with modern clefs; two historical and analytical essays: Lewis Lockwood's "Notes on the Text and Structure of the *Pope Marcellus Mass*" and Knud Jeppesen's "Problems of the *Pope Marcellus Mass*: Some Remarks on the *Missa Papae Marcelli* by Giovanni Pierluigi da Palestrina" translated by Lockwood into English; and views and comments of the writers Giovanni Battista Martini, E. T. A. Hoffmann, Richard Wagner, August Wilhelm Ambros, and Giuseppe Verdi. Partially annotated classified bibliography of about 30 entries; no index. Series: *A Norton Critical Score*.

HENRY PURCELL (1659–1695)

486. Zimmerman, Franklin B. *The Anthems of Henry Purcell*. New York: [American Choral Foundation], 1971. 65 p.   ML410.P93 Z48

Special issue of the *American Choral Review*, Vol. XIII, nos. 3 and 4. Gives historical overview of the styles and practices of Purcell's time and discusses Purcell's motet anthems, cantata anthems, and oratorio anthems. Provides a classified listing of Purcell's anthems, giving title, voicing/instrumentation, and date of composition. Also provides selective list of Purcell's anthems available in modern editions. Musical examples; bibliography of 35 writings; no index.

MICHAEL TIPPETT (1905–1998)

487. Theil, Gordon. *Michael Tippett: A Bio-Bibliography*. New York: Greenwood Press, 1989. xiii, 344 p. ISBN 0-313-24270-4   ML134.T5 T5 1989

Would have been perhaps more suitably part of Greenwood Press's *Bio-Bibliographies in Music* series. Consists of brief biography, list of works and performances, discography of Tippett as composer and conductor, and annotated bibliography of writings by and about the composer. Appendices: chronological and classified lists of compositions; honors and awards; ballet and television productions; and resources. Expansive index. Series: *Music Reference Collection*, no. 21.

VIII

Choral Music Web Sites

488. *American Choral Directors Association*

http://www.acdaonline.org/

Official Web site of the American Choral Directors Association (ACDA). Provides information about *The Choral Journal*, an ACDA publication.

489. *American Guild of Organists*

http://www.agohq.org/home.html

Official Web site of the American Guild of Organists (AGO) and *The American Organist*.

490. *Association of British Choral Directors*

http://www.abcd.org.uk/

Official Web site of the Association of British Choral Directors (ABCD).

491. *Association of Canadian Choral Conductors*

http://www.islandnet.com/~ibullen/accc/

Official Web site for the Association of Canadian Choral Conductors (ACCC). Links provided for the following organizations:

Alberta Choral Foundation

http://www.musicalberta.com/acfframe.html

L'Alliance régionale des chorales de l'île de Montréal

http://www.cam.org/~arcim

BC Choral Federation

http://www.bcchoralfed.com/

Choirs Ontario

http://www.choirsontario.org/

Nova Scotia Choral Federation

http://www.chebucto.ns.ca/Culture/NSCF/nscf-home.html

Saskatchewan Choral Federation

http://www.musiceducationonline.org/scf/scfindex.html

492. *British Choirs on the Net*

http://www.rodcuff.demon.co.uk/choirs/

Attempts to list all known British choral Web sites.

493. *Choir and Choral Music Web Ring*

http://www.webmusic.se/ring/

Provides access to more than 300 choir and choral music–related Web sites.

494. *The Choir Links Page*

http://www.abc.se/~m9850/TheChoirLinksPage/

Provides links to hundreds of choirs categorized by type. A sampling of categories used: boy's choirs, children's choirs, church choirs, girls choirs, gospel choirs, male choirs, philharmonic choirs, show choirs, student (university) choirs, women's choirs, and youth choirs. Maintained by John Wilund.

495. *ChoirWorld*

http://www.choirworld.com/

Information available in English and German. Provides links to approximately 1,500 choir Web sites.

496. *Choral Finland*

http://www.and.fi/kuorosuomi/english.htm

Provides links to approximately 150 Finnish choirs and vocal ensembles and links to a few Finnish choral music information sites. Supplies information about Finnish choral music publishers and choir associations and about the Finnish Choral Directors's Association (FCDA). Site primarily in English with some information in Finnish.

497. *ChoralNet: The Internet Center for Choral Music*

http://www.choralnet.org/

Provides information pertaining to the choral profession, including searchable databases for choral repertoire, pedagogical tools, reference and research materials, choral performance, education and professional development, and links to choral Web sites.

498. *The Choral Public Domain Library*

http://www.cpdl.org/download.htm

Official Web site of the Choral Public Domain Library (CPDL) and its newsletter. Maintains an archive of sheet music in public domain.

499. *Choristers Guild*

http://www.choristersguild.org/

Official Web site of the Choristers Guild, an "ecumenical organization of directors of children's and youth choirs and publisher of music and related materials."

500. *Chorus America*

http://www.chorusamerica.org/

Official Web site of Chorus America and the quarterly publication, *The Voice of Chorus America*.

501. *Deutscher Saengerbund*

http://www.saengerbund.de/

In German. Official Web site of Der Deutsche Sängerbund in Schlagzeilen (The German Singer Federation in Headlines), boasting 1.8 million members worldwide in over 20,000 choirs.

502. *Europa Cantat*

http://www.europacantat.org/

Official Web site of European Federation of Young Choirs (EFYC) and its publication, *Europa Cantat*.

503. *The Hymn Society in the United States and Canada*

http://www.bu.edu/sth/hymn/

Official Web site of The Hymn Society in the United States and Canada and its quarterly journal, *The Hymn.*

504. *International Federation for Choral Music*

http://www.choralnet.org/ifcm

Official Web site of the International Federation for Choral Music (IFCM) and its publication, *International Choral Bulletin.*

505. *Japan Choral Association*

http://www.jcanet.or.jp/ (Japanese)

http://www.jcanet.or.jp/inter/JCA_guide.html (English)

Information available in Japanese and English. Official Web site of the Japan Choral Association (JCA) and its quarterly publication, *Harmony.*

506. *MUSICA International Database of Choral Music*

http://www.musicanet.org/

Database of choral music repertoire and pedagogic materials.

507. *Musica Russica: Russian Choral Music*

http://www.musicarussica.com/

Web site of the publisher Musica Russica. Besides serving as an online catalog of materials for purchase, this site also provides links to other publishers of Russian choral music, to Russian and Slavic choirs in the United States, and to Web sites related to Russian culture and music.

508. *Pepper Sheet Music Online*

http://www.jwpepper.com/

Online catalog of a variety of music, including choral octavos, choral cantatas and musicals, and resources for elementary school music.

509. *Royal School of Church Music*

http://www.rscm.com/

Official Web site of The Royal School of Church Music (RSCM), its *Church Music Quarterly* and *Sunday by Sunday* publications, and of *RSCM Music Direct*, its sheet music retail business.

510. *Royal School of Church Music America*

http://www.rscmamerica.org/

Official Web site of the Royal School of Church Music America (RSCM America), providing links to its many branches.

511. *Stabat Mater Dolorosa: The Stabat Mater, a Musical Journey through the Ages . . .*

http://ourworld.compuserve.com/homepages/HvanderVelden/

Privately owned Web site maintained by Hans van der Velden. Annotated discography of approximately 100 settings of the Stabat Mater dolorosa and Stabat Mater speciosa texts. Provides brief information about the composer, the date of composition, performing forces, duration, textual variations, publication information for the recording with a list of performers, and other notes as needed. Identifies 400 other Stabat Mater works not recorded on CD. Also, presents the text of the Stabat Mater dolorosa in Latin followed by translations into 15 languages and the text of the Stabat Mater speciosa in Latin and English.

512. *Yahoo! Entertainment:Music:Vocal:Choirs*

http://dir.yahoo.com/entertainment/music/vocal/choirs/

Provides links to more than 200 professional and amateur choral performing groups and organizations. Also provides links for various choral subjects, such as youth choirs, women's choirs, men's choirs, and choral-related Web directories.

513. *Zam'ru: The Jewish Choral Music Database*

http://www.zamir.org/db/

Web site maintained by the Zamir Chorale of Boston. Database of published Jewish choral music.

Subject Index

Numerals are filed before letters, not as though they were spelled out. Initial articles in all languages are ignored in filing. Hyphenated words are considered as separate words in filing. Citations provide annotation number.

ABCD (*see* Association of British Choral Directors)
ACCC (*see* Association of Canadian Choral Conductors)
ACDA (*see* American Choral Directors Association)
AGO (*see* American Guild of Organists)
APVE (*see* Association of Professional Vocal Ensembles)
A cappella choir movement, 360
Adam, Adolphe (1803–1856): Bibliographies of music literature, 450
Adler, Samuel (1928–): Choral music, 454
African-American composers
   Analysis, 368
   Bibliographies of music, 38, 154, 155, 157, 368
   Bibliographies of music literature, 38
   Biographies, 157
   Cantatas, 384
   Discographies, 157
   History and criticism, 368
Agostini, Paolo (1583–1629): Masses, 412
Ambros, August Wilhelm (1816–1876), 485
American Choral Directors Association, 62, 169, 176, 488
American Choral Foundation, 166
American Guild of Organists, 167, 489
American Musicological Society, 18
American Revolution bicentennial, 1776–1976: Bibliographies of music, 151
Analysis (*see also entries for individual composers*)
   13th-century music, 428
   14th-century music, 421

Author Index

Entries are given for all authors, including joint authors, contributors, and editors. Names of translators are excluded. Citations provide annotation number. Numerals are filed as though they were spelled out. Initial articles in all languages are ignored in filing. Hyphenated words are considered as separate words in filing.

Martin, Frank. *"Golgotha,"* The Composer's Point of View: Essays on Twentieth-Century
    Choral Music by Those Who Wrote It, 452
Marty, Martin E. *Church Music and the Christian Faith*, 237
Marvin, Jameson. "The 'Conductor's Process'," *Five Centuries of Choral Music: Essays
    in Honor of Howard Swan*, 196
———. "Music of the Renaissance: A Wealth of Literature for the Male Chorus," 78
Mateer, David. "John Baldwin and Changing Concepts of Text Underlay," *English Choral
    Practice, 1400–1650*, 308
Mathiassen, Finn. *The Style of the Early Motet (c. 1200–1250): An Investigation of the
    Old Corpus of the Montpellier Manuscript*, 428
Matonti, Charles J. "Discovering Principles for the Composition and Use of Contempo-
    rary Liturgical Music through the Study of Selected Requiem Masses," 441
Matthews, David. *Anthony Milner: A Bio-Bibliography*, 451
May, James D. *Avant-Garde Choral Music: An Annotated Selected Bibliography*, 72
May, William V. *Pronunciation Guide for Choral Literature: French, German, Hebrew,
    Italian, Latin, Spanish*, 280
Mayer, Frederick D. "A Selected List of Music Suitable for Use at the Junior High School
    Level," 176
McChesney, Richard. "Music for the Chorus without Tenors," 176
———. "Music for the Inexperienced Choir," 176
———. "Music for Two-Part Women's Choir," 176
McConnell, Harlan. *Key Words in Church Music: Definition Essays on Concepts, Prac-
    tices, and Movements of Thought in Church Music*, 316
McCoy, Jerry. "Literature Forum: New Literature for College and University Choirs," 75
McCray, James Elwin. "The British Magnificat in the Twentieth Century," 411
———. *The Conductor's Manual of Choral Music Literature*, 191
———. "A Survey of Published Magnificats for Treble Voices," 410
McDonald, Arlys L. *Ned Rorem: A Bio-Bibliography*, 451
McGowan, John Bailey. "Sixteenth-Century Polyphonic Settings of the Latin Hymn *Te
    Deum Laudamus*," 447
McNeil, Albert J. *The Chorus Handbook: Chorus 101: The How-To Book for Organizing
    and Operating a Professional or Volunteer Choral Ensemble*, 195
McRae, Shirley W. *Directing the Children's Choir: A Comprehensive Resource*, 218
Meckna, Michael. *Virgil Thomson: A Bio-Bibliography*, 451
Meggett, Joan M. *Music Periodical Literature: An Annotated Bibliography of Indexes and
    Bibliographies*, 13
Meier, Bernhard. "Die *Octo Beatitudines* in der Vertonung von Adrian Willaert und
    Orlando di Lasso," *Chormusik und Analyse: Beiträge zur Formanalyse und Inter-
    pretation mehrstimmiger Vokalmusik, Zweiter Teil*, 293
Menk, Nancy. "Literature on the Women's Chorus," 176
Mennin, Peter. *"Symphony No. 4: 'The Cycle',"* The Composer's Point of View: Essays on
    Twentieth-Century Choral Music by Those Who Wrote It, 452

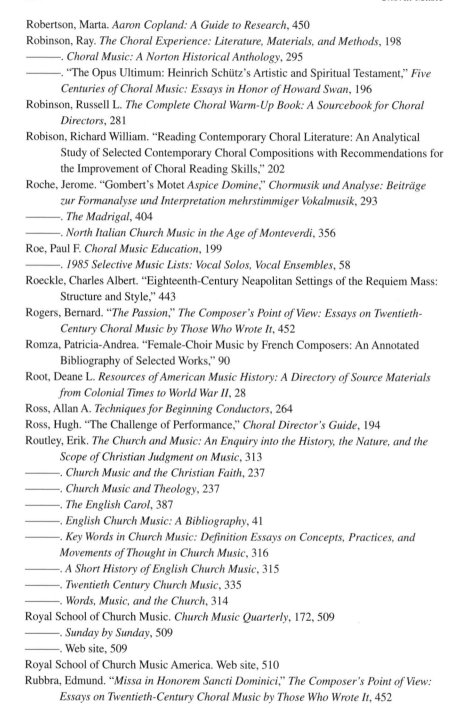

Turner, Ronald A. *A Study Guide to Anthem Literature: History and Performance Practice*, 378
Tyler, Linda L. *Edward Burlingame Hill: A Bio-Bibliography*, 451

Ulrich, Homer. *A Survey of Choral Music*, 319
Urrows, David Francis. *Randall Thompson: A Bio-Bibliography*, 451

Vagner, Robert. *A Selective List of Choral and Vocal Music with Wind and Percussion Accompaniments*, 113
Valentin, Erich. *Die evangelische Kirchenmusik: Handbuch für Studium und Praxis*, 340
———. *Handbuch der Chormusik*, 130
Van Camp, Leonard. "A Bibliography of Choral Music for Six-Part Mixed Voices," 176
———. "A Bibliography of Choral Music for Three-Part Male Chorus," 176
———. "A Bibliography of Polychoral Music," 176
———. "A Bibliography of Rounds and Canons," 176
Van der Velden, Hans. *Stabat Mater Dolorosa: The Stabat Mater, a Musical Journey through the Ages. . . .* Web site, 511
Vassalli, Antonio. "Circolazione letteraria e circolazione musicale del madrigale: Il caso G. B. Strozzi," 397
Vidali, Carole Franklin. *Alessandro and Domenico Scarlatti: A Guide to Research*, 450
Vinquist, Mary. *Performance Practice: A Bibliography*, 21, 22
Vinton, John. "A Selective List of Choral Compositions from the Classical Period in Practical Editions," 176
Vogel, Emil. *Bibliothek der gedruckten weltlichen Vocalmusik Italiens: Aus den Jahren 1500–1700. Enthaltend die Litteratur der Frottole, Madrigale, Canzonette, Arien, Opern etc.*, 50
Vollen, Gene E. *The French Cantata: A Survey and Thematic Catalog*, 51
Volz, Carl. *Key Words in Church Music: Definition Essays on Concepts, Practices, and Movements of Thought in Church Music*, 316
Von Ende, Richard Chaffey. *Church Music: An International Bibliography*, 40

Walker, Diane Parr. *German Sacred Polyphonic Vocal Music between Schütz and Bach: Sources and Critical Editions*, 139
Walker, Paul. *German Sacred Polyphonic Vocal Music between Schütz and Bach: Sources and Critical Editions*, 139
Ward, Robert J. "Compositions for Speaking Chorus," 176
Ward, Tom R. *The Polyphonic Office Hymn, 1400–1520: A Descriptive Catalogue*, 142
———. "The Polyphonic Office Hymn from the Late Fourteenth Century until the Early Sixteenth Century," 359
Warland, Dale. *The Chorus Handbook: Chorus 101: The How-To Book for Organizing and Operating a Professional or Volunteer Choral Ensemble*, 195
Wasson, Weyburn. *Twentieth-Century Choral Music: An Annotated Bibliography of Music Appropriate for College and University Choirs*, 74

Title Index

Entries are given for all titles, including separately titled essays within monographs. Periodical titles are selectively included. Citations provide annotation number. Numerals are filed as though they were spelled out. Initial articles in all languages are ignored in filing. Hyphenated words are considered as separate words in filing.